Alexander Johnstone Wilson

The Resources of Modern Countries Essays Towards an Estimate of the Economic Position of Nations

Vol. 1

Alexander Johnstone Wilson

The Resources of Modern Countries Essays Towards an Estimate of the Economic Position of Nations
Vol. 1

ISBN/EAN: 9783744730853

Printed in Europe, USA, Canada, Australia, Japan

Cover: Foto ©Thomas Meinert / pixelio.de

More available books at **www.hansebooks.com**

THE
RESOURCES OF MODERN COUNTRIES

ESSAYS TOWARDS AN ESTIMATE OF THE ECONOMIC POSITION OF NATIONS AND BRITISH TRADE PROSPECTS

BY

ALEXANDER JOHNSTONE WILSON

REPRINTED, with EMENDATIONS and ADDITIONS, from FRASER'S MAGAZINE

IN TWO VOLUMES

VOL. I.

LONDON
LONGMANS, GREEN, AND CO.
1878

PREFACE.

With the exception of the chapters on China and Japan, and on Turkey and Egypt, and also part of the chapter on our Minor Possessions, the following essays were in substance printed in 'Fraser's Magazine.' They have been revised throughout, however, and much new matter added, with a view to bring them as near as possible to the present date.

When these essays began to appear in the autumn of 1876 this country was hoping that the end of the period of trade depression was at hand. That this hope has hitherto been unrealised is by many believed to be in part due to the feverish state of mind into which all Europe has been thrown by the war between Russia and Turkey. Under the influence of the fears engendered by that war, trade has certainly gone from bad to worse, and the strain upon this country's mercantile resources has been very great. But we are now again hoping that the end is nearly reached, and that with the return of peace trade will once more revive.

I should be sorry to be considered a mere prophet of evil, but I believe that the roots of the decay in at all events our export trade lie deeper than any mere war scare. To me it seems indeed probable that the return of peace may only serve, for a time at least, to bring into stronger relief than ever the extent to which we have discounted the future, and that we would therefore do well to refrain from the indulgence of sanguine expectations. The nature of our relations with foreign countries is changing, and the trade outlook of the future by no means clear, even were peace now assured for a generation, which it by no means is.

That being so, I venture to hope that the considerations set forth in the following pages may not be without their use. I make no pretence to have exhausted the subject—it is too vast and intricate for any individual to hope to exhaust it; but I hope that I have at least said as much as may suffice to aid its full discussion, and I shall not regret should such discussion or the logic of events prove that I have taken too gloomy a view of the situation.

In one part of the horizon there is even now a hint of brighter prospects than existed when I revised my essays at the end of last year. The United States Congress is about to consider proposals for a reduction in the tariff, and, should these proposals become law, they will materially change for the better the position of our American trade. This prospect is, however, darkened both by the uncertainty of congressional politics, and by the signs of political divergence which are again becoming unmistakably visible between the heterogeneous sections composing the American Union, and we can at present only hope doubtfully.

My thanks are due to Mr. A. F. MURISON and the Rev. GEO. JOHNSTONE, for the help they have afforded me in reading the proof-sheets.

LONDON: *February 1878.*

CONTENTS

OF

THE FIRST VOLUME.

CHAPTER		PAGE
I.	THE TRADE PROSPERITY OF THE PAST AND PRESENT GENERATIONS IN THIS COUNTRY .	1
II.	THE ECONOMIC POSITION OF INDIA	47
III.	CHINA AND JAPAN .	115
IV.	THE UNITED STATES .	140
V.	RUSSIAN PROGRESS .	212
VI.	TURKEY AND EGYPT	271
VII.	AUSTRO-HUNGARY AND GERMANY	296
VIII.	FRANCE AND BELGIUM	347

THE RESOURCES OF MODERN COUNTRIES.

CHAPTER I.

THE TRADE PROSPERITY OF THE PAST AND PRESENT GENERATIONS IN THIS COUNTRY.

We are passing through a commercial crisis of a very peculiar and complicated kind. It differs superficially from previous crises with which the present generation is familiar in being less sharp but more prolonged. It is in some cases concurrent with, in others supplementary to, similar crises in other important nations with which we have intimate trade relations, and has been accompanied by remarkable collapses of national credit, the full effects of which have yet to appear. These and other causes still combine to render the prospect of a speedy trade-recovery dim, and to make any estimate of the actual position of this country difficult. During all times of mercantile trouble, when credit suffers painful contraction and business diminishes in volume, the popular mind is ready to accept the gloomiest views on the position of the country. The common cry is that other nations are beating us in the race for wealth; that our manufactures no longer hold their own against those of foreign nations; that people abroad are learning to do without our iron and coal, and growing able to make their own machinery; so that, if we might accept the common view, the fate of this country is sealed. The present crisis or period of trade recoil shows little exception to the rule in this respect. Once more the so-called croakers have obtained the ear of the nation, and any piece of news likely to bear out the worst views of the future is eagerly seized upon and its significance probably stretched to the utmost. Thus a few months ago we were entertained with descriptions of the manner in which the United States is distancing us in the making of iron and steel, and competing in our home markets with cotton goods; we have been told that our railway companies are actually buying foreign coal, and foreign locomotives to burn it in; foreign tariffs are flung in our faces; and we have been over and over again assured that free trade will prove the ruin of the nation, because we give everything and get nothing—unfetter the trade of every other nation, whether they free ours in return or not. These and many other facts, notions, and arguments find widespread acceptance at a time like the present, and even when not accepted in their entirety they colour men's minds with despondent ideas. What gives more force to such statements is the feeling that our trade crisis has not yet reached its acute form. The evil day has been only staved off, not surmounted, and the long stagnation through which the country has already passed is, it is felt, merely leading us up to a settling day when the bad securities hidden away in banks and by merchants must come out and find their level, the losses unconfessed be revealed, and, in short, the general balance sheet of at least the last decade of speculation and progress, be struck amid perhaps widespread ruin. We have had such crises before, however, and have survived, and it may be that the one now so long looked for will come and pass as before. It would hence be unwise to take the feeling of the moment without reference to all the facts, and at once predict the impending decadence of English trade.

I propose, therefore, to make some examination of the facts bearing upon the present situation at home and abroad, in order to arrive, if possible, at the truth regarding the prospects and dangers, or advantages, of this country as a great manufacturer and trader. The complicated forces at work will render this survey rather a wide one, and at best far from complete; but enough may be brought together to enable impartial readers to form a sounder conclusion on the drift of events than can be obtained by listening altogether to the dictates of the passions and fears begotten directly of the time. The subject is all the wider, too, that it will involve the bringing together of some data wherewith to form a judgment on the credit, progress, capacities, and position of the principal foreign nations which are now admitted competitors against us or which threaten immediately to become so. It will not be possible, however, to enter so deeply into the whole subject as could be desired ; and, before entering on it at all, there is a certain preliminary work to be done, without which any estimate of the present situation would be comparatively without value. We must go back and take note of some of the successive steps of progress which the trade of this country has taken within, say, the last forty years, in order that we may learn on what that progress has been based. The nature of the growth of the wealth of England within little more than a generation is of the utmost importance to an understanding of her future position. Many nations have risen to great wealth only to sink again, after the lapse of a few generations, into poverty, insignificance, and oblivion. Has the recent history of England, or of her economic policy, been of a kind to warrant the conclusion that she also is going the way of all the earth, and that the period in which we now are marks the first recession from the culminating point in her career? No question could possess deeper interest at any time ; and just now it is beyond measure important that we should know what we have been doing and how we stand. I shall, therefore, in this preliminary chapter briefly trace the leading events in our recent commercial and industrial history, and try to indicate the leading elements in our present abounding wealth.

The present generation is familiar enough, in a general way, with the chief features of the marvellous growth of wealth which has taken place within the last forty years; and the old men of our day can call to mind times in curious contrast to the present. Yet the memory of the old state of things is rapidly growing faint, and it may not be amiss to remind the reader, therefore, of the position from which the generation now passing away started. Young people do not realise how very modern our trade expansion has been, and cannot see, therefore, how many of the issues of it have yet to be worked out. The past forty years—all their outburst of fabulous wealth and Titanic energy notwithstanding—have been perhaps only a sowing time. In the history of the world, the epoch which to us looks so long and so mighty in results may count for but little. If we look back no farther than the past century, we shall to some extent see the newness at least of much of what we now boast. In a hundred years the population of these islands barely increased as much as it now does in a decade; trade was small and circumscribed; locomotion difficult. Less than one hundred years ago the population of England was computed at under

10,000,000 souls, or not within 2,000,000 of half its present total. As recently as the beginning of the present century the estimated annual make of iron was less than 200,000 tons. Our ancient cotton and woollen industries were only creeping into importance towards the latter part of the eighteenth century, when the inventions of Arkwright, Hargreaves, Crompton, and Dr. Cartwright were beginning to tell on the cost of manufacture. Everything was slow, quiet, unprogressive; and the social disturbances of the closing years of that century, and opening ones of this, did little, apparently, to break the sleepy spell. The outburst of energetic life and fecundity, both of invention and of race, came to all appearance suddenly into being less than fifty years ago, and the nation seemed to sow and reap in little more than a generation more than it had done in all the previous ages.

It was in part only seeming, however; and the intimate connection which can be shown to subsist between the bustling reproductive present and the slow vegetating past, ought to make us careful not hastily to assume that we can yet judge of the effects of the labours of the present and the passing generations. For it would be wrong to conclude on the mere trade figures that the past centuries had but little to do with the outburst of prosperity and 'progress' that characterises the present time. In the history of the nation they are united indissolubly. The slowly adopted improvements, the patient industry and saving habits of the manufacturing population of England, unquestionably prepared the way for all that followed, and made it easy for us to take the lead in the world when the new order of things came upon it. Not only so; but the social and political events of the past bore, if possible, more intimately still upon the advancement of the present. The wars and conquests of England in the West and the East first of all placed her at the head of modern empires, and in part displaced the monarchies of the older world with their despotisms. By our colonisations and blundering but on the whole successful wars in North America, we possessed ourselves of the mismanaged territories of Spain and France; and our advance in India checked the growth of the Dutch empire, stopped there also the foreign aggrandisement of France, and helped to blot out the political and commercial significance of Portugal. When the wars of the French Revolution began, the foundations of a great empire had already been broadly laid; and when it ended, England stood out as the power which had almost alone grown greater in the struggle. During this long conflict we had not only maintained all our own acquisitions, but had added to them the supreme dominion of the empire of India and the possession of South Africa. Our position in the Mediterranean had been consolidated by the possession of Malta. We had laid hold of the French colony of Mauritius, as an outport and depôt in the Indian Ocean, and secured the road to China by getting a foothold in the Straits of Malacca. While all these territorial advantages fell to us, the Continental turmoil had also thrown more and more into English hands, in spite of our then bad navigation laws, the general conduct of international trade. Napoleon had made leagues against us, had sought to shut us out of Europe, with this result only, that one after another the maritime power of Continental nations had been broken, and their traders almost swept from the seas by our privateers. Dutchman, Dane, and Spaniard, Frenchman and Venetian, all ancient competitors of England, fell before her; and, when the sword was sheathed in 1815, it was no exaggerated boast to call her mistress of the seas.

These facts should never be lost sight of in any consideration of the causes which have led us to where we now are. Without these preparatory steps, both in domestic industries and in foreign wars and conquests, England would not, with all her material advantages, have been so entirely the gainer by the progress of the last forty or fifty years as she has so far proved to be. It has not been hitherto a question of others distancing us in the race, because we have had the racecourse almost entirely to ourselves. Our old rivals were either crippled or driven from the field, and there is the more need to remember this because the time immediately following the war was one of severe domestic suffering, and of much retrograde legislation, conceived with a view to lessen, if possible, that suffering. The peace of 1815 found England well-nigh exhausted. Her National Debt, funded and floating together, had risen to 840,000,000*l*., involving an annual charge of 32,000,000*l*., which had to be borne by a sorely impoverished population. In order to raise the necessary supplies recourse was had to increased fiscal burdens; and between 1815 and 1820 over 1,000,000*l*. in new customs duties alone were, after deducting the remissions, imposed upon the imports of the country. The worst of all the laws which then restricted trade, however, were those relating to the exports and imports of corn, which the younger men of to-day have well-nigh forgotten. They blocked the way to all industrial progress. During the eighteenth century, and indeed for a long period anterior thereto, a blind and short-sighted policy had been pursued with regard to this great food staple, under the prevailing notion that it was the duty of the State to protect the home agricultural interests, irrespective of all others, a notion still very strong in rural England. But it was not until the beginning of the present century that these bad laws began to press with their full cramping power on the trade of the country. Then the ever-shifting provisions for dealing with the corn trade began to tell, because the population of the kingdom was fast growing out of the capacities of a backward or ill-regulated home production to supply it with food. A bad harvest occurring in 1816 tended to aggravate the mischief caused by the high duties levied on imports, and the practical prohibition which they put on any import of corn below a given price. Many enlightened persons in this country saw the evils of this false system; but the landed interest was too strong and blind to admit of reform, and for many years the country had to submit to a protective 'sliding scale' of duty under which, as the price of corn went up, the import duty decreased, and *vice versâ*. By an Act passed as late as 1828 it was arranged that 62*s*. per quarter should be taken as the centre point, as it were, of this scale. When corn was at that price the import duty was to be 24*s*. 8*d*.; and when it rose to 69*s*. the duty fell to 15*s*. 8*d*. Should the price rise to 73*s*. per quarter, then the duty fell to 1*s*., its *minimum*. It is difficult nowadays to realise the torture which such legislation as this imposed on the trader who, by a mere fall of 2*s*. or 3*s*. in the price of a quarter of wheat, might find himself, through the action of this sliding scale, compelled to stand at a loss of 17*s*. or 18*s*. owing to the additional duty which fell to be paid. With a growing population, and an increasing tendency in that population to gather round manufacturing centres, the misery which was often entailed by this practical prohibition of food imports is not to be described. It gave rise to discontent, and sometimes to incipient rebellion; to riots often, followed by ill-judged interference of the authorities, such as the rick-burnings and chartist *émeutes* that followed the passing of the Reform Bill. Yet it was not till after long years of agitation by John Bright, Richard Cobden, and other leaders of the Anti-Corn Law League, that the landed party gave way sullenly, and assented, amid the most gloomy predictions of impending ruin, to the repeal of the sliding scale altogether, and the virtual abolition of all corn laws by the substitution of a fixed duty of one shilling per quarter.

Thus recently was one of the most oppressive pieces of fiscal legislation that man could have conceived withdrawn; and not until 1849, when the new law came into force, could the industries of the country be said to be anything like unfettered. Then indeed they bounded into vigour and expansive life. Yet twenty years more passed before this shilling duty—the last rag of land-owner protection—was itself flung aside, and the import of corn became perfectly free. Slight as this duty was, there can be no question that it sometimes told injuriously on the import of corn, and to the advantage in a selfishly exclusive way of the landed interest, as against the working population of the country. This will be understood when it is remembered that, on the wheat and flour imports of 1875, this shilling duty would have yielded a gross income of 1,383,000*l*., and that since then it would have been more.[1]

But many other changes had in the meantime taken place, all tending more and more to throw off the shackles of trade, and to enable the energies of the people to have the fullest, freest play. Up to 1820 the reactionary fiscal policy to which we have alluded affected all departments of business more or less. Duties that looked light, but whose effect was crushing, or at best harassing, were imposed here, there, and everywhere. With 1820 there came a change, however; and between 1821 and 1825 we find a clear 4,500,000*l*. worth of duties knocked off the tariff, with no loss at all to the revenue, but, on the contrary, a gain of nearly 2,000,000*l*. From that time forward, with the single exception of the period 1836 to 1840, when there was an increase on balance, in the customs duties levied, of nearly 1,000,000*l*., the knocking off of fetters went on until, as we find from a table in that admirable work, Tooke and Newmarch's *History of Prices*, by 1855 '13½ millions of duties, or two-thirds of the entire customs revenue, had been remitted, and the produce was still within 1¼ million of the amount at which it stood before a single remission had taken place.' These changes have all to be taken into account in coming to any just conclusion regarding the present position of

[1] Report of Her Majesty's Commissioners of Customs for 1875.

the country, or in estimating the progress which it has made; and, if we continue the statement to the present time, we shall see the freedom under which we now exist more clearly still, as well as how very modern it is.

As late as 1840 our customs tariff was described in the report of a committee of the House of Commons as 'presenting neither congruity nor unity of purpose;' as 'often aiming at incompatible ends,' seeking both to produce revenue and to protect interests in ways incompatible with each other. There were no fewer than 1,150 different rates of duty chargeable on imported articles, very few of which had been imposed on any recognised standard; and the committee gave a list of 862 of such articles which were subject to duty, seventeen of which then produced 94 per cent. of a revenue amounting to 23,000,000*l.* No less than 147 of the articles enumerated as subject to duty had not apparently been imported at all, for they yielded nothing. The articles which yielded the greater part of the revenue are enumerated as follows: Sugar, tea, tobacco, spirits, wine, timber, corn, coffee, butter, currants, tallow, seeds, raisins, cheese, cotton, sheep's wool, and silk manufactures; and this mere enumeration reveals to us what a gulf there is between a generation ago and to-day. The present customs tariff contains less than two dozen articles all told, and including those on which duty is imposed to countervail the excise charges on internal products. The ordinary import articles on which duty is charged number only seven, and from the present list sugar, butter, tallow, timber, seeds, cotton, wool, and silk goods have disappeared. Yet the gross revenue from customs was but about 4,000,000*l.* less in 1876-7 than it was in 1840 with nearly 900 articles on the list, and this too though we are in a time of great trade depression. The effect of this freedom from burdens can hardly be measured, however, by a mere statement of the wonderful elasticity of our revenue, strong testimony although that be to the increasing wealth of the community. These remissions of taxes have added incalculably to the power which we in this country possess to govern the markets of the world, as we shall by-and-by take occasion to demonstrate when we come to deal with foreign tariffs.

Here, then, is in outline another great step which this country has taken in what may be called the negative elements of progress. The reforms came slowly, and were often the result of protracted struggles; but they did come, and following all the preparatory steps which the nation had taken—mostly by a kind of blind chance—told most effectively on her commercial and industrial position.

But there are yet other hindrances, the removal of which has to be noticed, and which, till removed, cramped England very seriously, viz. the navigation laws and the great trade monopoly of the East India Company. These acted most injuriously on the enterprise and trade of the country. The principle of the navigation laws was essentially the same as that which lay at the root of the corn laws and of all legislation designed, as it was thought, to benefit and protect home interests from the effects of foreign competition. They date from a very early period, and took as long to remove from the statute-book of the realm as the corn laws did. It was not till 1651, however, that the ridiculous determination to foster home navigation as it was thought, and attack the prosperity of other countries, took a complete and definite shape. In the end of that year a law was passed, the object of which was to cripple the trade of the Dutch, then rapidly approaching the zenith of their commercial prosperity. By that law it was enacted that no products of Asia, Africa, America, or Europe should be imported into this country in other than British ships. As regards Europe some slight modification was made a few years later, specified articles being substituted for countries in all instances save Russia and Turkey; but the modification was worth little. As a piece of revenge against the Dutch this law had little effect; but as a means of hindering the prosperity of England it was the most ingenious device that could have been framed, and, had Holland had within herself the resources and wealth which were possessed by England, the effect of such short-sighted policy might have been to place England to-day almost as much out of the running as Spain. Holland was internally poor when measured by her ambitions, however, and ultimately overstrained herself in the effort to keep the lead. Yet, as it was, we lost a good deal of foreign trade through the operation of the law, because we had not got the shipping nor the resources that were necessary to maintain it; and by-and-by, as other powers rose in the world, they began to retaliate upon us with laws as exclusive and as destructive to us as ours were to them, until, had matters gone on in this spirit of retaliation, every country would have in the end become perforce self contained; there would have been no international trade, only universal exclusion and dead-lock. Fortunately, retaliatory measures brought this country somewhat to reason, and did for us what plain sense appeared quite unable to accomplish. It took longer time, however, to accomplish the complete deliverance of our mercantile marine from the baneful influence of 'protective' jealousy than to effect any other great free-trade reform. A tentative effort to lessen the evil consequences of confining the carrying trade of England to English ships was made in 1825 by Mr. Huskisson; but it was not till 1854 that complete free trade on the sea was granted by the abolition of any restriction as to the nationality of vessels engaged in the coasting trade of the kingdom.

Four years previously the abolition of all restrictions affecting foreign trade had paved the way for this final measure; and, by setting free the resources of other powers, had stimulated our own mercantile marine, and opened the way for a great expansion of business. For many years the policy of reciprocity had been advocated—what James VI. would have called the 'niffer for niffer' policy; but it proved a complete failure. Other nations would not make patched-up engagements of this kind; and it was not till England took the lead in granting freedom to commerce without conditions that other nations began to follow in her wake. The trade monopoly of the East India Company had been abolished in 1834 so far as home competition was concerned, and need not detain us now.

Thus, then, we have noted briefly the various steps and leading characteristics of the conquests and commercial reforms which, in this country, either paved the way for or secured the benefit of the great outburst of enterprise and influx of wealth which began in the second quarter of the present century. The various reforms constitute, so to say, the negative side of the modern commercial prosperity which this country built upon the foundations of her world-wide empire; and, in order to get a complete outline of the position which we at present occupy, we must now revert briefly to the positive side of the subject; we must find out where the great modern wealth has come from and on what it has been based. Freedom of trade no doubt did much to call wealth and enterprise into being; but in what did this wealth consist?

Happily the leading features are not difficult to trace. Although the foundations of the great manufacturing industries of this country lie far back in the past, their development, like the growth of free-trade principles, is quite modern, and dates in reality from the day when George Stephenson won the competition at Liverpool, with his locomotive 'the Rocket,' settling thereby the question of railroad travelling by steam beyond dispute. The mere stimulus to all kinds of mining and manufacturing industries which this victory and the subsequent railway operations gave, was itself enough to cause the trade of this country to press forward by 'leaps and bounds.' Since November 1830, it may be said to have done so; and the mere fact that England was the originator of the railway systems of the world, and that she contained within herself almost boundless materials wherewith to construct and equip those systems, would itself suffice to explain the pre-eminence which from that day to this has been unquestionably hers. The great natural resources of the country were first employed in supplying the materials for home development, and then gradually the wealth thus acquired by digging in the bowels of the earth was utilised in tempting or leading other nations into a career of 'progress' similar to our own. In spite of the many losses which individuals suffered in the early days of this progress, the nation grew steadily richer, and its stores of realised wealth increased almost with every new enterprise that it took up. It might drive some few individuals to despair, or ruin whole groups in their efforts to find the particular moiety of capital which they had subscribed to a particular railway; but the ruin of these was not felt in the general tide of prosperity. Year by year the amount of property assessed for income tax grew in value, hardly pausing for the panics and widespread ruins of 1847, 1857, and 1866. In 1848 the swelling exports of the country dipped under the weight of the commercial depression from about 59,000,000*l.* to 53,000,000*l.*; but in 1849 they jumped about 10,000,000*l.*, to over 63,000,000*l.* Since then, with only brief dips, the upward movement of reproductive industries has been continuous up to 1874. Each year the realised wealth of the one before told, as it were, in swelling the working power of the nation, and in enlarging its business capacities and the scope of its credit. A bare statement of the fact that for the first five-and-thirty years of this century the imports of this country never were above 50,000,000*l.* per annum, and the exports never above 48,000,000*l.*, according to the 'real value' computation, and that by 1870 the one had risen to 303,257,000*l.* and the other (exclusive of re-exports) to 200,000,000*l.*, tells us something of the immense stride which the business of England has made in the interval. Slow creeping gave way to haste; patient building up of fortunes to huge enterprises in which millions were staked, and lost or won in a single throw. These figures tell, however, but a small part of the story, and we have also to remember the enormous stimulus to increase in population which this activity gave, if we are to understand the leading features of this modern trade expansion. The producing power of the community was augmented in all ways with the invention of new modes of locomotion, and the fast-thickening population tended to congregate more and more by the great centres of trade and manufacture. Thus the population of Lancashire, which was only some 800,000 in 1811, had risen by 1871 to 2,800,000 odd. That of Yorkshire (all divisions) was in 1811 under 1,000,000, and in 1871 was about 2,400,000. But the changes are most conspicuous in the growth of the population of cities. The population of London is now more than double what it was in 1831, and nearly fourfold that of the first year of the present century. Liverpool had about 494,000 inhabitants in 1871; in 1831 only 202,000. Birmingham has increased from 184,000 in 1841 to 344,000 in 1871. Bradford had only 67,000 in 1841; and in 1871 had 146,000—more than doubled in thirty years. So with Newcastle-on-Tyne, the figures being 70,000 odd against 128,000 odd at these respective dates; and instances might be multiplied—the tendency being evidently towards the massing of population in great centres of business; a tendency which, apart from all questions of modern sanitary improvement, appears to have had a most stimulating effect on the growth of population, partly no doubt because it implied a wage-earning power never before reached. This massing and the great facilities with which the people were fed by the new modes of conveyance and through the freedom of imports which a prevalence of free trade allowed, had a strong influence upon the producing power of the industries of the kingdom. The tendency on the whole was to reduce waste of energy and waste of time to a *minimum*, and hence to lower cost of production and the wear of human life. The internal trade of the country was thus quickened as inevitably as the external; and, although wealth tended of course to accumulate most with the great capitalists who had the fortune to lead the van in the new order of things, it was impossible for them to keep it all to themselves. Gradually the gains of the great railway and coal and iron syndics of the country began to tell on the comforts of the masses. As luxury grew, wants grew, and with wants new employments and an ever-broadening basis for trade to rest upon. With every new store of savings, and every fresh return from old invested savings—the staying power of the country—

and the area of its permanent and necessary wants tended to grow, offering a solid barrier, as it were, below which no mere dip in the tide of progress could go.

Side by side with the increased produce of the country, the increased manufactures, and the increasing wealth, there were growing up facilities for intercommunication with all parts of the world, and with that an increasing tendency to emigration. The home hives were constantly throwing off young swarms, which, settling now in America, now in Australia, now in Africa, became so many new centres of demand, so many links in the trade chain that we had bound round the world. In 1871 the population of Canada, the Australian colonies, and of South Africa and the West Coast of Africa, with the various islands possessed by England in the African seas, was upwards of 7,000,000; and the European portion of it, which formed the majority, had more than doubled in the last quarter of a century. Most of these colonies did also a much greater business than their mere population would lead one to expect, and did most of it with home. The rich gold discoveries in 1848 in California, and in 1851 in Australia, the new stimulus given by them on all sides to the rapid development of business and the rapid dissemination of modern improvements, have all had an enormous effect in enlarging the dealings of England with her colonies and dependencies, as well as with the United States of North America. To the last-named, for example, we exported 11,000,000*l.* worth of goods in 1848 against 7,000,000*l.* the year before, and the total rose to 23,600,000*l.* in 1853; reaching, with many dips and severe fluctuations, the highest figures ever touched in 1871, when our total exports were 40,700,000*l.* It was not till 1847 that the total exports of the United Kingdom to the Australian colonies first exceeded 1,500,000*l.*; but in 1852 they rose (mainly by the purchasing power which the new gold from New South Wales and Victoria imparted) to nearly three times that amount, and next year increased at a jump to 14,500,000*l.* From this high level, reached through the power of the new-found gold, there was an immediate falling away; still the figures never again fell much below 10,000,000*l.*, and in 1874 rose to over 19,000,000*l.* We might go on swelling the list by speaking of countries nearer home, such as France, but these are the more striking examples.

If our exports rose rapidly, still more so did the imports. To an increasing degree, as the fast growing population of this country centred in the manufacturing and mining districts, we became dependent upon foreign nations for our food; and from the manner in which we were making all nations our debtors it was becoming more and more easy for us as a nation to buy our food from them. It is not to be supposed that the yield of our own land was growing less—quite the reverse. It was, on the whole, steadily increasing under the improved modes of agriculture which were being introduced; but that was not enough. We had become a manufacturing nation instead of an agricultural one, and we were richer, and lived higher in consequence, and we had also more mouths to feed, therefore we spent more abroad. It is worth observing regarding our imports how thoroughly their totals have continually belied the old mercantile theory that a nation was rich only in proportion to the gold it stored away. Since 1860 up to the end of last year the declared value of our imports of foreign and colonial produce exceeded that of our exports of British produce and manufactures in the aggregate about 1,125,000,000*l*.; yet, in the face of this seemingly overwhelming adverse balance, we have gone on growing richer and richer. How can this be? Well, in the first place we do not keep all our imports: we re-export a certain quantity—latterly, from 45,000,000*l*. to 60,000,000*l*. worth a year; and these re-exports must be taken as a set-off against the heavy adverse figure. Over the seventeen years which we have added together they may, perhaps, account for about 750,000,000*l*. Again, it should never be forgotten that, however accurate the prices now set down at the ports may be, they never represent the real state of the account. The prices of the imports from abroad are naturally set down at more than the original cost of the goods, and those of the exports at considerably less than the merchant expects ultimately to receive for them. According as his profit is 5, or 10, or 20 per cent. each way of the account is the real ultimate balance brought nearer the exchange of commodities, and their liquidation of each other, so to say, made more easy. Not only so, but the import figures are swollen by the addition of freight charges which of course only tell on the values of our exported goods at their ports of destination. And, finally, it should also be remembered that the rapid development of our internal wealth, the increase of our business as world-goods-carriers, and the profits which our merchants have derived from the import as well as from the export trade, have all enabled us to lend to foreign countries, so that they have within the last thirty or forty years become more and more heavily our debtors. As rapidly as the balance rose against them in this way, so rapidly did our command over all kinds of foreign products increase, and so much the less did an excessive import of goods embarrass us. In 1875, for example, after the great borrowings of foreign countries had nearly stopped, and, as a consequence, their purchasing power in some degree diminished, our exports of home produce were fully 150,000,000*l*. less than our imports nominally, while last year their excess was as much as 182,000,000*l*., and probably at the very lowest computation really were less by half these amounts after taking account of the profits and compensating re-exports. Yet we stand these heavy adverse balances without flinching, and may stand many more, because the world is still, and will long remain, heavily in our debt. The excess imports represent, in fact, to a large extent profit on our exports and foreign investments, and also to some extent the income yielded by a trade which finds no record in our Custom House figures at all. This trade may be called international, and its characteristics are so well described by the Commissioners of Customs in their report for 1877 that I cannot do better than quote their words:—

Owners of accumulated capital conduct operations of trade and industry in and between foreign and colonial countries, and require that the profits of such operations shall be remitted to them in the country in which they reside. Those profits so remitted can only be so as imports for which there are no corresponding exports, or at least exports made, if made at all, at a period so remote as to be no longer available for account and comparison. To illustrate this it is only necessary to suppose that the English owner of a coffee plantation founded long ago in Ceylon, who has hitherto found it the most profitable course to import its produce into England, whence it might be, after being sold, exported to France or Italy for consumption there, now finds it more profitable to send it direct to those countries through the Suez Canal. This trade would no longer in such an event directly affect the return of imports and exports of the United Kingdom, but the profit on the transaction—a larger one, probably, than before—would, assuming the owner of the plantation to reside here, be sent here represented by other goods—perhaps bullion, if that happened at the time to promise the best further profit on transmission—which would swell the amount of imports with no corresponding exports, or only such exports as were made years ago when the coffee plantation was founded. Hence it is not difficult to believe that the fixed and floating capital in foreign and colonial countries, belonging to Englishmen who have their domicile in the United Kingdom, carries on much of the trade between those countries, while it is only the profit of that trade, or the interest of that invested capital, which is sent to this country, and thus necessarily swells the amount of its imports and the excess of those imports over its exports.

The vista opened up by this paragraph is without limit unless we remember that this measureless preponderance of wealth and carrying power is an object of envy to other nations, and that the profits of this purely carrying trade are now being competed for by strong and eager, if much less experienced and wealthy rivals. But come of that competition what may, and let our hold abroad be lessened by our own extravagance in spending or by the further default of foreign nations, the course of our trade so far has abundantly proved that there is no form of wealth so useless as idle gold. We have strenuously used every form of wealth, and every fresh gain becomes represented as the means of making yet further gains and commanding ever wider markets.

On the other hand we must not forget, as Mr. Caird pointed out so forcibly in his recent address at the Social Science meeting in Aberdeen, that the value of our imports is now seriously swollen by the enormous quantities of food which we have had to buy abroad and by the increased price of corn. Since the last great outrush of industrial reproduction, we have, partly through the spread of luxurious habits it has induced, become more dependent on foreign supplies of food than ever, and especially since the series of bad harvests set in three years ago, a large proportion of the profits of the nation must have gone to pay foreign bread bills. Mr. Caird states that during these three years we have paid 160,000,000*l.* more on this account than in the preceding three, and we must be prepared during the coming year to pay more than ever. Corn is much dearer, and our necessities are fully greater than they have been in any of the recent bad years. This may not unlikely cause us to spend not the profits of our trade merely but a considerable portion of our savings as well, there being such a severe diminution in our export and general business. I cannot stop to enquire here what effect this state of affairs may have on the future of the country, but it must never be forgotten that the excess of our imports over our exports may become dangerous when it represents more than the annual gains of the nation from all sources, and that a long course of bad harvests might go far to cripple the nation or to revolutionise our social habits and agricultural customs. It is not yet an alarming fact that our imports have lately shown a remarkable tendency to increase in the face of declining exports; they were last year the largest ever known; but it does indicate a certain amount of extravagance, and if the demand for our home products does not speedily revive, it may become a serious danger. We might pursue this interesting enquiry to some length; but enough has been said to show the characteristics as well as the volume of the business we have been doing, and how little the lopsidedness of the account need alarm us if it be kept within prudent limits.

All these economic changes and forces, involving the continuously augmenting demands of the population at home, and the continued 'improvement' of countries abroad, have redounded, so far, to the advantage of England. She has been the pioneer in the march of material progress, and has furnished the means by which that progress could be attained by others as well as herself. Possessed of enormous mineral resources, which modern discoveries have called into manifold new uses, she has employed them to a certain extent, and this must never be lost sight of, in fitting out the world to be her rival. She has built steamships and railways for the great powers on the Continent, and lavished her substance, as it were, to bring them up to her level. For a time 'progress' might be almost said to be synonymous with the growth of English business and manufactures directed in great measure to this end ; and, whatever comes, a great deal of the ground we have thus occupied must, we believe, for a time remain to us, solely because there is no one else to take it up.

But here another question starts up. What has been the actual net result to England and her customers of this enormous increase of business within the past twenty-five or thirty years ? We have said that everything has been done to encourage trade, and that, all over the world, England has possessed herself of markets for her productions; but we have not yet seen how far this enormous increase in buying and selling has been placed on a sound footing. Have we, in other words, been growing richer proportionately with our increased business, and have other nations benefited by their dealings with us to the extent that their heavy payments to us every year ought to prove them to be? The answer which such questions require is a very long one, involving, as it does, the whole subject of international credit and wealth ; and we can here deal with but a small section of it.

As far as regards the trade of England, the prosperity and development have in one sense been *bonâ fide* enough. We have raised millions of tons of iron and coal where formerly we raised only hundreds and thousands ; we have wrought the products of our mines into innumerable works of utility, which have been scattered broadcast over the world, yielding a rich harvest of gain. In the early part of the century, as we have seen, the exports of this country were insignificant both in quantity and value, and in nothing more so than iron and coal. But after 1840 this was quite altered. In the ten years 1840 to 1849 inclusive, the total quantity of coal exported exceeded 22,000,000 tons, having risen from 1,600,000 tons in 1840 to 2,800,000 tons in 1849. The next decade to 1859 gives an export of 49,836,000 tons, and shows an increase from 3,352,000 tons in 1850 to 7,000,000 tons in 1859. For the third decade to 1869 the total export had risen to 92,600,000 tons, and was about 3,500,000 tons more in 1869 than in 1860, the figure for the latter year being 10,700,000 tons. Since then the progression has been almost without a break, till last year the total quantity exported rose to over 16,000,000 tons, all kinds of fuel included. The reaction has been, in point of fact, one of value, not of quantity, so far as coal has been concerned. The 14,500,000 tons exported in 1875 was worth only 9,600,000*l.* against 12,000,000*l.* for the smaller quantity of the previous years. Last year's greater export only brought 8,900,000*l.* odd. With iron the extraordinary increase in the volume of the exports is quite as remarkable, though not lately so expansive.

In the ten years to 1849 the total quantity of all kinds of iron, except machinery, exported was

4,600,000 tons, and had risen to 700,000 tons in 1849 as compared with less than 300,000 tons in 1840. From 1850 to 1859 the total quantity exported reaches over 12,000,000 tons, and had increased with but trifling exceptions from 780,000 tons in 1850 to 1,465,000 tons in 1859. The progress in the next decade was more remarkable still, a total of nearly 18,000,000 tons having been exported between 1860 and 1869 inclusive, and the annual quantity having risen from 1,500,000 tons in the former year to about 2,700,000 tons in the latter. The progress continued up to 1872, when the highest quantity ever reached in one year—3,400,000 tons—was exported. Since then there has been a falling off; but the lowest total touched since 1870—viz. 2,224,000 tons, the export of last year—is still above the total of 1868. Here also, as a matter of course, the values do not show the same regularity; but, on the contrary, have fluctuated severely, and are now much lower than they were two years ago. As a result of this the value of the export of iron, which in 1873 was in the proportion of about one-seventh of the total value of our exports, fell in 1876 to about one-tenth.[1] In estimating the true position and prosperity of English trade, however, it is, after all, to quantities that we have to look. A slight over-production one year may cause a sharp recoil in values the next; but if, on the whole, the

[1] Report of H.M. Commissioners of Customs for the year 1876.

consumption of our products goes on increasing, the fair inference is that business is radically on a sound basis—that of the real wants of mankind—and that depression in prices will pass off now as it has done before, when the world recovered from its fit of excess. It is urged, however, as regards iron, that, although the total weight has kept advancing with fair uniformity and has not receded in any serious amount during the past four years of dulness, the kinds now exported are different from what they were. Foreign nations want more raw or pig iron, and less manufactured, as they get out of tutelage and learn to 'do for themselves.' This is to some extent true: and accordingly, for three years, from 1871 to 1873, the quantity of pig-iron exported increased almost as steadily as that of railway kinds fell off; and since then, although both have fallen off in some degree, the decline in railway sorts has been much the most marked, until in 1875, less than 550,000 tons were exported, against 1,060,000 tons in 1870. The value figures of the export of machinery tell the same tale, and each year with increased emphasis. The statement, therefore, that people are now buying our raw iron to use in their own manufactures, and that one branch of our trade is rapidly being ruined by foreign competition, is, to some extent, a reasonable one. I doubt whether this be the true interpretation in all cases, however, but shall return to the subject when the condition of other countries comes to be examined. All that we have to do in the meantime is to show how marvellous the growth of the prosperity of this country has been since the making of railways became the fashion of the world. The future cannot, however, be judged by the past position of England alone.

I selected iron and coal for the purpose of illustrating the growth of our trade because they are our most important indigenous products and the most immediate sources of our great wealth; but the same kind of illustration is to be found in the statistics of our textile manufactures, to which we must briefly revert. In cotton piece goods, for example, our exports were only about 790,000,000 yards, worth 17,600,000*l*., in 1840—a higher figure that, moreover, than for either of the two succeeding years; but in 1874 they had reached 3,607,000,000 yards, of a declared value of 55,000,000*l*. There have been, of course, interruptions in this extraordinary progress; but they have never sufficed to check permanently the growing volume of the trade. The commercial panic of 1866, for example, had a most beneficial influence in extending it. For some years previously exports of cotton goods had been rather low, partly because cotton was both dear and scarce; but with the reduced prices of 1866 and succeeding years there came a marked revival—so much so, indeed, that the quantity exported in 1867 was upwards of 800,000,000 yards more than in 1865, and 1,000,000,000 more than the export of 1864, which of course suffered most keenly from the American civil war. The same statements apply more or less closely to the panics of 1847 and 1857, and give good augury for the results of the present stagnant condition of business, should there be no causes at work elsewhere to counteract the good effect here. The woollen manufactures of the country tell the same story. Exclusive of carpets the exports of woollen and worsted goods in 1840 barely reached 67,000,000 yards; in 1872 they had risen to 400,000,000 yards; and although they fell in 1875 to about 319,000,000 yards, and last year to 282,000,000, still either of these totals is higher than the highest previous to 1864 and about the level maintained up to 1869. That the depression is so great is of course matter for regret, but it has yet to be proved that these lower levels are to be permanent.

Obviously, as has already been shown, the import side of the account must have grown in a still more remarkable manner, and I cannot better illustrate this growth than by the table in the Appendix.[1] The rapidity of communication with all parts of the world which was established by means of steam, and the later development of electric telegraphy, and the extreme facilities which our internal communications

---

[1] Appendix A. Table extracted from the Report of H.M. Customs for 1876.

gave us, enabled us to buy, import, and manufacture rapidly all kinds of raw produce, to be re-exported at a profit which still again increased our command over the resources of other countries. The population is a working one taken altogether, although both the idle by force of circumstances and the voluntary drones are on the increase amongst us. The great majority therefore do something towards securing this harvest of gain. Therefore the import trade of the country has grown apace not for the staples of manufacture and for necessary food merely, but in an increasing degree for the luxuries which wealth alone can command. As tax after tax was lopped off those classes of articles suited for manufactures which went to constitute our principal foreign purchases, and as the industries connected with these raw produce staples, more and more unshackled, leaped forward to ever fresh conquests, the people recouped the national exchequer by increased payments on the articles of luxury or food still taxed. We therefore find that while the imports of such goods as raw cotton were comparatively stationary from 1840 to 1848, and had not quite doubled between the years 1854 and 1874, such an article of comparative luxury as coffee has increased in import nearly threefold within little more than the same period. Of all raw produce for manufacturing purposes whose import has increased, wool stands pre-eminent, its import having grown from 46,000,000 lbs. in 1842—the lowest figure in the decade 1840 to 1849—to over 119,000,000 lbs. in 1853, and to 344,500,000 lbs. in 1874; but even in this instance it would be rash to say that the increase has kept pace with the growth of a demand for pure luxuries, because this greatly augmented import is due in some considerable degree to the special circumstance that our own Australian and South African colonies are amongst the chief wool-growing regions, and that they tend naturally to send all their wool here to market, regardless whether it is ultimately bought for home manufacture or not. There has hence been an increasing tendency of late years for this country to become a sort of emporium for raw wool for the rest of Europe, just as Europe has had in the past to come to us (and as formerly it had to go to Venice) for many products of the East, of which the possession of empire there, and of the great mercantile navy of the world, made us almost the sole important vendors. With wool this re-export has consequently been much more extensive than with cotton or any other staple, as is shown by the fact that in 1840 we only re-exported 1,000,000 lbs. or so of foreign and colonial wool, whereas in 1874 we re-exported upwards of 144,000,000 lbs. The growth of a sort of middleman or brokerage trade in this article has been, moreover, steady and almost continuous; whereas in the case of cotton the fluctuations have been more frequent, and the progress less marked, continental Europe having, on the whole, more varied sources of supply for that article than for wool, and also a narrower manufacturing power.

Only one or two further characteristics of the imports account need be referred to here to show the spread of luxury amongst the people. The home consumption of such articles as tea has, like that of coffee, multiplied nearly five-fold in about thirty-five years, and the consumption of tobacco, wine, spirits, and various more or less expensive foreign products, has grown more rapidly than most of our branches of manufacturing industry. All this goes to prove both the enormous wealth of the nation and the distribution of that wealth over a widening class among the population.

I might pursue this investigation till it became unbearably wearisome; but enough has already been said to demonstrate the remarkable advancement of the nation in wealth and prosperity, and its increased and increasing command of the luxuries produced abroad in return for its toil and enterprise, for the riches it has found in the bowels of the earth, and the mechanical skill with which those riches have been turned to account.

As indicating the broad result we may say the total volume of the trade of England was, in 1873, 682,292,000*l*., of which 371,290,000*l*. were imports exclusive of bullion. This gives, per head of the population, an import of 11*l*. 11*s*. 2*d*., and an export of 7*l*. 18*s*. 10*d*. Since then the gross value has declined seriously on the export side of the account ; but the volume is still much larger than it was ten years ago, when the people in some places thought the country had reached the maximum of its prosperity. It is no wonder that in these circumstances the gross value of property and profits assessed in the United Kingdom has nearly doubled since 1854, the first year in which Ireland paid income tax.

The prosperity of this country rests, therefore, in one view of it at least, on a most solid foundation. What we have made is in the main our own, not borrowed. We have dug in the ground, and laboured in the workshop and the field, all the land through ; we have ploughed the sea with our ships and steamers with such success that all the markets of the world have been more or less opened to us. After all, we have no greater witness of our position as a trading nation than that afforded by our shipping. The total tonnage of British vessels entered and cleared with cargoes at home ports from and to the colonies and foreign nations has risen from 5,200,000 tons in 1840, to 39,000,000 tons in 1874 ; and such is the increase in our steamship business that its gross tonnage entered and cleared has risen in the same period from 663,000 tons to about 19,500,000 tons. In 1840 we had only 9,610 vessels engaged in the coasting and ocean trade, with a capacity of 720,000 tons. By 1874 that total had risen to 20,900 vessels, of an aggregate capacity of 5,900,000 tons, giving employment to nearly 204,000 men. These are startling figures, and need no embellishment. In all ways, therefore, there has been an unprecedented increase of the material wealth and resources of the country, such as, looked at by itself, leads us clearly to the inference that the present trade depression is, so far as we alone are concerned, merely an ebb of the tide. The material resources of this country are indeed capable of almost indefinite further expansion.

There are, as I have said, aspects of this question outside ourselves, however, which require the most careful scrutiny before we can commit ourselves to an opinion as to whether this indefinite expansion is likely to go on or not, nay before we can be sure that a much greater depth of depression will not be reached than now exists. We have not merely to ascertain that we have ourselves been working and growing year by year richer with unprecedented rapidity; but must also know how it has fared with our principal foreign customers, on whom, after all, our ultimate prosperity must depend. There have been frequent occasions in the short history of our modern progress when we have overrun our available resources at home, and have had to pull up short, to the grievous loss of many and the temporary disarrangement of business generally, but the great foreign demands on us have hitherto prevented these lapses from producing any very serious effect. After a few months everything has gone on as before, or faster than before. But the present trade depression leads us to the inference that the real source of it lies this time outside ourselves. For the first time almost since the new order of physical progress came to the fore, there has been a stoppage of foreign demand; not a mere temporary home check to business, the result of what is usually called over-supply and inflation. We had in 1875 some very remarkable trade failures in this country, it is true, over which business people moralised and shook their heads not a little; but compared with the great collapses of the past, they were, after all, insignificant. And the peculiarity of them was that hardly any of them touched the general public, or broke credit so severely as to cause the more acute symptoms of a panic. When Overend and Gurney's doors were found closed on Black Friday in 1866 the world, as it were, stood still; but there was no such standing still in 1875. The banks on whom the losses of the large and disgraceful failures chiefly fell were rich enough to stand the shock without flinching, and could have continued their accommodation to traders without perceptible stint, if traders had so desired. Notwithstanding all this, trade has kept falling away in a manner never known before to the same extent after any of the acute forms of modern panic. Whole classes in the country have suffered a gradual diminution in their available resources. There has been a shrinkage in the prices of leading staples which has beggared many and compelled numbers either to suspend business or face ruin. Loss upon loss has fallen on the thrifty, or apparently thrifty classes, through failures on the part of foreign borrowers, until the whole framework of credit within which our business has been conducted is strained in sustaining a dead weight that the long depression has laid upon it. Gradually this quiet kind of liquidation, this silent hidden impoverishment, has been progressing amongst us, until, as a banker one day said to me, it is impossible to tell who is solvent. Stocks of goods accumulate at business centres, production is curtailed, prices have fallen almost without pause, and money has become almost useless to the bankers in the legitimate walks of trade, yet relief comes not. On the contrary, fear and distress gather as it were to a head, and shrewd observers look for a settling-down of values to their true level which shall yet shake the nation to its very centre. Granting that the ruthless butchery now desolating one of the fairest lands in Europe has come as a paralysing force on the possibly reviving energies of the world, that is not enough to account for the state this country is in now. The world is wide, and our trade is wide as the world. Had there been wealth and energy enough elsewhere to work and produce, there would have been revived trade in some quarters and revived life here before now.

This slow wasting away is something that neither wars nor all the trade failures nor the bad harvests will account for, and we must search for the true causes in the general condition of nations. This is the inquiry which I propose to institute, and nothing need be said here further than that I believe there is abundant evidence to prove that the source of the decay in business lies in a degree not yet determined outside ourselves. We have no longer the unlimited markets for some of our products that we had formerly. Progress appears to have reached for the time its limit, if by progress we mean the increased production of English mines, English looms and lathes, in response to the renewed and swelling demands of foreign nations. An attentive study of the phenomena leading to and attending the present trade depression will, I imagine, show us that the stagnation the country now suffers from is a natural reaction from the former inflation, indeed, but also a wider reaction than any that has hitherto visited us, and one much more difficult to overcome. We may get out of this depression with undiminished prestige; but we can hardly get out of it soon, because every other country is now more or less involved in it, and it is just possible that when we do escape, the trade position of this country towards other countries may be in some ways decidedly altered. There may be perhaps greater competition, especially if our one preeminent power over customers ceases to operate—our lending power. This in the past has played a striking part in our advancement and in that of other countries, but will it be resumed and continue?

I propose, in order to answer this and other questions, to investigate with a certain detail the present position of those foreign countries that have been, and are, our customers and debtors; and therefore only remark here, in a preliminary and general way, that the great source of existing bad business appears to lie in the fact that we have conducted our foreign trade for the past generation on a widely-extended system of credit. By that I do not mean ordinary credit as between buyer and seller, but as between this nation in its collective capacity and foreign nations. With the exception of, perhaps, France, Belgium, and Holland, and, to a less extent, Germany, no foreign country has had in itself resources sufficient to buy and pay for the commodities that we have sold to them so freely. In order to do the prodigious business which we have done for the past thirty years, we had therefore to lend these nations the means to pay for our manufactures; and we have gone on, as a country, lending to other countries and for the benefit of particular classes of our traders and manufacturers with such an ever-increasing profusion as we grew wealthier, that we have ended by getting nearly all the world pretty well over head and ears in our debt. Hence it is not the failure of home traders like the fraudulent Collie, or the foolishly extravagant troop that followed in his wake, that causes our trade to languish just now; but the exhaustion and bankruptcy of nations—a bankruptcy of which we have not yet seen either the extent or the fruits as I fear we shall see them. It is not either by the mere failure of Turkey, Peru, and Egypt, or by the laying bare of such swindles as those of Paraguay and Honduras, that the mischief has been done; for these exercised, taken altogether, but a very minute influence on the huge volume of our business. The evil is far more widespread; and it therefore becomes a question of the deepest importance to ascertain what our real prospects are, and where we stand. How are those nations that have not yet failed, but which are heavily our debtors, likely to bear the strain of being flung upon their own resources should our credits to them cease? Are they poorer or richer to-day by all that we have lent to them and sold them? If poorer, what branches of our trade will, by their poverty, be most seriously and most permanently affected? and what prospects have we of new markets to take the place of the old, should they at no distant date have still further to contract their operations? Or if they are richer, have we in our haste to be inordinately rich put into their hands the means of vanquishing us in their own and other markets when a depression, which we shall assume to be temporary, has died away? These and hosts of other questions bristle round this subject. Readers will see at once that, as our trade is international, so it will require something like an international investigation to determine its soundness or otherwise, and its prospects in the near future. An investigation of that kind I cannot profess to undertake thoroughly; but in the chapters which are to follow I hope to contribute something towards a just appreciation of the position of affairs, and to help the formation of a sound judgment upon them by such facts and considerations as appear to me relevant to the subject.

CHAPTER II.

THE ECONOMIC POSITION OF INDIA.

It might form an interesting sequel to the previous chapter to endeavour to trace, *pari passu*, the growth of our trade and the expansion of British lending. Unfortunately we should thereby, after all, gain but a fragmentary view of the several foreign nations and dependencies to which we have lent. Our trade with them is not all the trade that they do; and however great a part the money we have given some of them may have played in expanding our business of late years, it cannot be taken as by itself sufficient to determine the vital expansive power in those countries. Our object is rather to find out what solid basis there may be in the past development of the leading nations that form England's customers, which would warrant us in supposing that the prosperity, say, of the past quarter of a century is to continue unabated. I must try to indicate, therefore, not merely the permanent trade capacities of such countries, but the accidental causes which may now be working for or against a further development, whether of their entire trade or of their trade with this country only.

I shall therefore proceed to offer some observations on the position of our more prominent customers, and I propose to begin with India for several reasons. In the first place India is, for certain classes of cotton fabrics, by far the largest customer we have; and secondly, it is the one country with a large trade, the development of which has been entirely in our own grasp. We can trace in it, therefore, without very much difficulty, the precise consequences of the forcing process which scientific discovery has made the fashion all over the world, and of which we have been the most strenuous advocates. Add to these considerations the fact that India has of late been very prominently before many people in this country through the 'silver question' and 'depreciation in exchange' controversies, and through its disastrous ever-recurring famines, without its true position, financially or economically, being well understood, and we have found more reasons than were necessary to justify the selection of this as the first country to be dealt with. England has had in India an unresisting industrious population of nearly 200,000,000 to work her will upon, and what has she done with it?

In no country, except perhaps the United States, has the modern doctrine that railways, telegraphs, and all scientific improvements, were the only roads to speedy wealth, had more unrestrained play than in India. Ever since the time of Lord Dalhousie the motto of the English rulers of the country has been 'material progress at any cost;' the development of the empire by means of railways, canals, irrigation works, model farms, telegraphs, and roads. High pressure has thus been put on wherever we directly ruled, and the Residents at the dependent native courts have in many cases carried the stimulus of this new spirit into the councils of the petty rulers whose hands they were deputed to guide. As a result of this, in less than twenty-five years India has been covered with a network of railways, which now reaches upwards of 6,500 miles, and a closer network of telegraph wires extending to some 35,000 miles, the whole representing an outlay of over 120,000,000*l*. The large sum of 17,000,000*l*. has been sunk within a very short period in irrigation works on the Indus, the Sutlej, and on the Upper Ganges, in Orissa, and at the mouths of the Godaveri and Krishna rivers, besides lesser works in the Bombay Presidency and in the Deccan. This sum is, I believe, also exclusive of outlays under the old East India Company never taken note of, and of some at least of the indemnifications paid to bankrupt private companies. While this has been going on, attention has also been given to the improvement of the agriculture of the country, to forestry, and to the introduction of new inventions, or new plants for cultivation, on all of which considerable sums have been spent by the Government. The intention of most of these works has undoubtedly been on the whole good. Military considerations probably had a good deal to do with the rapid railway building that went on after the Indian Mutiny was suppressed, and the directions taken by such lines as the Scinde, Punjaub, and Delhi, the Indus Valley, and several smaller undertakings, were given them for strategic reasons; while much of the telegraph communication established was admittedly for Government purposes. But with these deductions, one main object of the Government was, no doubt sincerely enough, the good of the people. It was hoped that a great outburst of wealth would follow the introduction of the iron roads, and that India would soon stand forward as the richest country in Asia, one well able to bear all the burdens laid upon her by her forced material revolution. She was, in short, to be 'developed' precisely as England has been Nothing could well be more instructive, therefore, than a study of the lessons of this artificial development.

It must, I fear, be admitted that the expectations which Indian officials have been accustomed to indulge in about the good they were effecting have been only moderately fulfilled. A great deal of the work on which so much money has been spent has proved so far almost completely devoid of profitable results. No distinct profit has accrued to either population or Government from most of the irrigation works begun in undeniable good faith as helps to the people, but indiscreetly expanded by officials who did not know sufficiently what they were about. There are also in connection with some of them singular instances of transactions very like jobbery. A company, for instance, called the East India Irrigation Company, tried to construct the Orissa works, and to make them pay, but failed, and the Government bought them up at a cost of over a million sterling, and it is calculated that about 2,600,000*l*. will be required altogether to complete these canals, which, when made, will not pay their maintenance expenses. The Orissa people do not care for irrigation, and will not pay for it.[1] The history of the Madras Irrigation and Canal Company is another instance too notorious to need detailing, and we merely call to mind the fact that the Government has to pay interest on some 1,600,000*l*. of capital guaranteed by it, and that the works constructed with the money are maintained at a dead loss. In other places, such as the Upper Ganges and the Sutlej Valley, matters have not been so bad. The water is more appreciated and the people seem better able to pay for it, so that some of the works yield a small net percentage on the capital outlay. As a whole, however, the irrigation works of the Indian Government are not prosperous,

[1] *Moral and Material Progress of India*, 1874, pp. 68, 69.

and do not yield in a direct or indirect form half the interest on their capital. So experienced an official as Sir John Strachey may be trusted on this point. In his admirable Budget speech, on introducing the financial estimates for 1877–78 last March, he gives the following summary of the results in some prominent instances :—

'The total capital outlay on Irrigation works in Lower Bengal up to the end of 1875–76 was 4,072,742*l.*; and not less than 1,494,000 *l.* will be required to complete the works that are in progress: the gross income from these works in 1875–76 was 23,043*l.*, and the working expenses were 52,249*l.*; there was a dead loss on the year's operations, independently of interest on borrowed capital, of 29,906*l.*; the net loss in interest and working expenses during the year was 203,700*l.*; and the total accumulated loss up to March 31, 1876, was 878,100*l.*

'The Orissa and Midnapore projects had cost, up to March 31, 1876, 2,482,039*l.*; and are so far completed that water for irrigation on a large scale has been obtainable for several years past: in 1875–76, these canals yielded an income of 17,953*l.*, while the working expenses were 41,406*l.*: including interest, the net loss on these canals was 122,567*l.*, and the total loss up to March 31, 1876, was 666,131*l.* The further works which it is proposed to undertake in Orissa will cost about 368,000*l.* more ; and no one, I believe, pretends that, within any time which can now be foreseen, there is the remotest chance, if things are left as they are, that we shall get any adequate return from this great expenditure.

'The Sône Canals in Northern Bengal had cost, to the end of 1875-76, 1,521,366*l*.; and more than 1,185,000*l*. will be required to complete them: they will be in the highest degree beneficial; but I am confident that there is not, under the present system, any probability that they will, for many years to come, pay the interest on the capital outlay: the income in 1875-76 was 5,090*l*., and the working expenses were 11,543*l*. I do not lay stress on these figures, because the works are not finished; but it is a curious and most significant comment on them to be told, as we have been on the highest official authority, that the value of the crops saved by these unfinished canals in the single year of drought 1873-74, was estimated at 480,000*l*.

'The lowest sum at which it is possible to estimate the capital outlay in Bengal on canals and local railways now in operation or in progress, exceeds 8,000,000*l*. After expending 4,072,742*l*. on canals, there was, as just shown, a dead loss to the Imperial revenues in the year 1875-76 of 203,700*l*. I do not wish to speculate on the results that would probably be obtained under the existing system when the total expenditure reached 8,000,000*l*.; but the prospect could hardly be more unsatisfactory; and in spite of all this, the works themselves are most useful and beneficial to Bengal.

'I might give similar, although less extravagant, examples from the works in other provinces; but I think that enough has been said to show that there must be something radically unsound in our existing policy.'[1]

These are very explicit and startling figures, and it is no wonder that Sir John questions the wisdom of the policy which has led to the results they indicate. These irrigation works, which entail an annual money loss on their mere maintenance, do not in some cases return any indirect benefit to the revenue in the shape of increased land revenue, and I fear are equally barren of good results as regards the people. The capital spent upon them is therefore a dead charge on the revenues of India in most instances, and I cannot see how this state of things is to be remedied. The imposition of a local water rate, which is now to be tried, will only add to the miseries of the people.

The case of the railways is at first sight not so bad. Some of them are, as I have said, not constructed with a view to pay. Like the barracks of the troops, on which India has been compelled to spend nearly as much as on irrigation works, they are part of the means necessary to enable us to keep the empire well in hand. Part of them have been built, however, with a distinct

[1] *Gazette of India Extraordinary*, March 15, 1877, p. 26.

trade object, and as all are expected to be of some use to traders I may fairly assume that the whole are monuments of a progressive age, of English ideas as to the best mode of making the best of the country. All of them, at any rate, have been severe burdens on the finances, and in this view ought to find justification in the results attained. Either the general trade of the country must be greatly enlarged and its wealth or revenues greatly increased, or the policy in this instance must also be mistaken. A study of the growth of Indian debt would by itself certainly lead to the latter inference, for it has increased in recent years at a most appalling pace. Mr. Smollett pointed out lately in the House of Commons that between deficits and excessive outlays on public works, the debt of India will have increased within the seven years ending next March by over 43,000,000*l*. This is probably an under estimate, since the outlay on the Madras famine may not unlikely exceed considerably the amount provided. But taking it as exact, this is surely a startling fact, and the worst of it is that this is by no means an isolated experience. Deficits, borrowings, famines, and extravagance have been so long the rule in India that the debt may be said to have been piling up in this fashion, with but few pauses, ever since we had anything to do with the country. The giant strides have been made, however, since it came under the direct control of the Crown, and before passing any judgment we must look both at the way the debt has grown and at the capacities shown by the country to respond to the temporary stimulus which the contraction of debt always gives.

The total debt, exclusive of the then small guaranteed railway capital, was only 59,500,000*l.* in 1858, when the Crown succeeded to the inheritance of the defunct East India Company, and ten years before it was only 49,000,000*l.*, big enough for the wealth of our dominions. The present amount of the debt in all forms is as near as possible 234,000,000*l.*, including the money raised in England and India during the current financial year. The charge for interest on this debt, funded and floating, and including the interest due under railway guarantees, is now over 11,000,000*l.* Ten years ago the total charge was a little over 6,000,000*l.* In 1858 it was only 2,500,000*l.*; and at the beginning of Lord Dalhousie's administration in 1848 it was 2,300,000*l.* Of this enormously increased burden the railways and canals nominally meet about 3,700,000*l.*, and the rest has to come out of the augmented taxes of the empire. A mere enumeration of figures in this way would by itself convey very little meaning, however, to the reader, who might well say, 'All this is probably true enough, but if India can bear these increased charges through her generally increased prosperity, what harm have they done?'

That is just the point. Can India bear these increased charges with ease, or do they by their rapid growth indicate a pressure upon her resources which is fast making this vaunted 'progress' a curse to her population and an intense danger to the stability of British rule? The English have had full scope for all their ideas in that vast country, and have gone on with expenditure, year, by year with unbridled liberality, but what is it all leading to? We must examine the signs of true progress to be found in the general state of the country in order to see. Apparently the testimony borne by statistics is conclusive on the question. The revenues of India look at first sight enormously greater than they were before all this modern turmoil began —quite equal, we should be disposed to say, to the increased burdens laid thereby upon the population. The gross revenue was barely 21,000,000*l.* in 1838, barely 25,000,000*l.* in 1848, had only risen to 31,700,000*l.* in 1858, and is now about 50,000,000*l.* That is a great stride in advance, and would seem to show that the country has benefited to a much greater degree by all that has been done for it than the mere yield of public works indicates. A closer look, however, enables us to see that this by no means altogether follows, for a considerable portion of the increase is due not so much to increased productiveness of the country now in our possession as to the revenues of fresh States that have been absorbed by the dominant authority, and to the fiscal development produced by frequent revisions of taxes. Lord Dalhousie, for example, brought under direct British sway, either by conquest, coercion, or diplomatic manœuvring, the rich province of Lower Burmah, the valuable territory of the Berars belonging to the Nizam of Hyderabad, the rich kingdom of Oude, and the fine corn-growing Punjaub, besides lesser territories like Nagpore, Sattara, and Jansi, all of which his successors have been busily working up almost ever since. Every now and then India has thus been blessed, or otherwise, with a fighting Viceroy, who has made it his boast and glory to effect such annexations and appropriations; and in order to understand what India has really gained in revenue by the improvements of recent years we must make considerable allowance for their yield. Let us begin then at Lord Dalhousie's day. He found the Punjaub half conquered when he landed in India in 1848, and played the part of a second Warren Hastings in his conquest of that and other territories. The gross revenue was then, as we have seen, under 25,000,000*l*., about half what it is now. But the provinces and States we have enumerated above, and which Lord Dalhousie added to British dominions within a few years, themselves account for more than 14,000,000*l*. of the subsequent increase, taking last year's return as a basis of comparison. The exact figures I cannot give, because territories are mixed and to some extent re-shuffled since 1848, but I believe this to be a moderate estimate. This leaves us about 11,000,000*l*., therefore, as the increase upon the revenues of the old provinces of the British dominions, and even this is partly gathered from the resources of a much extended empire. It also is subject to several further important deductions. There is, for example, a great increase in the interval between 1848 and now in the returns from opium, which cannot fairly be called an increment of Indian revenue at all. The opium revenue is derived from China just as much as if we levied the duty on it in Chinese custom-houses and put it in our own pockets. We had put a fancy price on opium when it was still a contraband article in China, in order to obtain from it the income which China by making the drug contraband had virtually refused; and when we forced the legalisation of the traffic in 1862, we took care to compel the Chinese to levy a duty low enough to enable us still to secure for our Indian revenue the larger part of this profit. What we lost in price by their duty, we more than gained by the extended consumption which the last war with China enabled us to secure for the drug through the new ports opened to English trade, and consequently the opium revenue has increased and has been maintained at a high elevation in recent years after a quite astonishing fashion. For the year ended March 1875, it reached a gross amount of 8,557,000*l*., and in 1858–59 it was only 5,000,000*l*. to 6,000,000*l*. There is therefore an augmentation of fully 2,500,000*l*. gross under this head which is due solely to our greater hold over China. This is but one example, and another may be found in the augmented salt tax. By the extension of our territory, and the wider hold that it gave us over the salt-producing lakes of Rajpootana and the mines of the Punjaub, we have been able to establish a stricter customs line, and to control much more fully the contraband consumption of salt. Smuggling exists still, and must exist while we levy duties of such enormous weight in some provinces on one of the prime necessaries of human existence, but it does not exist now in the degree which formerly prevailed, and we may not unfairly ascribe a third of the increase which has taken place in recent years in the salt revenue to the action of this control. We have, in Madras and Bengal at least, both levied higher duties and exacted those duties more thoroughly, and it seems likely that a greater yield than ever will now be obtained from the salt traffic of the interior through the arrangements which have been made or are about to be made with the native States of Rajpootana. The power to levy taxes more effectually, however obtained, cannot in fairness be taken to indicate a growth in the prosperity and elasticity of the revenue due to the 'development' of the empire. Adding these items together, and after making all due allowances, we shall be near the truth in saying that the real increase in the revenue of India which we could ascribe *bonâ fide* to its materially increased prosperity, does not exceed some 5,000,000*l.* or 6,000,000*l.* in the past five-and-twenty years. I am disposed indeed to think that a close investigation would prove this to be a generous estimate, for there is another important consideration which Mr. Fawcett brought out in the observations he made in the House on Lord George Hamilton's last Budget speech. It was to the effect that the method of dealing with the gross amount of Indian revenue adopted by Indian officials is most misleading, inasmuch as it includes cost of collecting revenue. Unnecessarily extended territory and multiplied taxes induce a great increase in this cost when taxes merely are in view; but when we consider also that this 'gross' revenue includes many public works whose return is often more than balanced by the outlay, the delusiveness of the figures becomes enormous. Mr. Fawcett places the net income at 40,000,000*l.*, or nearly, and says that it has not increased in recent years at all, and in saying this he is, I think, quite within bounds. It is true that we must allow something for the natural increases in the revenues of such provinces as the Punjaub and Oude, which did not at first yield anything like what they do now, but we shall see better what these mean if we examine a little more particularly the chief item of revenue—that from land. No test of the wealth of the country could be so closely indicative of its true position and progress, if we except the province of Bengal where the permanent settlement made by Lord Clive no doubt interferes with the powers of the Government to put the screw on in proportion as it sees signs of more spare cowries in the hands of the peasantry. Bengal is, however, by no means exempt from 'improving' taxation, its low land revenue being cited as a justification for the imposition of local cesses and water rates on the poverty-stricken ryots, who besides gain nothing from the low land rent owing to the English blunder of turning the zemindars into proprietors. Everywhere else, except in Bengal, the land tax or Government rent is the barometer of progress.

I shall not go back beyond 1860, the date when Mr. James Wilson went out to put the finances of India in order after the Mutiny had been quelled, as I wish to have a period of almost fixed territory and unbroken repose to deal with. In that year we find that the gross yield of the land revenue was 18,757,000*l.*, and for the year ended March 31, 1875, it is put down at 21,296,000*l.*, an increase in fifteen years of only 2,539,000*l.*, or say 13 per cent., and obviously but a proportion of this increase can be claimed as due to the increased wealth of the population. Surveys have been made in many parts of the country, and a more close and rigorous system of assessment adopted, so as to obtain fuller revenues, and these must be credited with their fair share of the increase. Indian officials themselves admit this to be the case, and I do not wish to deny it, or that the area of cultivation has in some districts considerably extended, so that the Government has obtained more numerous land rents. This is of course inevitable, and is due more to the increase in population natural to a long peaceful administration than to the development of the resources of the country in the cant sense of the term. Indeed, I cannot find in the land revenues any trace at all of *native* development, meaning by that the growth of wealth and a wealthy class. Where Europeans have taken to growing tea, as in Assam, or the cinchona plant, as in Darjeeling, cotton, as in the Berars, or indigo, as in Tirhoot, there is no doubt a distinct development, but that it does not always nor often benefit the native population is proved by the frequent famines and by the revolt of the miserable indigo cultivators against the rapacity of the English planters some ten years ago. The revelations then made were a significant commentary on Indian progress, and worthy of the worst days of West India slavery. In the same way, when the Government grows or fosters the growth of opium, it reaps the profit, not the native ryot, and when Europeans grow cotton the 'development' and the wealth are still exotic, not native. So with land revenue; it indicates to some degree increased cultivation, not increased rent-paying capacity, but after all, that does not amount to much, as will be seen if we take averages instead of single years for comparison. Thus in the five years 1860 to 1864 the average gross land revenue was 19,365,000*l*., in the five years 1865 to 1869 the average was 19,924,000*l.*, and in the five years ended 1874, 20,955,000*l.* The average of the last five years is therefore only 1,590,000*l.* higher than for the first five, although in every district almost of any importance except Bengal there have been revisions of assessments. There can be no doubt either that these augmented assessments press very grievously on the mass of the people, so grievously that in not a few instances they have barely enough left to live upon, and may perish with the first breath of misfortune, if left unaided by the Government.

On this point I shall here present the testimony of two witnesses, one native and one foreign, who speak with some authority and experience. I shall begin with the latter, and give some extracts from a pamphlet on the Indian Budget of 1876–77, lately published by Mr. John Dacosta, an old and experienced Indian merchant, which deserve careful reading, especially as he quotes official statements and admissions singularly at variance with the rose-water views and assertions made by Lord George Hamilton when he introduced the estimates for that year :—

In the Bombay Presidency, the Revenue Commissioners' reports show that 10,880 acres of cultivated land in Surat, and 25,035 acres in Guzerat, were abandoned in 1872 and 1873; that, owing to a decrease in the cultivation, chiefly in the Kaira and Broach districts, there was a decrease in the revenue collected in the Northern Division in 1874, although an enhancement had been made in the rates; and that, while the unfavourable year 1871-2 was followed by two exceptionally propitious seasons, the depression of the people, as manifested by the relinquishment of their fields, had continued. A minute of the Government of Bombay records, about the same time, that 'the Government has read with much concern the opinion expressed by the Collector of Sholapore, as to the undue pressure of the revised rates, in consequence of which a large quantity of land has been put up for sale in default of revenue, much of which found no purchasers.' From Poonah, the official reports state not only that 'the amount of land revenue unrecovered was very considerable; but that, in order to realise the amount actually recovered, it was found necessary to sell up many occupancies.' Moreover, a memorial was addressed to the Governor-General last year by some three thousand landholders in the Bombay Presidency complaining that the enhanced demand upon them for land revenue was out of proportion with the productive value of the land; and that, owing to their inability to satisfy it, many had been deprived of their estates, cattle, and other movable property, while the ryots or cultivators were on the verge of starvation. In the North-West Provinces things are in an equally critical condition, and the revenue officers themselves have called the attention of the Government to the matter. The Commissioner of Allahabad, adverting to the administration of Futtehpore, remarked that the revenue or land tax was heavy in many parts; that the imposition of a ten per cent. cess fell heaviest on the villages which were least able to bear it; that many villages broke down, and many more were threatened with ruin. From the collector's report it appeared, moreover, that many zemindars or landholders who had failed to pay up the revenue were imprisoned; that their personal property had been sold, and that a large number of villages or estates had been attached for arrears of revenue.

The *Pioneer* (the organ of an important official section in India) remarked, about the same time, with reference to the Bundelkhund district, that, 'if speedy relief were not given, the entire social order would be in danger of dissolution; that the people were crushed by misfortunes, the landowners were hopelessly involved in debt, the population was diminishing, the land was going out of cultivation, and the cattle and farm stock were deteriorating.' Mr. Halsey, the collector of Cawnpore, in his pamphlet on the settlement of that district, says that the margin left for the cultivator's subsistence is less than the value of the labour he has expended on the land, and describes the condition of the people in the following words: 'The district has the benefit of water communication by both the Ganges and the Jumna; it is intersected by the East Indian Railway, and is partly traversed by the Ganges Canal; yet the land is only worth five years' purchase, and the state of the average cultivator is one of hopeless insolvency and misery.'

The Lieutenant-Governor of the North-Western Provinces states, moreover, in his administration report, published in 1873, that while travelling he was forcibly struck by the wretched condition of the Lullutpore district; and goes on to mention that 'many estates had been so depopulated and so much land had fallen out of cultivation, that the assessment, previously moderate, had become very severe.' The difficulty of collecting the land revenue in those provinces was shown in the same report by the number of cases in which coercive measures had to be taken. The *dustuks* or summonses issued for the recovery of the land revenue amounted—

In 1868–69 to 81,891
   1869–70 ,, 98,885
   1870–71 ,, 101,146

The difficulties of the zemindars led them to press their ryots, and a considerable increase ensued in the number of suits between landlords and tenants, as the following figures, taken from the same report, will show:

>In 1869–70 . . 53,331
>1870–71 . . 60,405

Some of the revenue officers reported on the baneful 'effect of such suits in setting class against class;' and the Lieutenant-Governor recorded the following significant remark in his official report: 'The antagonism of classes whose interests lie so closely together, and *who have hitherto been connected by so kindly a bond,* is one of the greatest political dangers of the day.'

That is a remarkable statement, and, were we to take it as only partially true, one that cannot do other than modify popular notions of the wealth of India. The inevitable conclusion is that the masses in India lie in poverty-stricken helplessness, and that they have as yet reaped no direct benefit from the taxes they pay. Still more striking and emphatic on this point is the second testimony which I have promised to cite, that of Mr. Dadabhai Naoroji. He read some papers at Bombay last year on the poverty of India, in which some very striking figures are adduced to show that the masses of the population live absolutely on the verge of destitution. The sum of this testimony is that the total yield of the land from all sources, the produce of mines, the annual value of manufactures, is only an average of 40s. per head for the entire population of British India. This is, to be sure, only an estimate, but the statistics cited by Mr. Naoroji in support of his total seem to be reasonably satisfactory. As regards the products of agricultural land alone, the following table and observations may be given in the form in which he has drawn them up.

Provinces	Value of the Produce of Cultivated Land	Population	Produce per Head
	£		Rs.
Central	16,000,000	9,000,000	18
Punjab	36,000,000	17,500,000	21
North-West	40,000,000	30,000,000	14
Bengal	96,000,000	67,000,000	15
Madras	36,000,000	26,500,000	14
Bombay	40,000,000	11,000,000	36
Oude	13,000,000	9,500,000	14
Total	277,000,000	170,500,000	

Such is the produce of India in a year of good harvests, in which any second crops will be fully included. I have not taken the produce of grazing-land or straw or kurby, though the cattle required for cultivation and stock need not only all these grazing-lands, but also a portion of the produce of the cultivated land, such as some grains, fodder, and other produce. From the above total of 277,000,000*l.* it is necessary to deduct for seed for next year, say, only 6 per cent., that is, allowing sixteenfold for produce of land. The balance will be about 260,000,000*l.*, as the produce of cultivation, during a good season, for human use and consumption for a year. If the Government of India would calculate this production correctly, it would find the total a good deal under the above figures.[1]

Mr. Naoroji complains with great justice of the

[1] *The Poverty of India*, a paper read before the Bombay Branch of the East India Association on February 23, 1876, by Dadabhai Naoroji, p. 21.

extreme looseness of nearly all Indian official statistics. It is one of the most difficult things in the world to find an intelligible meaning in them, and inferences from such figures as are to be had about the yield of agricultural land can only be made with hesitation. Still from what can be gathered as to the ruling price of food grains in various districts, the rate of wages, and the known yield of crops in certain instances, a fairly accurate deduction may be made. I am disposed on the whole to think that Mr. Naoroji has erred on the safe side. If so, it is easy to comprehend how small the tax-paying power of the Indian people must be. It cannot be measured by any European standard of which we have cognizance. At least 150,000,000 of people must live from hand to mouth, quite unable to save means for days of adversity, sure to be instantly brought to starvation when the harvest happens to be bad. Does not such a statement as this make plain to us one of the chief causes which make famines now so constantly recurrent in India and so disastrous, or need we wonder that an authority like Sir John Strachey should declare that they must not be treated as abnormal accidents in Indian affairs? Is it in the least astonishing either that taxes cannot be increased in amount, or that the land revenue now levied in Madras and Bombay entails great misery on the population? To take 21,000,000*l.* of hard cash from a rural population whose total crops do not represent much more than 260,000,000*l.* at the outside, is surely not a promising task. The slightest increase in an assessment may mean and does mean abject misery, and I think, therefore, that at all points I am justified in maintaining that the land revenues of India have grown more by the extended area over which they are levied than by the free yield of augmented rates. In the four years 1874 to 1877 the Government will have given back at least 15,000,000*l.* to the people in the shape of famine relief, and, large as that sum is, it by no means measures the excessive pressure of this tax in many districts. If the testimony of the land revenue is thus unequivocal as to the real progress of the people of India in wealth, that of other branches of revenue is equally so, though not exactly in the same way. The salt taxes, for example, may increase in yield through the wider area of their application and their stricter levy, but they certainly have not done so through the greater ability of the people to pay them. This year's yield is now more than double what it was in 1860, yet in some parts of the empire the consumption is less now than it was before taxation was so high. In Madras, for example, where, according to the laborious official compilation already quoted,[1] 'the revenue has been increased by raising the price,

---

[1] *Moral and Material Progress and Condition of India*, 1874, p. 8.

the increase of profit was considerably less than the degree in which the tax was augmented, and the sales have actually diminished.' In Bengal the same thing has, I believe, been going on. Mr. Dacosta says: 'A ton of Cheshire salt, which the people of England may buy for 10s., pays 8l. 17s. 3d. of duty before it is admitted into Bengal, and with freight and other charges costs 10l. 10s. to the people of the country. At this cruelly high price the consumption is much restricted. No salt is used in agriculture, the cattle are stinted of this invaluable condiment, and the poor along the sea-coast use salt earth scraped from swamps washed by the sea, while in inland districts the scrapings of saltpetre pans are what thousands of families are reduced to consume. Much disease is said to be engendered by the scarcity of pure salt, and the trade in salt fish, which might supply a cheap and abundant article of food, is hampered by the high duty.'[1] Lord George Hamilton, in his speech on the Budget of 1876-77, sneered at Mr. Dacosta's pamphlet as 'aboriginal,' or something of that kind equally pertinent, but he had no other answer to the facts thus advanced, and Sir John Strachey admits their truth in his speech already cited, though unable to suggest a present remedy. There is, I very much doubt, no denying them, and these salt duties thus give a fair enough idea of the degree

[1] *The Indian Budget for* 1876, pp. 13, 14.

to which the Indian Government is pressed for means, as well as of the misery which must prevail in the country when this prime necessary of life is the only indigenous source of revenue which can be drawn upon by the pressure of more stringent fiscal regulations and higher taxes. The increase in the yield from drink is as nothing in comparison. Excise and forestry receipts are taken together in the 'statistical abstracts,' and they have barely increased at all since 1869. Close comparisons throughout the sixteen years under review are, however, not possible because of the shiftings which taxes underwent in the earlier period. Customs form another branch of revenue which has been almost stationary for six or seven years, which has not increased indeed, to any perceptible degree since 1862, when sundry remissions and readjustments came into force, and that too in spite of the number of necessaries on which duty is levied. Almost the same may be said of stamps, which do not yield 400,000*l.* more now than they did in 1869, and only about 1,100,000*l.* more than in 1862, although many devices have been used to force the revenue up. Every item of revenue of any importance therefore indicates that the Government is working at the highest possible pressure. No more taxes can be imposed; there is in the country urgent economic necessity that not a few should be remitted or reduced.

Notwithstanding readjustments of land cesses, additional percentages on salt dues, and the adoption of every conceivable expedient, the gross revenue of India has been practically almost stationary since 1868. It was then 48,534,000*l.*, and has never been higher than 51,414,000*l.*, while for 1876–77 the regular estimate places it at only 50,570,000*l.* Sir John Strachey expects to realise 52,000,000*l.* in the present year, taking the rupee at the conventional 2*s.*, but I fear the result will not come up to expectation, for the yield of the land tax in Madras and Bombay must be seriously affected by the famine.

While this is so, the liabilities of the country have been growing at a tremendous pace. If we strip away the meaningless and misleading distinction between 'ordinary' and 'extraordinary' budgets, we shall see better what the real state of the account is since 1868. That distinction ought never to have been made in the manner it has been, because the Government of India cannot treat its accounts like a railway company, and what it calls reproductive expenditure on capital account is and can be no such thing in ninety-nine cases out of the hundred, as the term is usually understood. When such items as the famine outlay get classed in this extraordinary account, the absurdity of it becomes apparent at once and is not lessened by the balance-sheets of the canals or State railways.

In the last four years, owing to the famines, the deficit has been much above the average since 1863. For the three years ending in March next it is estimated at about 13,000,000*l*., and will probably be a great deal more, the Government having borrowed upwards of 8,000,000*l*. this year already, while the 'regular estimate' deficit for 1876-77 is placed at upwards of 6,000,000*l*., the Bengal famine having cost 1,600,000*l*. more than was estimated. Now, independent altogether of the size of the deficit, there is something alarming in the fact that there is a deficiency at all, and that it is normal in spite of the great pressure which the financial system inaugurated partly by Mr. Wilson has brought to bear on the population. Instead of abolishing these deficits by an addition of about 11,000,000*l*. to the gross revenue since his day, they are only occasionally reduced, and the prospect of their continuance for an indefinite period appears to be calmly if not flippantly contemplated by the home authorities, because they are so enamoured of those magic words 'reproductive expenditure.' The term is utterly delusive, and no prudent financier would think of lugging the vague credit 'indirect benefit' into his accounts. Capital cannot by any possibility be wisely spent in this free-handed style for indirect results.

This objection cannot, as I have said, be made in one sense against all the railways, but yet the annual charge which they lay on the revenues of the country shows that they have been pushed on far ahead of its rate of development, and that as a consequence of that they have probably retarded progress as much as they have helped it. The most enlightened Indian administrators may be said to have almost admitted this. Sir John Strachey, for example, asserts that many of the State railways are not expected to pay at all. The only great lines which are now paying with some steadiness all their charges and more out of revenue are the East Indian, the Great Indian Peninsular, and the Eastern Bengal. But when we come to analyse this apparent soundness, we find that a considerable part of it is due to the Government business done, for which Government pays out of the taxes, and to such accidents as the Bengal famine. We find, for example, that their net earnings from the Delhi assemblage last year were 90,000*l*.; and the Bengal famine may be said to have almost alone enabled the East Indian line to pay an excess on the guaranteed dividend in 1874–75. There is of course a certain general development of trade. The number of passengers carried by all the lines has doubled since 1865, and the weight of goods also, but then so has the mileage of the lines. But there has not been that rapid progression which people expected who reasoned from the experience of countries like our own, or like France and Belgium.

Hence up to the end of 1875 the net amount paid by the Government as interest under guarantees to the several private railway companies was nearly 26,000,000*l*., a sum that ought in strict book-keeping to be added to their capital expenditure. For the five years 1869 to 1873 it averaged 1,551,000*l*. per annum, and was practically the same at the end of the period as at the beginning, notwithstanding that about 1,000 additional miles of cheaply made lines had been opened from which much was expected as 'feeders.'[1] Since 1873 there have been better returns, and Lord George Hamilton last year announced to the House that for 1876–77 the deficiency on the guaranteed railway interest would be reduced to 1,260,000*l*., or nearly 900,000*l*. less than in 1872–73. For the current year it is expected that there will be a check given to this reduction owing to the money ceasing to come in from special windfalls of traffic such as arose last year from the burlesque at Delhi. Altogether the increase of the last three years has been due to adventitious causes of this kind, and very little of it to the development of permanent traffic. Mr. Juland Danvers states, for instance, that the East Indian, Eastern Bengal, and Punjaub and Delhi Railways carried 913,000 tons less grain in 1875 than in 1874, when the Bengal famine caused a large demand. Thus the great prosperity of these lines was due entirely in 1874 to the

[1] Mr. Juland Danvers' report on Indian Railways for 1873.

Government freights; and the Government in fact first paid away in freights to the companies money which it had borrowed, and when the latter showed a large profit made by such payments, called it the result of satisfactory progress in the trade of the empire. At present the most reasonable inference would be that the trade could not support the inflated level of two years ago; and we fear it cannot be denied that the guaranteed railways of India must continue to cost the Government a good many millions before they are all independent, and no one can tell when in the distant future they will return to the Government all the money thus drawn from the general taxation for their maintenance. The principle of their construction was indeed a vicious and ruinous one, as is proved by the statement of Lord George Hamilton in 1876. He said that the Government was able to construct the State railways at a cost of 4,300*l.* per mile without the Agra bridge at Rajpootana, and 5,600*l.* per mile with it, whereas the private guaranteed railways had cost 10,000*l.* per mile. And Mr. Danvers (Government Director of Railways) says in his report for 1875-76 that the estimated cost of constructing the State lines now projected is little over 5,000*l.* per mile. Part of this excessive difference may be set down of course to the broader gauge of the guaranteed lines, but that by no means accounts for it all, and the broad gauge was itself a piece of wanton extravagance. A good half at least is due to bad engineering and reckless extravagance and jobbery, under shelter of the Government guarantees. And it is partly because these railways have been so preposterously dear in proportion to the state of the country and population that they have cost and will continue to cost the State so much money under the indiscreetly given guarantees. While they do so they must be considered almost as much retardant of general prosperity and development as the reverse.[1] We cannot tell, indeed, what the real position of the country is toward these railways. An account of how much the Government pays to the companies every year for the carriage of troops, stores, officials, and material for the State lines, would enable us to see more clearly how far they are really resting on the developed resources of the country. All we can at present say is that in the second half of 1875 the East Indian Railway gross traffic receipts were less by about 35,000*l.* than for the corresponding half of 1874, and that, although passenger receipts were increasing, those from merchandise had been falling off steadily for three half-years. This is the principal railway of India, and might be taken as a test but for the

---

[1] It is significant of the poverty of the Indian population, and by consequence of the folly of burdening them with means of communication too costly even for most parts of the United States, that the average rate received for carrying a passenger one mile on the East Indian Company's system is considerably under $\frac{1}{3}d$. This too in spite of the enormous proportion of high-fare Government and European traffic which the annual flight to Simla of itself entails. The exact figures will be found in Mr. Juland Danvers' report for 1875-6, p. 33.

enormous Government business that it does. It is fair to say also that the Great Indian Peninsular showed for the last half of 1875 an increase, but it was owing chiefly to the passage of the Prince of Wales and his retinue over the line; and this line is also usually upheld to no small extent by the movement of Government officials or the Government goods traffic. The Madras Railway, on the other hand, barely maintained its position, and the Eastern Bengal receipts showed a considerable falling off in the last half of 1874, though they were higher in the first half of 1875. We need not pursue this point further. I have said enough to demonstrate that the railways, like the canals, are still a burden on the State and likely to continue so, and that calling the expenditure on them reproductive is therefore talking nonsense. They do not altogether, and allowing for every adventitious aid, yield more than $3\frac{3}{4}$ per cent. on their capital, much of which is guaranteed 5 per cent. by the Government. But even these figures do not represent the actual Government loss, owing to the fact that those lines which earn an excess on the guaranteed interest obtain half the money for distribution among their shareholders. The amount of such excess came to 1,776,457*l.* for the whole of the year 1875, of which more than 1,500,000*l.* was earned by the East Indian Company mainly from Government business, and from the savings due to its low rate of working expenses. I think enough has been said then to show that the traffic of the Indian railways bears little testimony to the increased wealth of the natives of India.

There is just one other observation, however, which may appropriately be made here. It relates to the direct influence of the railways in producing famines. It is, I fear, beyond question that the construction, maintenance, and working of all these lines has induced an enormous consumption of Indian timber. Not only is there a large annual demand for wood for sleepers, very little of which is met by imports from abroad, but the great difficulty in obtaining coal on all lines, even till lately on the East Indian, has caused much timber to be used as fuel. The forests of India have therefore been felled in the most reckless way, and till recently no regard has been paid to their preservation or renovation. Nay, so fast has the timber disappeared that no replanting could have kept pace with the destruction. There can, I fear, be no doubt whatever that this stripping naked the face of the land has conduced to droughts, and it is not at all unlikely that, as a consequence, famines may now continue to be more prevalent than they were of old. In this view of matters the case against railways is infinitely stronger than any that could be urged against canals. These might have been a dead weight on the country, but they would at all events have left the trees standing as well as provided the means for averting calamity when it threatened. But the railways have stripped the country in nearly every way, and their over-rapid extension has made it impossible now for canals to be made in number sufficient to remedy the mischief. It is doubtful whether the replanting of trees can be carried out to the needed extent in some parts of the country with any hope of success. Those who have brought India to this pass, in blind disregard to consequences like these, have really much to answer for.

A more general inquiry, and the one bearing most closely on our subject, presents itself in the general trade returns of the empire. What indication do they give of the progress it is making and of its ability to go on standing the load of fresh burdens which are year by year being laid upon it? The weight of that load is of course officially denied, and Lord George Hamilton, as the mouthpiece of the India Council in the House of Commons, claimed that while the debt has been in some three years increased by 13,000,000*l.*, the net charges upon the country have been lessened by 1,200,000*l.*; but this is nonsense. This result is due mostly to the windfalls of the famine traffic to the railways, as I have already pointed out. The fixed debt charges have been lessened by one thing only, the redemption of the Old East India Stocks. That there has been a reliably permanent decrease is simply impossible while borrowing goes on apace from year to year. The state of the normal trade of India is therefore a matter of the highest importance, for if that trade bears the same testimony as the canals, the land revenue, and the railways, the gravity of the situation will be demonstrated beyond the possibility of dispute. True, this testimony is not altogether direct regarding the position of the people, for it is not the people who benefit in any material degree from the external trade of the empire, but its English possessors who absorb the profits. Still for my immediate purpose as well as in a less direct way for its value as testimony to Indian progress, the Indian trade returns are of the utmost value.

Taking these returns, then, from 1860 downwards in periods of five years, we find the following results:

Years	Gross Imports, Merchandise, &c.	Treasure	Total
1860 to 1864	119,857,000*l*.	85,158,000*l*.	205,302,000*l*.
1865 to 1869[1]	158,484,000*l*.	88,089,000*l*.	246,573,000*l*.
1870 to 1874	161,279,000*l*.	41,323,000*l*.	202,602,000*l*.

Years	Gross Exports, Merchandise, &c.	Treasure	Total
1860 to 1864	210,733,000*l*.	5,113,000*l*.	215,846,000*l*.
1865 to 1869[1]	279,314,000*l*.	9,009,900*l*.	288,323,000*l*.
1870 to 1874	281,177,000*l*.	7,951,000*l*.	289,128,000*l*.

Between the first and second periods here given there is a marked improvement in the gross values of both the exports and the imports, but between the

[1] It should be remembered that, owing to a change in the date of making up the accounts, the financial year 1866-67 contains only eleven months.

second and third there is no such improvement. The export figures are all but stationary, the total imports have sensibly declined, and when we look at the years in detail we find that, so far as regards the exports, the total of 1874 was below that for 1871; while the totals for merchandise alone have never been so high as in 1864, 1865, and 1866, when India was enjoying to the full the prosperity due to the American war. The export of merchandise was worth some 13,000,000*l.* less in 1874 than 1865. The figures for 1875 and 1876 of merchandise alone exhibit increases in the totals of both imports and exports, but the exports are still a good deal below the level of 1871–72, a time of 'abnormal inflation.' The excess of exports over imports, including everything, was last year as much as 16,000,000*l.* nominal, the average being about 12,000,000*l.* Although these most recent figures indicate a gradual increase in the trade, they must not be taken as conclusive that India is making great progress. There is in truth no such decided sign of development of Indian trade as we have a right to expect after all the money that has been lavished in bringing the productive powers of the country to a high pitch. Some raw staples which India produces are rising in importance, but others are declining or fluctuating, in both price and quantity, from year to year. Last year there was, it must be remembered, an abnormal stimulus given to the exports by the state of the exchange, but we have yet to see whether that stimulus will leave any permanent effect. At present the probabilities are that it will not, for India has great difficulty in holding its own with some of its staples, such as jute, indigo, and cotton. Much is no doubt expected from the export of wheat, which has lately developed rapidly; but when peace is restored in Europe this export may fall off, as it will do in any case whenever Europe has a fine harvest. On the whole, then, the exports of India give no satisfactory assurance of the rapid development of the empire.

But if the exports give this impression, still more do the imports, which are after all the greatest test of the growing wealth and resources of a community. These are decidedly lower in the last quinquennium we have given than in the previous, and when looked at in detail, and taking merchandise by itself, cannot be said to have substantially and permanently increased since 1869, when the highest level was touched. It is indeed evident that that portion of the import trade which depends on native demand is almost stationary, while articles required by the Government for its public works, or to meet the wants of its starving subjects, are imported in larger or smaller quantities pretty much according as the borrowings are large or small. This probably accounts for not a little of the increased imports shown in the last two years; this and a growing tendency on the part of Europeans to embark in enterprises within the country. It is certain, at all events, that the market for English staples of manufacture is not now an active one and has not been so for some time. India has not applied such lavish amounts of capital to railway building lately, for example, because less has been done by the private companies, and so the import of iron and manufactures has notably declined. On the other hand, the famines have entailed very heavy imports of corn, which may latterly be placed against that decrease and probably more than counterbalances it, if it indeed be a decrease, for what is not wanted to make new railways may be more than needed to maintain the old. While one year with another the import trade in goods is thus almost at a dead level, and certainly not going forward by leaps and bounds, the import of treasure has fallen off to an enormous degree; and as this is so intimately bound up with the general question of the position of India economically, it is worth while to examine the account with some particularity.

India has for long been a very large consumer of the precious metals and chiefly of silver, so that she has absorbed on balance between the years 1835 and 1866 about 200,000,000*l.*; but the great annual import did not begin till 1855-56, when the large railway building schemes of Lord Dalhousie first caused a demand for wages, &c., which loans in London were able to supply. Nearly two-thirds of the guaranteed railway capital appears to have been thus spent. In subsequent years the cotton prosperity, already alluded to, gave such an impetus to the export trade of the empire that there was an enormous balance of trade in its favour; so, as the people had no mercantile or, as we might say, civilised wants inducing them to import goods, or rather, perhaps, as the profits of their great trade did not go into the pockets of the people but into that of the English traders, the imports of bullion rose to 20,500,000*l.* in 1863-4 and to 26,500,000*l.* in 1865-66, from which point they fell away as suddenly and sharply. The state of this part of the import account for the past few years cannot be better shown than by the following table, extracted from the report of the Committee of the House of Commons on the Depreciation of Silver, lately published:

From 1868-69 to 1871-72 the surplus of gold imports into India was . . 16,500,000*l.*
From 1872-73 to 1875-76 ,, ,, 7,500,000*l.*
From 1868-69 to 1871-72 the surplus of silver imports into India was . . 23,500,000*l.*
From 1872-73 to 1875-76 ,, ,, 9,500,000*l.*

It is thus evident from the mere fluctuation of the bullion account that Indian trade has, for some reason or other, much less favourable a hold on foreign markets now than it had some years ago. India's position is in almost every way the reverse of that of England, with which we dealt generally in the introductory chapter. She had no great foreign investments, no large colonies, no wide-spread carrying business, and very few native manufactures worthy of the name or capable of commanding an export trade. The balance to be settled between the totals of her export and import trade is, in consequence, more a simple matter of cash than with most countries. If she sells a great deal more than she buys, her foreign customers must pay her the difference in silver or gold. Now at first sight an evident nearer approach of the two sides of the merchandise account to a level, as indicated by a cessation of larger bullion imports, might be taken as a sign that India was growing richer, and able to buy more; and, had we not studied the figures of her trade, that might have been the conclusion we should have jumped to, especially after hearing all the far-sounding talk about prosperity, progress, and what not. But we have seen that the merchandise figures are, in recent years, all but stationary, so that the indebtedness of other countries to India cannot be said to have materially varied, and the gain of the last two years is likely to be partially neutralised by the falling off this year and next. In the net bullion imports given above, the period of cotton-growing inflation is not included, and there is therefore no abnormal cause for the excess of the first period over the second to account for the enormous difference between the two. We are consequently driven to seek other explanations. To my thinking, they are not difficult to find. The main, if not the sole, cause of the stoppage of a bullion import by India undoubtedly lies in the fact that the Government of India has in recent years been compelled to pay increased amounts in England, while, at the same time, borrowing on account of India has not been quite so heavy except in the two years of famine, 1874–75 and 1877–78. This is best understood by the statement made by the House of Commons Committee in their report on silver. It points out that, through a slight increase in the import figures, the balance to be remitted to India has been reduced somewhat of late years; but, while that is so, the India Council have been driven year by year to increase their drafts for money due here on account of the Indian Government. This is how the account stands.

Between 1868–69 and 1871–72 there were remitted to India in treasure 40,000,000*l.*, and in Government bills 29,500,000*l.*, a total of 69,500,000*l.*; and between 1872–73 and 1875–76 the remittances in treasure were only 16,500,000*l.*, while the Government drafts had increased to 50,500,000*l.*, the two together making a total of only 67,000,000*l.* Thus, while the gross amount remitted has fallen off, on a comparison of years, 2,500,000*l.*, owing to the large famine borrowings and heavier imports of goods, the demands of the Indian Council have swollen 21,000,000*l.* In other words, the position of the

normal trade account of the empire, supposing it a
genuine outgrowth of the condition of the people, was
in 1875 and last year almost entirely neutralised
through the demands of the India Council here.[1] So
much so that, were it not for the trade of China, by
which a large proportion of the Council drafts are
ultimately utilised, it would of late have frequently
been almost impossible to remit at all. As it was, the
exchange rates fell in 1876 at one time so low that
they threatened a loss of 4,000,000*l*. to the Government of India on that item alone. The great increase
in the amount due by India on account of interest on

[1] The following table, extracted from the Report of the Committee
on the Depreciation of Silver, will show approximately the position of the
Indian trade account pure and simple. It will be seen that the vaunted
progress of the Empire has very little real foundation, and that the
margin to the credit of India tends to narrow in a dangerous degree to
the level of the India Council drafts:

Official Years	Exports (exclusive of Treasure)	Imports (exclusive of Treasure)	Excess of Exports
	£	£	£
1860-61	32,970,000	23,495,000	9,475,000
1861-62	36,320,000	22,320,000	14,000,000
1862-63	47,860,000	22,630,000	25,230,000
1863-64	65,625,000	27,145,000	38,480,000
1864-65	68,025,000	28,150,000	39,875,000
1865-66	65,490,000	29,600,000	35,890,000
1866-67 (11 months)	41,860,000	29,040,000	12,820,000
1867-68	50,875,000	35,705,000	15,170,000
1868-69	53,060,000	35,990,000	17,070,000
1869-70	52,470,000	32,925,000	19,545,000
1870-71	55,335,000	34,470,000	20,865,000
1871-72	63,190,000	32,090,000	31,100,000
1872-73	55,230,000	31,875,000	23,355,000
1873-74	54,980,000	33,835,000	21,145,000
1874-75	56,360,000	36,220,000	20,140,000
1875-76	56,210,000	38,515,000	17,695,000

her debt, and on the guaranteed railways' capital, as well as on account of the extravagant charges for her army stores, salaries, pensions, &c., payable in England, has therefore had just this outcome. The resources of the country are straitened to the utmost to make ends meet, and the purchasing power of the people of India consequently most materially reduced. What profits there are on their export trade which might otherwise escape the English traders go to meet the Government demand, which is thus sucking the country drier at every step of so-called progress at a rate that must soon make it an empty husk. It has become a dominant and imperative necessity that the exports should always largely exceed the imports; and whenever the latter come nearer than a given point to the level of the former, commercial distress, depressed exchanges, and hampered trade must be the inevitable result. Between public and private demands for remittance, India must practically pay this country yearly some 19,000,000*l.* or 20,000,000*l.* at a moderate estimate, of which almost 16,000,000*l.* is on Government account; and she has nothing but her excess of exportable produce in the long run with which to pay this prodigious annual drain.

The extreme fall which lately took place in the value of silver is a fit enough illustration of the way in which this economic position takes effect. It has been the fashion to ascribe all this fall to panic, induced by the over-production in America, and the bad management of the German Government intent on its ambitious schemes for remodelling its currency on the basis of the richest nations. But, obviously, we have only half the truth in statements of that kind. Silver has in fact fallen in price, not so much from over-supply as from decreased demand. The investigations of the committee appointed to look into the subject proved clearly enough that, except from Germany, there had as yet been no over-supply, and it also proved very distinctly that India no longer took the quantity of the metal that it used to do. Leaving out the years of the cotton famine, we find that the net absorption by India of this metal was about 28,500,000*l.* from the years 1866–67 to 1869–70 inclusive, and for the next four years 10,600,000*l.*, while for the two years up to March 1876 it was about 6,000,000*l.*, most of which was absorbed in 1874–75 under the operation of the famine loans. The heavy drafts on account of the famine and other loans of the present year will no doubt have the same effect, but this is no sign whatever of a real improvement in the state of the exchange. That will be kept up merely by the cessation of the sales of India Council bills. For the time being the charges of the Indian Government in England will be met out of borrowed money and silver may be largely remitted from England, but directly this borrowing comes to an end the exchanges will go back to their previous uneasy see-saw, and the difficulties of the position will be aggravated by the increase which has meanwhile taken place in the burdens of India. In the year ended March 1876 the absorption of bullion only amounted to 1,555,000*l.*, and were it possible to conceive of India ceasing to borrow, it might not merely cease altogether to take silver, but probably have to submit to a drain the other way. The India Council had to borrow a large amount last year in order to keep the exchange from going to perhaps 1*s.* per rupee. No wonder, therefore, that the Indian exchange fell to a low figure that loan notwithstanding, and that grave alarm was excited for the future of the empire. No more terrible proof could, in short, be given that it is suffering from our hurried and ill-advised efforts at progress than this constantly increasing depression in the rate of exchange unless upheld by loans. At this moment men's minds are at ease again; the exchange has risen and clouds have passed away; but what would it have been had the Government not borrowed here and in India to an unusual extent, or had it not taken power to issue temporary bills in England expressly for the purpose of tiding over the summer difficulties, in the hope that when harvest came the India Council might be again able to draw on the produce of the empire for the means of paying off these bills? The sensitiveness of the exchange till the Secretary of State got power from

Parliament in June to issue his loans gave a sufficient answer to that question. We must wait for the return tide again, however, to see how the exchanges will stand the dead weight of the continuous Council drafts, after the present huge loans have been exhausted, before deciding that the danger is all gone and business likely to be advancing and prosperous — the Indian revenue unhampered with the necessity of borrowing so many millions to make good the loss on exchange. Treasury bills only postpone the evil day at the best, and it is not at all unlikely that a deluge of Council drafts coming on the market at a time when merchants were busy moving the produce in autumn might still upset the exchange and produce commercial disasters. The position is well stated in the report of the Parliamentary Committee above mentioned, and offers a remarkable contrast to the airy optimism of the ordinary official history of the financial situation. This is what it says:

Before the Indian Mutiny the total disbursements at home ranged, very roughly speaking, between 4,000,000*l.* and 5,000,000*l.* sterling. From 1860–61 to 1866–67 they ranged between 9,000,000*l.* and 11,000,000*l.* Now they stand at about 15,000,000*l.*, and to the precise extent to which India must thus remit funds to the Home Government, she has so much less to receive in merchandise or silver. Her powers of importation are reduced to that extent. Taking the receipts from the railways, it appears that during the 10 years 1860–61 to 1869–70 the Indian Government received, as a balance to be paid out in India, 35,000,000*l.* from the

Guaranteed Railway Companies, or, on an average, 3,500,000*l*. a year. In the year 1870-71 the amount received was 2,250,000*l*., and in 1871-72, 1,200,000*l*. Since then the receipts from this source have been practically closed; nay, more than this. In 1872-73 the railways received from the Government in London 530,000*l*. and in 1874-75 nearly 800,000*l*., in place of paying an annual average of 3,500,000*l*. in the previous period. In round numbers, therefore, the Government had to provide 4,000,000*l*. a year more than in the previous period, by other means. These other means were either drafts on India, or loans raised on its own account at home. In 1874-75 about 5,000,000*l*. was raised by loans, and in that year only 10,840,000*l*. was drawn, but in the two previous years the drafts amounted, as has been shown, to between 13,000,000*l*. and 14,000,000*l*., and in the first 10 months of the year 1875-76 to 12,360,000*l*. It appears that they would have nearly reached 15,000,000*l*., but for the difficulties experienced in selling bills in February and March.

We need only add further on this point the significant fact that the loss on exchange alone has been latterly equivalent to fully 10 per cent. additional debt charge on the revenues of India, and that, since 1865 at least, the amount of the loss has been steadily on the increase. In that year it was only 43,000*l*., and rose to close on a million in 1874; it was lower in 1875, thanks to the large famine borrowings, and last year, owing again to the extensive borrowings which Indian officials always sanguinely hope to do without and always rush into more and more inordinately on each new occasion, the actual loss was only about 700,000*l*. The same soothing influence will operate powerfully now, and it may always be trusted to adjust the balance for a poverty-stricken land, whether Germany deluges the London market with silver or not. Till no financial legerdemain can longer hide the true state of the case from the English people, or till the unwieldy superstructure of debt topples over of its own weight, all may be made easy for the Indian officials by this ready borrowing. But for the natives of India the situation is a most gloomy one. Year by year they find the struggle for life harder and harder, and as the 'improvements' begotten of debt, of much wasteful extravagance and official stupidity or corruption —for, strange as it may sound, there are Anglo-Indians who can be corrupt—extend, so also does the 'famine area.'

This exchange barometer is a very significant one, then, and would startle us all were it allowed to tell all it could, for it gauges roughly the labouring condition of Indian trade as well as the extent of Indian poverty. As to the trade, there can be no question that the constant borrowings to hide the true state of Indian finance have a most injurious influence on the business of the country in several important ways. For one thing, trade is carried on altogether on a false basis; more is imported into India than, left to herself and paying tribute as she does, she could pay for; and every now and then a fall comes in the exchange, raising prices in India, increasing exports, and adding therefore to the difficulties of the people. It must always be remembered that to the natives of India the possession of a large export trade is in some important respects a most questionable benefit, and that an artificially stimulated trade can hardly fail often to prove a curse to them, because what benefits it yields go to their conquerors, not to them. Prices rise without being followed by wages, and the profit of the advance goes either to the money-lenders into whose grasp we have given nearly all that portion of the people whom we do not squeeze directly ourselves, or to fill the pockets of the English merchant, indigo grower, cotton and corn speculator, and people of that class, who go to India to extract fortunes out of the natives as fast as they can and often are not over-scrupulous as to the means. For the poor this is merely a process of stripping, however disguised by clap-trap phrases. Were the trade of India all in the hands of the natives, stimulants such as are now applied to it would probably induce great poverty, much hardship to large classes, and occasional famines; but worked as India is, for the benefit of the foreign invader, and for that alone, the trade is a thing altogether exotic, unhealthy, and injurious, inasmuch as, whether large or not, the profits are English not Indian. On the present basis, no matter if the trade of India doubles in the next ten years, the bulk of the population will be in misery and hanging often on the verge of starvation, as much in the hands of money-lenders, and as deeply in debt to the English *exploitants* of the country as now. They may well be worse off than they are now.

This silver question is therefore a much more important one than the currency theorists who demand a gold coinage have any idea of. Gold coinage indeed! why, but for our loans there might soon be imminent danger that India would have no coins at all of metal finer than bronze, and these very loans hasten that consummation at the very time that they stave it off. What with the profits of the merchants, the remittances on account of the preposterously costly Indian Government, and the transmitted earnings of English officials in India, the whole empire writhes and strains under an intolerable burden. Its trade is not its own but its conqueror's. Nothing, surely, could be more unsound or financially and politically more dangerous.

Strictly speaking, the political dangers are hardly within the scope of this work, but I may be permitted to say a word upon them in passing, more especially as the trade of India cannot be supposed to be secure if we are storing up for ourselves political troubles by the manner in which we are draining the empire of its strength.

Lord George Hamilton is in the habit of speaking with a fine courageous explicitness of the 'great development of the productive powers of India,' and no doubt there has been development, but it is development at present neutralised, and more than neutralised;

it is development based on debt and supported by as needy and frequent recourse to the money-lender as any spendthrift could set the example of, and therefore it is development which must before long, I believe, inevitably force on us, granting that we retain India, one of two alternatives—either we shall have to enter on another career of conquest and annexation within India in order to get the revenues of the tributary states, which now pay us little, into our own hands, or England must presently step in and relieve India of some part of the pressure of her debt. These tributary or feudatory states own over a third of the total area of India, and control nearly a sixth of the total population, yet contribute only 725,000*l.* to the Imperial revenue, although they enjoy some of the most important benefits of our rule, such as immunity from foreign attacks, freedom to trade, &c. That the Government of the empire can go on in the future as it has done in the past, is a sheer impossibility; for the pressure of taxation upon the people is heavy enough to cause the idea of a new rebellion to find strong support; and every year finds us weaker, because nearer to a state of chronic bankruptcy. The danger of losing the great income from opium constantly increases, for example, side by side with the growing burden. An *émeute* in China would probably cut it off at once, and leave us face to face with an enormous deficit such as the present five or ten million doses of borrowing administered every other year could never fill. I am not writing in an alarmist frame of mind, but from sober weighing of the facts of the position, which facts the official intellect may, with its schemes of progress in the abstract, be too ready to ignore.

Our financing in India has become a monstrous danger which weak words cannot conceal. And what after all are we doing there? What strength does our position give us? what reserve force or pre-eminence among nations? The fashion is to speak of India as the brightest jewel of the English crown, the great source of our strength, a mine of wealth to the nation, and so forth, but the fashion appears to me a very foolish one when the whole subject is carefully looked into. Ever since the mutiny it appears to me that our position in India has been a precarious one, and that the holding of it is costing this country more in mere human lives and abstracted English labour than it can afford. We have to maintain a large army there to keep us from being surprised from within or without, and the administrative staff grows year by year more expensive, until it has become patent to every unprejudiced observer that the empire we now hold cannot long bear the burden. We lend the money to help to postpone the evil day, but it will come all the more for that, and when we have to take upon ourselves the swollen debt of this empire where will the profit be? A book might be filled with examples and proofs of the dangers of our position in India from this point of view alone, and of the ostrich-like folly of our conduct, but I may not do more than indicate the broad conclusion. But it is easy to denounce and predict, the question is, what are we to do? Give up India forthwith? That we dare not do, was it for no other reason than that we have brought the country into a condition which totally unfits it for deliverance. We cannot suffer India to fall back into the grasp of the Mahommedans, who elsewhere have made fertile lands barren wastes, and life itself a disaster to those they oppressed. We cannot leave but we must retrench, alter utterly our treatment of the country, and get the full conception of the ends whither we are now going driven into the heads of our administrators.

The borrowings of India on the score of public works will have to be rigorously stopped. Every thousand pounds added on account of these works to the interest-bearing debt hastens by so much the inevitable catastrophe. The clamours of Indian railway directors for the completion of this line or that, in order to open up a new district for their profit, as well as of restless officials for millions to spend on pet projects of irrigation and land improvement, ought to be unheeded when they involve more debt. Furthermore, there ought to be a close overhauling of the whole public service involving a much wider admission of natives to positions of trust, and a sharp reduction in ornamental posts or in the expense involved by the oppressive centralisation with its multitudinous exactions on the time of district servants. The total expenditure must, in short, by this and by all means, be brought within the limits of income. That will not cure the evil, which is now too deep, I fear, for such mild treatment; but it will at least give time for a true appreciation of the position, and let the governors of India know what she can really bear and do—a great step gained. Were no loans allowed to be raised for the purpose of eking out a loss on exchange, or to avert a famine, they would soon realise the fact—patent enough to all who have their eyes open—that India has been living these five-and-twenty years at least beyond her means, and is doing so practically as much now as ever; that we are taxing her till her people starve; and that her very trade, augmented though it be, supplies us with an index to her exceeding great poverty.

With this opinion regarding the political dangers and necessities of India, it is almost unnecessary for me to indicate what I expect the course of our trade therewith to be. I have already spoken of it as inflated and as strained, and these assertions hardly need proof. Our exports to India have been inflated by the money we have lent her to the extent of many millions, and her exports to us have been strained by the rapidity with which English sojourners in her, for them, uncongenial climate have wanted to make their fortunes, and by the incessant requirements of a most expensive Government, by far the most steadily expensive that India ever had. But should the artificial support be withdrawn from one side of the account it would also tend to reduce the strain upon the other, and supposing economy possible, we might in this view look for a smaller interchange of commodities than has lately been customary. I am probably assuming too much, however, in thus talking of Indian Government retrenchment, for I do not believe that anything short of a catastrophe will ever make that Government seriously think of retrenchment. There are too many traditions, too many departments, too much self-seeking and jobbery, against any such idea. If matters go on as they do now, therefore, we may not unreasonably expect that the trade of India will stand nearly at its present level when the people of India die by millions of famine and pestilence. There are not wanting signs that they may do so, and at all events the trade of 1877-78 is not likely to at all equal that of 1876-77.

And as regards England at all events, I am disposed to believe that the Indian demand for foreign goods is likely to be smaller for some time to come than it has lately appeared to be. Not only is India less able to buy and rather glutted by a supply by no means wisely regulated, but her internal means of production are steadily increasing under the shelter of her slight import tariff. English capitalists and a few others are building mills and setting up machinery in its three old presidencies, until the Indian-made cotton fabrics are now obtaining a large share in supplying the wants of the people. Mr. O'Connor in his last report on the trade of India states that the number of spindles now running in the mills of India is now over a million and the number of looms over 9,000. The success which this indicates must seriously affect the export trade in cottons from Manchester. It is not a success that specially benefits the natives of the country, nor would it be possible but for the Indian import tariff.

The duties levied are not nominally very high as a rule, for the simple reason that the population could not buy the goods at all were they dear, but they are just as hampering to the natural development of trade in a poor country as high ones in a rich. The facts brought to light in the agitation which went on early last year amongst the Lancashire cotton manufacturers, and which has by no means as yet subsided, offer a very good illustration of this. These manufacturers contend strongly that the five per cent. import duty charged on their goods in India is proving the ruin of their trade. What with this and the loss on exchange, those manufacturers who had been striving to establish an exotic kind of industry in cotton manufactures in Bombay are able to beat the English makers, and must, in time, take away their trade. I give the following summary of the Manchester people's argument from the 'Times' of March 7, 1876:—

So far as regards India, it is pointed out that the productions of Indian mills are supplanting those of our home mills. Certain kinds of goods that the Indian mills can make have been exported from this country to India in decreasing quantities year by year, while shirtings, which as yet India does not make, have been sent from here in ever-increasing quantities. Thus, the average exports of 'domestics, gray T cloths, and drills' from this country between the five years 1852 to 1856 was $9\frac{5}{8}$ millions of lbs., while between the four years 1871 to 1874 it had fallen off to $4\frac{1}{4}$ millions. In the same periods the export of shirtings had increased from 1,310,000 lbs. to 3,480,144 lbs. Statistics as to Indian mills and productions, as well as relating to the effect of the Indian import duty, bear, however, most vitally on the question at issue, and are, besides, the most interesting. From them we learn that the capital invested in mills in India had increased from Rs. 22,085,000 in the middle of 1874 to Rs. 38,685,250 in November 1875. A mill in India of 60,000 spindles and 1,000 looms would cost 200,000*l.*, and the same in England 100,000*l.* The English mill has the advantage in depreciation, interest, and coal, while the Indian mill would have the advantage, so long as its business was confined to the home supply, in transit charges both ways. It would have to bear the cost of increased interest and depreciation to the amount of 12,500*l.* per annum as against the English mill, and would be at a disadvantage of 8,500*l.* in fuel, making together 21,000*l.* The saving, however, of 15 per cent. in the charge for double transit would amount to 45,000*l.* on a 300,000*l.* production, so that, after all, the balance of advantage on the side of the Indian mill, granting equality of production, would be 24,000*l.* This calculation relates to coarse cotton goods, which Manchester appears inclined to admit that India can beat her in making, duty or not. Shirtings, it is contended, are not yet quite in the same position. The make of an Indian mill of similar cost would be only 100,000*l.* worth of these, instead of 300,000*l.*, and the balance of advantage secured by being in the country where the cotton is grown would only be about 4,500*l.*, a sum which, possibly, English manufacturers might be able to neutralise. But the 5 per cent. duty here comes in and imposes another burden, calculated at 6,000*l.*, on the English goods, and suffices to turn the scale in favour of India for even that class of cotton goods which she has not as yet successfully produced. She is protected in this manufacture till able to stand alone. It is no wonder, therefore, that mills in India have increased from 11 in 1870–71 to 41 in 1874–5, and that the imports of machinery to India should be steadily growing. The most enlightened among those in Lancashire who agitate for the repeal of the Indian import duty on cotton appear to recognise as inevitable the ultimate triumph of India in the competition for the supply of cotton manufactures to the Indian empire, but think that this triumph should not be assisted by artificial props such as this import duty, which they do not consider a necessity for the Indian exchequer.

There is no doubt much force in what is here urged, and what applies to a large article of import such as cotton goods applies almost equally to many others. The taxes impede trade and hinder the development of exports from this country to India, whilst at the same time they give a hectic prosperity to exotic industries in India. Coming on the top of a rate of exchange always in an abnormal state as against the currency values in India, five per cent. duty may be particularly retardant. At the same time the duty is punishing India by producing to some extent the same effect as excessive exports only in another way. The price of goods is raised to the people without at the same time their wages, for protective tariffs on imports invariably tend in the long run rather to depress wages than to raise them. This tariff is in any case against the British exporter to a certain extent, and coupled with other causes may help to lower the bulk and value of his trade with India for some time to come. Were there no tariff against this country on cotton goods the increasing indigence of the people, the over-speculation of the past few years, and the frequent derangement in the exchange must make our export trade to the East unsatisfactory. But economists tell us that things are very favourable for our doing a good stroke of business in buying Indian goods in India to sell elsewhere. The exchange, which retards imports to India, stimulates exports from it, because a merchant can buy in India with a metal which has there an exaggerated value compared with what it bears in other countries, and therefore obtain a larger quantity of goods at a cheap rate in proportion. It works, in other words, most powerfully on the side of the Government and the various 'developing' agencies it protects. But then the question comes to be—what can India sell in augmented quantities? At present she produces a few staple articles of great use to us and to other nations, but is the demand for them likely to increase as fast as the operation of this law might require? That question is difficult to answer fully, but the indications of past trade returns give to some extent a favourable answer. India may yet be capable of forcing to a considerably higher level of exporting capacity, and great things are at present predicted of her coming wheat trade alone. Last year the tea trade was also greatly stimulated by the less rate of exchange and the badness of the Chinese crops, and her standing in respect of linseed, indigo, jute, and cotton is on the whole fair. Nowhere, however, is there any sign that, apart from artificial stimulants, Indian trade would develope rapidly; and in some important respects she is not unlikely to find in future a glutted market. To have unlimited scope there must be an unlimited market, and India has not got that by any means. On the contrary, some of the most important articles of export are keenly competed with and beaten by other sources of supply, such as cotton and indigo. Her opium export is threatened by native products in China, and she is a long way yet from the supremacy in either tea or wheat. The latter is perhaps the most dangerous of any exportable staple for a country to rely upon, because the demand for it must always vary according to the quality of the harvest in importing countries. Hence, however cheaply India can grow corn—and I am told that wheat can be had in the North-West Provinces for from 14s. to 16s. per quarter in good years—it would, therefore, be the height of folly to rest much hope on her always finding a market for it equal to the exigencies of the annual drain upon her resources. If we do not want the corn and if nobody else does, what matters it how cheap it can be bought in India? So with other staple articles, India cannot sell beyond the capacity of the foreign markets, be the exchange ever so much against her. Attempts to do so these last few years have only had the effect of glutting these markets, and thus it will always be. Both sides of the trade account are injured by the false state into which they are brought by the action of the Government, and how or when the injury is to be repaired I dare not venture to guess till signs have been given that the action has been suspended. It is a sound economic doctrine, no doubt, that when the exchanges go against a country exports are stimulated, but it is a doctrine of limited application only, as the traders in India have ere now found out. An unhealthy stimulus of whatever kind must, in the nature of things, lead to reaction. Then again there is one Indian staple export threatened at the present time almost with extinction—that of jute. This fibre has not at all realised expectations, and both the quantity and value of the export of India have decreased seriously during the last four years. What the empire can get immediately to take its place is more than I can tell. Not only so, but supposing every market in the world eager for Indian produce, its capacity of supply cannot be relied on while whole provinces are devastated by frequently recurring droughts.

On the whole, therefore, we cannot take a great deal of consolation, I fear, from this sound economic doctrine. India will no doubt have to try her best to reduce the exchanges by diminished imports and increased exports for years to come, but the country is possessed of few means for doing the latter, at least with a rapidity sufficient to avert mischief. We in this country do not realise yet how difficult it is to apply sound economic doctrines in all their fulness to a country so poor, so adventitiously placed, so nursed and coddled and squeezed and stimulated, all in the same breath, as India is. The one cardinal fact that all this is done for the foreigner who holds the country vitiates almost every simple inference. We cannot say definitely what India is capable of or what she can bear, all is so forced and artificial. Nor do we understand the poverty of the resources of India, or the sickly way in which foreign capital behaves too often when transplanted there. The history of some of our Indian banks in the past might teach us a lesson of moderation in our attempt to say what Indian trade will do in the future. As to the other remedy—the lowering of Indian imports—that is one which, as I have shown, the position of affairs must speedily bring about. Depressed exchanges, growing native poverty, and vexatious customs tariffs may be left to work their natural results in this case with an absolute certainty that Indian imports will soon decline if the Indian Government ceases to borrow. Here, however, the borrowing policy of the Indian Government steps in, and increases the confusion and distress into which purblind financing or worse has brought the trade of the empire. By the artificial wants which the Government schemes create, there is set up an artificial import which year by year aggravates the situation and renders any balance of accounts more and more an impossibility. Since 1857, well on to 100,000,000*l.* of the total goods imports of India has consisted of such things as naval and military stores, metals, machinery, coal and coke, railway and telegraph materials, carriages, &c., nearly all of which must be considered an artificial demand which borrowings have almost entirely created. The total extent of this inflation exceeds of course the total sum of the Indian debt of all kinds. Sooner or later this artificial system of creating progress by means of huge debts must be abandoned, and when it is the imports of India must decrease by some millions per annum. But that this decrease will itself now right the position I very much doubt.

I should say then, to sum the matter up, that the prospects of an increase or even substantial revival of our trade with India are decidedly not good, whatever they may be with the East generally, because the economic condition of India is not itself good. The country is poor; in some places over-crowded with population, and in many districts over-taxed. It is deeply in debt abroad, and the earnings of its reproductive works, where they have any, go to enrich the foreigner, not the native population, lessening thereby the purchasing power of the latter. The money or produce goes away out of the country to pay tribute money and foreign profits and does not fructify at home.

The loan system now threatens to bear very bitter fruit. If, as unless in their astonishing infatuation those who govern India are bent on bringing the country to a crisis full of danger to themselves and to all their plans, we stop these loans, then with them for some time we must stop also a considerable portion of our Indian trade. Without borrowing India cannot buy as she has done. Add to these considerations the fact that the import duties of necessity imposed hinder the growth of our vast cotton goods trade with India, usually amounting to from 18,000,000*l.* to 20,000,000*l.* per annum, or nearly two-thirds of the whole that India buys from us, and we shall see that the outlook for the future is decidedly not satisfactory. Far more attention is therefore demanded by the situation of affairs in India than the English public has yet given, or than they can be expected to give when everything

Indian is usually contemptuously relegated to the closing days of the parliamentary session, to be dealt with in the dog days, and amid a choke of public business such as usually signalises the industry of Ministers and Parliament at that trying period, unless there should happen to be an urgent need for power to borrow, when with difficulty a quorum may be got together a little earlier. If we do not want to lose not merely our Indian trade but India itself, we shall have to alter radically her whole financial administration.

I have dealt with but very few of the more prominent features of Indian finance and trade, but in what I have said I believe the key to the position of the empire may be found. The popular ideas which prevail in this country about India are totally erroneous, and the conceptions of our work there which flow from these ideas are full of danger. For us India has always been a place to grow rich by. Its capacities have been utilised to that end : we rule the country, when all is said, for that sole object. Let Englishmen once realise that we are now working this great field at a loss; that the energies of the country are strained in order that a few may make fortunes off the labours of a poor, patient, and wonderfully docile people, and their whole attitude towards India will change. Let it be known that we are not civilising India but exhausting it ; that we are not elevating the races there but debasing them;

that the trade of India is not for its people but for ourselves; and that year by year our rulers there are piling for us a fearful account which will one day have to be settled, and I believe there is yet enough manhood amongst us to cause the national policy to be reversed, to make us set this great dependency free. To one looking quietly at the facts, seeing the misery we create—a greater misery because a more constant than much native misrule, the debt we are heaping on an unresisting people, the hate we are generating, and the real ghastliness of our beneficence, the cant of the day is unspeakably revolting. Like the Spaniards, we have called on our priests to bless our tyranny and we mouth unctuous phrases about our humanity, while we wring our millions from a labour-worn and hungry people. Keeping a population nearly ten times that of England low in the dust, close to the confines of want, we flare up on occasion into spasmodic public-subscription benevolence and render back a microscopic percentage of our gains to save from starvation some few of the millions thus destined to die, talking the while of the mysterious visitation of Providence. The Queen sends her paltry hundreds and her commiseration, parsons harangue about our good-heartedness, and the whole nation, reading the long lists of donations in the newspapers, feels itself great beyond description, a pattern to all the peoples of the earth. It never strikes us that we may be the cause of these terrible famines, that we are sucking India dry as one sucks an orange, that all the grandeur of our empire there is grandeur based on wrong and oppression. Heaven grant that we have no rude awakening from our delusions, but I confess I have my fears. And this at least may be said, that if England does not soon release India from the greater part of her debt-burden, India will by-and-by again rise against us in an agony of endeavour to fling us out of her bosom. And when another rebellion raises its head it will find us much weaker in some ways than the last. It will fall on an empty treasury, and will not be suppressed except at a cost to England in money and blood great enough to sweep away in a year the gains of a century. Whether rebellion comes or not, the force of events will in time, I believe, compel us to surrender India and the Indian debt together, unless we prudently lift the load from her shoulders now.

CHAPTER III.

CHINA AND JAPAN.

Before passing on to review the position of the western nations with which we have close relations, it will, I think, be well to make a few observations regarding China and Japan. With the former we have long been on intimate and somewhat peculiar relations, and the importance of the latter as a source of trade is, if not at present on the increase, still considerable.

I have already in dealing with India pointed out the supreme importance of the Chinese opium traffic to its revenues. Without that traffic India would now be hopelessly bankrupt, and, independent of any trade relations which England may have with China, this opium trade is therefore of the very highest importance.

It would take a book were I to write the complete history of our curious policy in regard to this noxious drug, and of the frauds on China, the corruption in China, and the countless iniquities it has caused; but I hope a brief reference to the leading facts of the situation will here suffice. Everyone at all acquainted with the history of the English in Asia knows that the highest authorities in China have always strenuously opposed the opium traffic, and that until forced they never sanctioned its admission into the country. The trade was contraband up to 1862, and the opium used to run the gauntlet of Chinese customs boats up the Canton River in defiance of all national rights. Englishmen gloried in the iniquitous defiance of law and of course made colossal fortunes in the trade, perhaps about the most ill-gotten gold that Englishmen ever pocketed. We not only defied the laws by carrying on this traffic, but we corrupted Chinese officials and weakened the internal administration of the empire by the heavy bribes which we either paid their officials or were content that they should exact. Not only that, but we kept in bondage, and keep in bondage to this day, large numbers of ryots in Bengal whom we treat precisely as the indigo planters did their slaves in Tirhoot, only with a little more regard for decency, or as the village money-lender does when he gets an unfortunate community into his grasp.

A trade of this kind carried on under these conditions materially heightened the tendencies of the Chinese to quarrel with us, and unquestionably it had a good deal to do with our various Chinese wars. We managed to beat the Chinese, and at last compelled their Government to allow opium to be entered at the treaty ports as a recognised article of import at a fixed duty of thirty taels per picul, and we established ourselves in Hong Kong as a means of more securely seeing that this and other mandates put into the treaty were obeyed. Since then, as I have already said, our opium trade has, to all appearance, flourished apace. We sell a great deal more now than we did a dozen years ago, and in one point of view made a very lucky stroke for India by that treaty stipulation.

There is another side of the subject, however, which is too readily overlooked, and it is this. By compelling the Chinese Government to step aside from its old attitude towards this traffic we destroyed in a great measure its power to prevent the growth of the poppy within its own dominions. There is good reason to believe that opium has been known for ages in China, and some assert that it originally found its way thither from India long before Europeans meddled there, but until within the last fifteen years the Government effectually prevented its cultivation except to a small extent in outlying provinces such as Yunnan. Since the last treaty with England, however, this has been all changed, and poppy cultivation may be said to be almost unrestrained. A home competition has thus grown up which threatens our Indian monopoly most seriously. But for the fact that the Indian opium —the Malwa especially—is much stronger and that its flavour is an acquired taste with the higher classes in China, it might be impossible even now to compete against the native product at a profit sufficient to make the business worth the while of the needy Indian Government. As it is its sales have been nearly stationary and the Indian Government has a large stock on hand, while the use of the drug has been, on all reliable testimony, growing in China to an alarming extent. I might give an overwhelming amount of testimony on this head from our own blue books on the China trade, but one or two extracts will be sufficient. Thus, for example, Consul Edkins reports from Newchwang in 1875 a 'most remarkable falling off in the import of opium. There can be no doubt that this is mainly due to the increased production of the native drug. In my report for the year 1872 I noticed the cultivation of the poppy in the Kérin province, in the neighbourhood of Ninguta. There can be no doubt that the cultivation of the poppy is extending throughout this district, and in that portion of Mongolia which lies nearest to us. The cultivation is still illegal, and the authorities are unable to raise revenue from the native drug, for an extra tax, which is levied on poppy-sown land, most probably goes no further than the pocket of the collector. The value of a picul of native opium is about 300 taels (say about 98*l*.). The quality is said to be improving. The drug is eaten as well as smoked. I have myself been in company with a Manchu sportsman who took nothing during the day but a pill or two of his own home-grown opium. The cultivation of the poppy is sure to spread, for the crop is most profitable in ordinary seasons. Unless the Indian Government can promptly reduce the duty on Malwa opium so as to permit of the foreign merchant laying it down here at a cost of 300 taels a chest, it will soon totally cease to be bought by Chinese in the north. Only one-fifth of the opium used by the Chinamen is foreign, i.e. 80 per cent. is native, and as the quality of the native drug improves, the disproportion will increase.'[1]

Consul Medhurst, of Shanghai, a most intelligent and capable witness, bears the same testimony, and in his report for 1872 points out how the high price of the foreign drug stimulates home production. The whole north-west and west of China is, he says, practically independent of our trade for the supply of opium. For various reasons, however, he was not then of opinion that the consumption of the Indian drug would materially decrease. It is so much stronger flavoured than the native kinds that those who smoke it cannot brook any other. But subsequent events seem to have modified this opinion, and in his report written in the latter half of 1876 he makes some statements of a very ominous kind in view of the position of India. I cannot do better than state the case as it now appears in his own words :—

Despite the increase throughout all the provinces of China

---

[1] Commercial Reports from Her Majesty's Consuls in China, part ii., 1875, pp. 110-111.

of the habit of opium-smoking, and which has for these previous three or four years hindered any reduction of the import of the Indian drug, the large quantities that are now produced in Manchuria and Western China have during the past year very sensibly affected the trade: and those merchants engaged in it are very despondent about the future. Indeed, they assert the year has been one of disappointment to them, the prices realised having been such as barely paid ordinary interest on the capital employed. Of course the general despondency of trade in China during the year has had its share in bringing about this state of things. Competition, moreover, has been keen among the importers, and this, coupled with a failing demand, could produce no other result. The greater number of the provinces now grow nearly sufficient opium to supply themselves. Down the Yangtsze and from Newchwang such quantities are now being brought and placed on the market at so low a price in the ports open to foreign trade, as materially to diminish the consumption therein of the foreign drug. Wealthy people, as a rule, habitually prefer the latter article; but large quantities of it, especially Malwa, are now sold adulterated with the cheaper sort, and that itself is much doctored with cardamoms, sugar, and spices, to disguise its rough flavour and increase its sale.

Such is the present state of affairs, and according to the usually received law of supply and demand, the trade will gradually die away into nothingness, or such reduction will take place in its value here as will enable it to compete with that produced in China; and if it be desired to induce the Chinese to abandon their present practice of making the cultivation of cereals give way for the growth of the poppy, which, notwithstanding the interdict that from time to time has issued from the Central and Provisional Governments, has of late extended so alarmingly, this reduction must reach to certainly one-half. Temporary resuscitation will doubtless occur, but in the face of the constantly diminishing demand it is impossible to hold out any hope in the future of the import of opium into China becoming again a prosperous branch of commerce. The decrease in the consumption of Patna, that is of opium of the most approved manufacture, is remarkable, making it very doubtful whether the assertion of those who state that confirmed smokers who are well to do and accustomed to use the best drug, will have it at any price, can be sustained. While the prospects here and to the north are considered by those interested in the trade as so discouraging, it must be admitted that the total import into Hong Kong, through which port the whole of China is supplied with the Indian drug, has not sensibly diminished.[1]

This is a long extract, but it sums up the subject fairly, putting, perhaps, the best possible face on the situation. I own that the signs thus manifested of the spread of the growth of the poppy in China seem to me most ominous, not only, as I have already pointed out, for the finances of India, but for the future prosperity of the Chinese race. Formerly we did at least this good by the high taxes we imposed on the drug before it left India—we made its use the luxury of the rich, and our supply was altogether so small that it hardly affected the health or morals of the nation. But now, although we still draw a huge income from the sale of this dangerous narcotic, we no longer remain the dominant source of supply, and the Chinese are rapidly becoming adepts in the preparation of a drug nearly as strong as our own, while its use in some form now permeates the land. Nemesis seems to be

[1] Consul Medhurst's Report for 1875-76, China Reports, No. 1, 1877.

about to overtake us, in short, through the very means which we took to extend, legalize, and secure our trade. The dangers of the present condition of the finances of India, and the precariousness of one at least of its staple exports, are together brought before us by facts like these with a force that cannot be denied.

Unsatisfactory as the position of the opium trade may be, it is not much more so than that of the general trade between the United Kingdom and China. Both the import and export sides of this trade are at present in a very unhealthy state, and the losses of the past four years must have been enormous. As I write Mincing Lane is full of complaints about the unprofitableness of this year's ventures in tea. Merchants have bought recklessly in China and shipped recklessly, with the result that heavy losses have to be faced in the London market, which is glutted at the commencement of the season by the excessive supply. This state of affairs has been brought about in part, it is said, by the grand style which old habit has made second nature to English merchants in doing business in China. They try to trade now as they did before they had rivals and as they did when a season's speculations might realise a man a large fortune, and when luxury, a large staff, and the most profuse expenditure could be easily maintained. Now, however, the Chinese merchant is both better informed and able to play off his customers one against another, and

Englishmen have competitors from America and from Germany who appear to be often able to get as against them the best of the bargain. Nowhere so much as in China, moreover, has the electric telegraph worked such a complete revolution in favour of speculation by the small man with little or no capital but some credit; and merchants of the old school, possessing large means perhaps, now find themselves jostled and it may be beaten by the small man who works through bankers' credits or who buys on his own responsibility, but whose operations are backed by the purely financial firms who operate through anyone whom they think likely to enable them to turn over their money at a profit. This sort of trading engenders often the rashest competition, and more than any other breeds disasters. Prices are run up in the keenness of competition or on some passing phase of the home market communicated through the cables, and by-and-by everyone finds that he has bought too much and at too high prices. Operations by telegraph are in some ways the most unsafe of all, and a condition of business like that prevailing in China, where there are far too many usurers, far too many merchants, and far too many merchants' *employés* fighting for the business, makes it doubly a dangerous one. I believe much of the loss which this wild trading has entailed within the past five years has yet to be accounted for, and that when our next financial storm comes, old houses whose capital is exhausted, and financial middlemen and banks whose credits have been foolishly squandered by little operators with nothing to lose, will become bankrupt. There is no trade where a deceptive method of lending and a constant abuse of a foolish credit system have played more havoc than in our trade with the East as a whole. The ball is now kept rolling, but every now and then we see a house go down exhausted, and one day will be unable to express our astonishment that so many grand but empty fabrics have continued to stand till now. In some ways our trade with China is the least satisfactory of all. Our exports thither are not carried on prudently, and our imports are as ill-regulated as they could well be. What, for example, could be worse than the present situation of the importers of tea to whom I have already referred? Not only does our market suffer from glut but also from the great deterioration which has taken place of late years in the quality of the dried leaf. An eager haste to be early in the market, a fierce competition between different lines of tea steamers, and reckless buying, have combined to overstrain the primitive methods of preparation clung to by the small Chinese growers, and as a consequence the quality of Chinese tea has become often intolerably bad. It is a demoralised trade in China as well as here, and I see no prospect of a return to a better state of things. Consul Medhurst of Shanghai, in his interesting report for 1875–76, goes so far as to say that the Chinese tea trade is ruined unless foreign capital and organised methods of cultivation are introduced into the country—a remedy which does not at present seem likely to be applied. The tea trade of China is therefore altogether in a most unsatisfactory condition, and in the meantime must go from bad to worse.

In its decadence India has, to be sure, a great chance, and the cultivation of tea there and in Ceylon may grow till it compensates us; but that will not satisfy either the exigencies of India or our own. If the opium staple export from India goes to the wall and the China tea import to England as well, what hope can we have of a speedy renewal of healthy progress in our general trade with China? No other commodity that she has now to offer is likely to take the place of tea in any important degree. The silk trade is nearly as bad as the tea trade, and losses incurred in it have been hid away or plastered over till it is altogether hollow. Not only are other silk-producing countries able to make headway in competing with China, but the fashion of the world has for the time discarded silk as a constant and a principal article of dress, and silk is no longer in high demand. China is rich in soil and in climate and working powers, and may find other great staples such as cotton, flax, indigo, tobacco, sugar, and corn, but she has not done so as yet, and till she does we must pronounce her export trade in a precarious condition so far as England and India are concerned.

We shall have, at all events, financial disturbances before it can give signs of improvement.

Nor is the condition of the Chinese import trade any better, at any rate as regards the import of British goods. China is our second best customer for plain cotton fabrics, coming next to India, and the loss of her trade, or any part of it, would be assuredly most seriously felt. Several causes, independent of the financial position and of our own folly, combine to render our hold of the trade and our power to expand it much less assured than it was a few years ago. Chief of these appears to be our own dishonesty. We have in the greedy, unscrupulous competition which modern business habits have introduced into all departments of trade, made and sold to the Chinese bad heavily sized fabrics to an extent that has discredited our productions as against both the coarser but cheaper and stronger home-made tissues and the better made cottons of the United States. The Chinese are large growers of cotton, and probably about four-fifths of the entire consumption of cotton cloths are still of home manufacture, in the interior of China at all events. Whatever depreciates the character of our goods must necessarily perpetuate the disposition to prefer the home-made fabrics to ours. In time, however, this mischief of dishonest fabrics would perhaps cure itself by the ruin of the mischief-makers, were there no other element of danger to fight against than native competition. But both the Americans and the Dutch, and to some extent the Germans, now compete with us in the Chinese markets, and though none of them make much way, both the Americans and the Germans appear to compete with at least a promise of success. So far as America is concerned, it is entirely our own fault if it is more than a promise. While the Americans try to trade on their present economic basis, not all their ingenuity in inventing labour-saving appliances, their energy, and their apparent advantages as growers of the finest cotton in the world, can enable them to beat free traders like ourselves out of the Chinese markets unless we behave like fools and rogues. I am not inclined therefore to set very serious store by such shouts of triumph as this one, which caught my eye lately in a leading American mercantile journal:

In our articles with regard to the export of cotton goods from the United States we have frequently called attention to the condition of the trade in China. Up to this time the total export to China of the United States and Great Britain combined would scarcely supply more than six per cent. of the population; but the trade is a constantly growing one, for hand-made goods can never stand against those made by machinery. The latter will inevitably supplant the former, and with an accelerated speed as time progresses. Now, the question we have often asked, and ask again to-day, is, what country shall furnish the new spindles which will be required to supply this increasing trade? The answer comes up to us from China itself—'America;' for the Chinese have at last become sufficiently acute to prefer cotton to clay. This preference our articles have before this shown to exist, but just now it is being expressed with strong emphasis. We have received this week from Liverpool the Shanghai circular of Mr. P. Maclean, and his description of the condition of that market is decidedly cheerful. He states that the holders of English manufactures have had but a sorry time of it since the issue of his last report. The dignified title 'selling' can be applied only to the business of a few; the great majority, to borrow an auction expression, have had to 'give their goods away,' and numerous have been the attempts wherein the British merchant has signally failed to secure even auction prices. There are times, he adds, when no amount of worrying or blarney, and scarcely any concession, will move the obdurate Chinaman to do business. But when Mr. Maclean begins to report about 'American goods' he clears up the difficulty, showing us the whole situation. These are his words: 'American goods, on the other hand, have been fairly saleable, and the tendency of prices (jeans only excepted) is against buyers. It may not be deemed out of place here to direct attention to the fact that the trade in American cottons with China is expanding very rapidly. The quality is greatly superior to the generality of stuffs that come out of Lancashire; it is more honest and enduring, and so, although the first cost to the consumer is higher, eventually it is the more economical manufacture.'

This certainly is agreeable information and good evidence of facts we have been constantly enforcing upon the attention of our readers. And what is true of China is true also of South America. These markets want our goods and we have them to sell. In quality they are admittedly superior. But we must be enabled in price also to compete with the most favoured nations. Heretofore we have frequently stated the position of the American producer in this particular. The result of it all is that our manufacturer can furnish the goods even now in his mill as cheaply as England can; and with some changes in our revenue laws, it will cost him still less to produce them. This, however, is not all; goods made, satisfactory in price and quality, constitute only one factor in the problem; the next is to have the facilities for laying them down, at a market where they are wanted, with as little cost as our rivals for transportation.[1]

And so on. The fact of the competition existing is not alarming but the reverse if we are stimulated to remove the cause for the taunt about the difference in quality, which is, I fear, at present to some extent true. As I shall demonstrate in the next chapter, America is not now in a position to compete with us effectually on any other ground than greater honesty. We can make varieties of fabrics, all good of their kind, if we choose, which she can in no way come near.

The most serious difficulty of all which besets our export trade to China is, however, the official difficulty. At the present time it is not unlikely that our shipments of cotton goods to China would be larger than those to India, were it not that a corrupt officialism makes foreign trading into many parts of the empire an impossibility. We have never, for example, been able to get our goods through the provincial customs barriers without payment of arbitrary squeezes which have nearly made trade impossible. Treaty rights have been systematically and totally disregarded, and after paying customs dues and transit dues at the ports, we have constantly found the officials in the interior

---

[1] *New York Commercial Chronicle*, June 30, 1877.

levying black mail on their own account from he native merchants.

The moral character of the Chinese official class is probably as low in some respects as any on the face of the earth. They neither respect pledges nor appear to possess intelligence enough to give system to their selfishness; their minds cannot conceive what constitutes justice and fair-dealing, and their arrogance grows in proportion to our forbearance. Ruptures with China are therefore always probable events, and after a time became almost necessary to our existence there as traders in any shape.

Two years ago this country was agitated with the prospect of having to punish Chinese official cruelty and treachery once more, and the storm blew over, I fear, only for a time, to come up again when provocation once more reaches the unbearable point. No trade, however necessary, can be secure which is carried on under conditions like these, and in spite of the opening of further inland ports, and of fair promises, I fear we cannot hope to see our merchandise overrunning China at a very early date. We may indeed see a very different sight.

Some concessions were made over the Margary affair, which may, however, do temporary good. The Chinese evidently felt that they had gone too far, and, as usual, became as fawning as they had before been truculent; and it is possible that a quiet steady trade free from over speculation, from heavy losses, might be done with the country for the next year or two should our overstrained credit not break down in the meantime. An extended trade cannot be looked for in present circumstances in any department, and if China loses her tea trade or becomes impoverished in parts nearly depopulated by the famines said to prevail in several provinces, we may look to see a most serious falling off in many directions. It must not, as may easily be supposed after what I have said, be taken as a healthy sign that our imports from China in 1876 were about the largest in value that they have ever been, reaching 16,300,000*l.*, for they were swollen by, amongst other things, the excessively high price of silk, a price that indicated unhealthy speculation. This article is more liable to fluctuate in value and quantity than any other, and gives us no reason to predict so high a level of prices this year. Our exports to China, on the other hand, were last year a million lower than they had been in 1875, and showed a falling off in the value of best woollens and cottons which there is reason to fear will not be made good in 1877. Our exports of cotton were indeed obviously excessive, the condition of the country being taken into account, and the slightly increased facilities which the new treaty ports opened were expected to give have proved of little or no value. China is not conquered by the foreign trader when he gets to a port; it remains nearly as inaccessible to his zealous huckstering as ever. Projects are entertained of opening up China by railways, and we occasionally hear most tantalizing accounts of the surpassing wealth and value of her iron and coal deposits; but these visions and projects seem to me utterly delusive in the present state of the Chinese empire. Only in very few regions would railways be at all likely to pay in a country like China, better provided with water communications than any other in the world; and whether they paid or not, it would be impossible at present to get foreign capital to embark in undertakings so little likely to be tolerated. There looks to be more feasibility in the projects spoken of for establishing manufactories of cotton fabrics as in India; but these also would probably result in ruin to whatever foreign capitalists made the venture. The truth is the Chinese are morbidly jealous of everything foreign, and especially of foreign success. They have, in every instance when foreign traders appeared to be gaining advantage over them, schemed to destroy these advantages. They have barely tolerated the experimental Woosung railway, and have the utmost jealousy of the American steam-boats on their unrivalled Yang-tse river, so much so that a native steam-ship company, said to be heavily subsidised, is striving to grasp the traffic for native profit. This jealousy no doubt in part accounts for the dogged resistance to treaty obligations already alluded to—a jealousy born of insatiable greed and unfathomable vanity. It is only fair, however, to say that the Chinese common people do not exhibit these qualities towards foreign enterprises and institutions. They are naturally peaceable and teachable enough, and only become savage when their ignorant fears and prejudices have been worked upon, as was the case last year at the opening of the new treaty port of Kiungchow.[1]

In these observations I have only offered roughly the more salient features of the position of the China trade and of the English there. I have said sufficient, however, to show that the position of that trade is not at present satisfactory as regards either India or England, except in so far as the bad qualities of teas now shipped from China are favourable to the rapid extension of tea-growing in India. The opium trade, if not really in danger of immediate extinction, is at least threatened with that danger, and a change in the tastes of opium-smokers, or an improvement in the qualities of Chinese sorts, may soon effect a revolution destructive to nearly one-sixth of the gross revenue of India. As regards our home trade with China, it is at present very unhappily situated, partly through our own faults of immoral trading, our competition and recklessness, but also from the character of the Chinese administration, which is inimical, with a slow, sullen, but ever-living

[1] *Vide* Acting Vice-Consul Ford's report where he describes the popular tumults and the alarms and stonings to which the Europeans were at first subjected in consequence of the many calumnies which had been current about their polity (*China Papers*, No. 1, 1877).

hostility, to all foreign enterprise and trade. I do not therefore look in the near future for any material extension of our trade in that region. On the contrary, it will at best be about stationary and often unprofitable, or it may recede to a very serious extent.

Turning to Japan, we find the position if possible still more difficult to gauge. The modern order is so new in Japan that we are affected at the outset by fears about its endurance, and the insurrections by which it is being shaken, though perhaps ultimately unsuccessful, help to strengthen these fears. Japan has indubitably completely changed front in less than a generation, and from being the most exclusive of countries has become the most slavishly imitative. This rapidity of change points in itself to a weak changeableness of disposition which does not permit us to rely on the national character. In the meantime, however, we do a considerable trade with the country, exporting direct nearly 2,000,000*l.* per annum from England, and carrying on a substantial business between its ports and some of our own dependencies. But the principal export trade of Japan is not with us but with China and the United States, and it is hardly probable that we shall make much headway against either competitor. Nor does there seem to me to be great scope for our competition, so far as English goods, at all events, are concerned. Japan is much more likely to offer a field for Australian than for English manufactured goods, and the Australians may yet contest the supremacy of the United States with effect. Americans have at present a large part of the manufacture of Japanese teas in their own hands, and the supply sent to the United States is increasing year by year. Americans and some Englishmen have also taken to work Japanese coal mines with such success that Japanese coal is rapidly superseding both Australian and English in the principal Chinese depôts. Should the Chinese fail to recover their position as tea-growers, it is indeed not improbable that we may find a substantial portion of the Japanese crops in our home markets, but hitherto only small parcels have been offered here and our traders appear to give them little encouragement; but unless India succeeds in meeting our wants to the full this may not long continue the case. I do not, however, anticipate that our trade with Japan will ever be an extensive one, although at the same time we should be foolish to neglect it, because an absorption of only two or three millions' worth of British goods every year must always be a valuable support to our trade position in China. Neither is there any reason why English capital and enterprise should not be more and more used with happy effect in developing Japanese resources. That would be a profitable thing for this country whether the products of Japan come to our shores or not. Our position is as yet incomparably superior to that of any other nation in the far East, and we should do good to all concerned by peacefully teaching the Japanese to make the best of their resources. Russia as a trader cannot touch us there, and all the outcry about Russian aggression in Japan, which prevailed two or three years ago, was based on a very mistaken conception of the situation. France makes no headway anywhere in that region in spite of her advantage in China and her possessions in Cochin China. We have Australia to back us there, and India, besides the supreme trade position in China, and with only America and some Germans in any real sense competitors, need not, unless we are negligent, fail to have a powerful if not dominant trade influence in Japan. But it is a pity that we cannot shake ourselves free of opium, which, however profitable an article it may have been to India and to unscrupulous English merchants, is a great drag upon our more honourable and beneficial trade; already it has done mischief to us in Japan and may yet do more.

At the present time, therefore, the prospects of our trade there are most difficult to indicate, and it will be prudent not to hope over much. There may be no storms in Japan and yet competition from San Francisco may beat us, if for no other reasons than that the Americans buy Japanese tea and we do not. Or there may be storms there as in China, and the whole position of the English in the far East be strained to the utmost. Of one thing we may at least be sure, that the loan-floating mode of stimulating our trade there is ominous of danger and perhaps of disaster. What good is done in China and Japan must be done by private hands and private means. Public loans, such as those Japan has twice floated here and such as China has several times raised amongst the foreign bankers and merchants in its treaty-ports, can do no good, unless it be a good to pay for gun-boats, Krupp cannon, and Martini-Henry rifles to fight us with. Neither the Chinese nor the Japanese Governments can employ money to sound purpose on civil objects.

The last Japanese foreign loan was indeed raised for a laudable object from a Japanese point of view. The new Government of the restored Mikado was much embarrassed by the many pensions which it had to pay to the dispossessed nobles and their retainers, and borrowed money here for the purpose of enabling it to capitalise these pensions. No doubt the measure afforded some relief to the national budget, as a fourth of the entire revenue was under the original agreement with the nobles and Samurai absorbed by the pensions. But this was hardly a justification for English investors risking their money even though they got ten per cent. for it, and the relief afforded was not nearly enough. The embarrassment of the Government has continued, and it is mainly owing to its successive reductions of the income or the rates of commutation allowed to these privileged subjects that rebellion is even now shaking the empire. I am by no means sure that the discontented classes may not triumph in time, if not now, and should they do so, there will in all probability be an end to progress and perhaps to foreign enterprise altogether, for a time at least.

A most interesting memoir on the finances of Japan has recently been drawn up by Mr. S. H. Mounsey, attaché to the British Legation at Yedo,[1] from which, amongst many other interesting facts, I gather that the debt of the Japanese Government is now over 29,000,000*l*., including the paper money in circulation. According to the budgets, the Government manages to make ends meet, but that is all, and changes in the mode of levying the tax on land, which yields from nine to ten millions sterling of the revenue, the total of which is less than thirteen, are not unlikely to produce deficits. When the expenses of the rebellion are added to the ordinary outlay deficits are for a time certain. Fresh issues of paper money and of Government bonds must be the inevitable result, and fresh trade and other disturbances may not improbably follow. It would be the height of folly, therefore, to lend more money to Japan; and I am not sure that the wisdom of previous lendings will be justified, although the loans are for short periods and loaded with heavy 'sinking funds.'

In any event, at present I cannot see that the

[1] *Embassy and Legation Reports*, part ii., 1877.

trade between England and Japan promises to be an expansive one. Like the rest of the world, Japan has made haste to mortgage her resources, and would have to suffer for that whatever her internal peace and order. But when to that danger is added the discontent of the old feudal barons and their retainers who have lost by the reinstatement of the Mikado nearly all their incomes, and of the peasant proprietors harassed as they think by the levy of their taxes in money instead of as formerly in kind; when we consider that everything is new and fluid in the Japanese order of government, that the past history of the country has been marked by sudden whirligigs of change, and that as yet, with all the force of the revolutionary era, the foreigners have not got any profound hold or any free entry into the country, we have grave reasons for abstaining from sanguine anticipations. We may be thankful if in the next few years we sell to Japan as much as we do now, and need not be surprised if we both sell and buy much less.

CHAPTER IV.

THE UNITED STATES.

There is no country with which England does business whose trade ought to be so important to her as that of the United States. The ties of race, language, and history that bind the two together are of the most intimate kind, and the service which each is capable of rendering the other is quite invaluable, so that the more they draw together in close business relationship the better it will be for both. This broad statement expresses the general truth and the general opinion as to what trade policy between the countries ought to aim at, but it is curiously and in many respects contrary to the actual condition of things. As matters at present rest, there is no branch of British trade about which more gloomy views prevail than surround our trade with the States. Many people can see no redeeming feature in the situation at all. The Americans have shut out all English manufactures by a ruinously high tariff, and inside this artificial barrier have so well succeeded in perfecting indigenous manufacturing industries, that were the barrier now knocked away many people believe that no more room would be found for foreign produce. The United States is, in short, bent upon becoming a self-contained country, capable of feeding itself, clothing itself, and of generally providing for the multiform wants of a high civilisation; and the despondent here at home say that success in the attempt is certain. By and by the trade of England with the States will be nearly all one way —we shall buy from them, but they will not buy from us.

This is truly a melancholy outlook; but before accepting it as an accurate precognition of events, it will be advisable to see in what degree the situation really corresponds to it now. And in order to do this I should like the reader to follow me into some particulars regarding the condition of the United States and their trade. It is unnecessary to say that the observations I make must be merely general, for the country is too vast, and the economic problems it is setting itself to solve practically far too mixed, scattered, and indefinitely stated as it were, to admit of a full and exhaustive *résumé* in the space at my command. A few broad features of the position are therefore all that I can offer.

Everybody is familiar with the extraordinary growth and unique position of the United States. They form at the present time an aggregate of territories peopled by about 40,000,000 from almost all races and nations on the face of the earth. On an English stock curiously mixed and variegated series of engraftings have gone on for something like a century, until now we have English, Irish, French, German, Russ, Spanish, Italian, Norse, Danish, Chinese, and Negro, all seething and toiling together in the building up of one great nation, or of many great nations. As yet the fusion is imperfect, the various nationalities but half-absorbed, while the country itself is too raw, too lately taken possession of, for divergent interests to have their full disintegrating force. Negro slavery abolished, unity is now more complete superficially, but rifts that may split the States in pieces are visible still and make one cautious in speaking of the future. The German has not yet learned to fraternise with the Irishman, the black is still at feud with the white; the yellow Chinaman is still on the confines of society, ever and anon threatened with summary expulsion; while North and South harbour the old hates, looking for a new chance of coercion or for revenge, and East and West hang ill together. But over all these struggling and half-digested fragments of races and nationalities the enterprising progressive spirit of the 'Yankee,' the native American of the North, distinctly dominates at present for good or evil. It is his civilisation which they must all conform to, and his ambitions which they must all share in and follow, or sink. The new generations that come to the front will be, in the North at least, imbued with his tendencies, share the prejudices of the 'glorious Union,' and be, above all things, citizens of the 'freest nation the world ever saw,' unless the forces now unquestionably fighting against their sway in the end shall prove the stronger. At present the consummation of a national unity is not reached, nor is it near at hand. There are still long struggles to come before the dream of the leaders of the people is fulfilled, if it ever be fulfilled. We are not, however, so much concerned with this aspect of the subject as with the fact that here we have a mixed multitude, partly composed of outcasts from all the civilisations of the Old World, and partly of vigorous spirits fleeing from an Old World decrepitude, scattered over what is practically a vast crude continent—a new country, the natural forces of which may be said to 'make for' a kind of barbarism and a primitive order of society. The country of the United States is as large as Europe, and all the population which occupies it might be gathered into the States of New England alone without overcrowding them. In the majority of cases therefore the forces of nature might be expected to prove too much for this sprinkling of men, and they have often in some respects proved so already. The pioneers of the West, whatever their nationality, have been to a great extent drawn back into a position of—if I might use the phrase—barbarised civilisation; become in many instances savages of the woods and prairies, often losing nearly all trace of their original state, except in so far as their former civilised habits lend aid to their new savagery. And there lies before the inhabitants of the States vast egions yet to people, almost boundless tracts to reclaim, which in the same fashion though in modified degree may produce the same mental changes—an isolation and separateness which no expenditure of flashy patriotism, no extent of 'travelling facility,' may be able to overcome. Oregon, for example, the 'gem' State of the Union, is as yet almost uninhabited, and many States, not so far from the governing heart of the country, are still not fully explored, far less peopled. Had it not been for the discoveries and appliances of modern science it is doubtful whether many central and western tracts could have as yet been reached at all. Men would have hugged the seaboards or the great water highways of the continent, and many generations might have elapsed before any but outlaws and restless adventurers could have been found in the far inland plains. The railway, far more than conquest or the pressure of emigration, has vanquished the Indian, and scattered the European population over the continent, from New York to San Francisco, from Charleston to Olympia. Nearly 76,000 miles of iron roads ramify all over the Union, and along these lines westward and southward settlements, villages, townships, and embryo cities are being scattered, until what was twenty years ago a waste wilderness of the Indians has often become the centre of a new civilisation, or the capital of a fresh State. Chicago is not much more than a quarter of a century old, and it has now over 300,000 inhabitants. By means of these iron roads, often endowed with millions of acres of land to tempt settlers with, the whole scattered population is also for the time being kept moving more or less in unison, or is at least, to some degree, prevented from dropping away into separatist tendencies such as the State system on which the Union is based and the isolation of far-divided territories would otherwise render inevitable. The railways and the telegraphs have here also proved levelling and binding in their tendencies, and have together changed the face of the North American continent, as well as many of the conditions under which the weighty issues of the future must be worked out. For all that, human nature and physical laws may yet prove too many for the Union. At all events, the ill-hinged together parts are but feebly held so far by their iron bands, and the crude States of the centre and west show ominous individualities of their own.

This brief general sketch may serve to bring us face to face with the real subject of this chapter. We see a great continent being laid hold of by mixed and more or less civilised fragments of races, all possessed in various degrees with the great impelling qualities of energy and intelligence. And the question comes to be, What are these doing now with this possession in a material point of view? Are they bringing out its resources in the wisest way, so as to benefit not only the possessors but other nations who must, many of them, lack what a country full of such varied riches can supply, or are they neglecting them or wasting them in order to chase chimeras and to realise the impossible? To answer these questions we must, as in the case of India, enter a little into the economics of the country and understand their drift. But I shall do so as lightly as possible, so as to spare the reader useless fatigue.

In the first place, it is an obvious inference that the true line to follow in dealing with such an unreclaimed territory as the United States is to cultivate and develope the land and its products as the safest road to wealth and national progress. Land here is, for one thing, the very cheapest commodity that a man could embark his capital in or devote his labour to. In many cases it may be had almost for nothing, and provinces almost have been for sale at sums which look to people in a country like England, where population presses and feudal and other burdens intervene, utterly ridiculous. For example, the Central Pacific Railway Company received a grant of land to the amount of 11,722,000 acres to assist it in building the line. Of this land the Central Pacific Company sold, up to October 1870, 127,626 acres, at an average price of about 10s. per acre, and the highest average price which has hitherto obtained has been about 28s. per acre. Instances of the same kind might be multiplied indefinitely, where territory of the richest description has been acquired in fee simple at prices which a Highland proprietor would esteem cheap for the most barren and useless precipices in his country. Cultivation can therefore be pursued as a rule with the least comparative initial outlay—a most important thing where hands count for more than capital—and it is to cultivating the natural products of the soil that the people of the United States should therefore, on a broad general view of their position, mostly devote their energies. In the main they have done this. They have done it almost in spite of their predilections. They supply Europe with the bulk of the raw cotton used in her manufactures, with a great proportion of the heavier tobaccos, with timber, and, above all, with grain. The United States have now become the greatest food-producing country in the world, and the singular advantages which they possess are illustrated by the fact that, except perhaps Hungary and our own colonies of Australia, there is no other corn-growing country which can be said at present to hold its own against them. In spite of the vast distances over which United States produce has to be carried ere it can reach the seaboard, and get shipped for Europe, in spite of trade restrictions, of which we shall speak by-and-bye, and of many disadvantages arising from the unequal distribution and command of capital, the farmers, the cotton and tobacco growers of the South and West can command the markets of the world

Since the Territories of the West and South were opened up, since California got over its gold fever and took to cultivate grain, Russia has, for example, been distanced altogether in the English market by America as a source of wheat supply, and what has been accomplished is nothing to what might be, did the American people direct all their energies, or but their main trade policy, towards the production of the most of what they can sell cheapest and at the readiest market.

Unfortunately this is just what they are not doing. A variety of causes have been for years in operation to direct the energies of the people into channels where their work does not pay so well, and where there is little or no chance of the results of it coming into active or general competition with the rest of the world for many a day to come. In the centres of business, in the East, and amongst the politicians and merchants of the Union, it has grown a sort of trade creed that the States ought at once to become a great manufacturing nation. The progress of such countries as England and France or Belgium has been watched by the speculative spirits in the Union with a keenness and jealousy quite unreasonable, but very natural, and the Americans have determined to imitate, and, if possible, excel in the same walks of industry. Possessing a civilisation inherited and imported from Europe, drawing in annually a considerable population familiar with the ideas and usages of Europe, nothing was more natural than that this ambition should find a stimulus in the new land to all appearance so wonderfully endowed with all gifts necessary to excellence. This ambition was in a measure fanned to flames by the speculation and apparent wealth which succeeded the Secessionist War, as well as by the pressure of necessities which that war created. In the great railway mania, which fell upon the States as it has fallen on all civilised nations, for ultimate good no doubt, however much for present trouble and loss to many, it was seen that the country was dependent upon Europe for most of its manufactures. The iron had to be imported—raw as well as manufactured—and in many ways the Union was, as the foolish phrase goes, at the mercy of the foreign merchant and manufacturer. This was represented as a situation too galling to be borne by a great and free country, which possessed within itself not only the materials, but the skill and the energy to make everything it wanted for itself. So the policy of Protection previously only upheld with some hesitation was vigorously developed after the close of the war, and under its shelter the United States have been for years striving diligently to become their own iron smelters and steel makers, weavers and spinners, their own tool makers and engineers, with what success we shall presently see. At present I need only observe that a sounder conception of the plain truths of political economy would have at once taught these eager manufacturers the risk they were running, for the very fact that the protection of a high tariff was necessary to their existence in any shape, should have revealed to them that they were straining the energies of the country towards ends for which they were not ripe, and towards which they could not therefore naturally flow. By protection, in short, American capitalists were doing their best to cause a poverty among the people which would by-and-bye react on themselves.

Besides the causes already pointed to, however, there were two influences which helped to blind the nation to the truth of the matter. One was the apparent abundance of capital, and the other the need of much national revenue. The abundance of capital was produced partly by the vast war expenditure, which had both brought a great deal of foreign money into the country on loan, and introduced a great quantity of paper currency, by which prices were generally inflated, and partly by the new railway enterprises, which also brought great amounts of foreign capital to the States. These all tended to make the nation look richer than it actually was, and helped to cause people to forget that the majority were still in effect only squatters in an unreclaimed country. On the other hand, legislatures were urged on by the necessity for increased taxes. The weight of the war debt was very heavy, and the resources of the Union were very limited to bear it. Owing to the peculiar organisation whereby the individual States composing the Union have almost the whole of the internal taxing power in their own hands, the central Federal authority is left with only the minor internal resources of excise taxes, stamps, and the proceeds of land sales in territories not belonging to or claimed by any State, and the customs. There were great difficulties, consequently, in meeting the demands of this new expenditure, amounting for some years after 1864 to, in gross, over one thousand million of dollars per annum. What more natural, therefore, than that the idea should find favour which seemed to shift the burden off native shoulders, and put it on those of foreign merchants and manufacturers? 'Let us at one and the same time,' it was in effect argued, 'encourage the development of home industries and levy a war tax on foreign imports. We shall thus help on the progress of the nation, and at the same time lighten the pressure of taxation on the community.' And it was done so accordingly with, for a time, the most astonishing results. Annual surpluses never failed, and the nation flourished and grew apace. Customs duties poured in beyond the necessities of the treasury year after year, until the debt of the nation began to be sensibly reduced, and the Protectionists were naturally proud of their policy. Free trade was at a discount and exclusiveness triumphant, so much so that many people have been driven seriously to doubt whether the Americans, 'with their usual astuteness,' have not been in the right, and advocates of a protective reciprocity, of 'countervailing' duties, and all that kind of thing, have actually been holding up their heads again here at home. It almost began to look, after all, as if the true way to make an industry flourish was to put a tax on it.

Time is beginning to show, however, at once the causes of this success and the transitoriness of its character. We must look at the subject with some minuteness. Mention has already been made of both the leading features that led to the adoption of this policy at the end of the war, inflation through paper money and the influx of foreign capital, and both these continued for a time to buoy up the apparent prosperity of the States. I shall take the latter first. During the years 1866 to 1875 inclusive, no less than 37,000 miles were added to the railways of the country, at the cost of, nominally, several hundred millions sterling. A great deal of money—how much I cannot say—but probably from seventy to a hundred millions, including bonds issued in the States, and brought to Europe afterwards, as well as loans raised here originally, was found abroad, in England and on the Continent of Europe; and with this money purchase was made of the raw and other materials necessary to be imported for the construction of these roads over and above what could be produced at home. As all these purchases paid heavy duties it was, therefore, to no small extent the free inflow of foreign capital which upheld the customs returns for many years. That capital thus sufficed to give a fictitious glow of prosperity to the country, which was made to look a country of boundless resource, able to import in any quantity, at any price, and to pay all that it owed abroad without difficulty while doing so. And what the foreign capital did not do directly was done by the extensive creation of paper credits in the States themselves, which the foreign money no doubt made easier. Railway bonds and shares were multiplied to an amazing extent, and made the means of carrying out enterprises, many of which ultimately proved a dead loss or all but a dead loss to their projectors. Add to these considerations the fact that through using little or no metallic currency at home, the States were able to export nearly all the produce of their gold and silver mines, which produce is estimated by the United States Master of the Mint in a paper sent to the English Committee on the Depreciation of Silver at about an average of 13,250,000*l.* per annum for the last eleven years, and we have the means of a temporary prosperity—real and sham—such as no other country ever enjoyed in so short a time. Except California, every State in the Union conducted its trade and paid its debts with 'certificates of indebtedness' which cost at the time merely the printing.

The staying power of the Union was thus for a time made great by a variety of means, and it could pay any price it chose for its whims without apparent suffering.

Taking all these causes together, therefore, we find reasons enough for the singular steadiness with which American trade stood the customs tariffs and everything flourished for a time. The effect of the great production of gold and silver cannot, indeed, be overrated from some points of view. But for the abundance of these metals, there must have much sooner been serious difficulties in the way of industrial progress. Prices would have risen enormously, and money at the same time have been unprocurable for the enterprises which have been successfully carried through. The very profuseness of borrowing must have induced earlier collapse, and the abundance of paper money would only the sooner have inflated everything for a sudden general crash. But in the eighteen years 1858 to 1875, Great Britain alone received on balance 127,000,000*l.* worth of the gold and silver of the United States, which were thus able to pay more readily in specie for their enormous foreign borrowings, and to find the means of maintaining credit through all the gigantic speculations and revolutions by which the country has attained its present material position.

The gold question is one altogether too abstract and wide to find treatment at length in this place;

but it must none the less be borne in mind that the precious metals have played a most important part in the material development of the States hitherto, and that the possession of them in great abundance is still a mighty factor in favour of the continued advance of the country in industrial prosperity. Were the United States to place their internal circulation again on a specie basis and still continue to export gold, they would continue to command foreign capital more freely than ever, and might not be hampered by the values difficulty as they are now. For a long time past the real cost of any given product must have been difficult to ascertain in the Union as in other paper currency lands, and the risk of loss from miscalculation proportionately severe. Whatever might be the relation of the metals to values in countries whose circulation was on a specie basis, that of the depreciated paper of the States was always so much higher. In giving the gold and silver to swell the cash resources of foreign nations, therefore, and in retaining the cheaper circulating medium for home use, the Union did not, as the 'soft money' party contends, benefit itself in the least. It only deluded itself for a time with a hollow show of paramount and all-compassing prosperity which collapsed at last and left the people face to face with the danger of a complete solution of the ties that hold a civilised business together and render its conduct possible. A narrow, depreciated, hard and fast paper currency then sat as it now sits on the trade of the country with a stifling weight.

But for a time the effect of both paper and metal was the same. The one helped speculators to secure what seemed enormous profits and to launch with a semblance of immunity countless projects, and the other helped to make the payment of interest on foreign debt an easy matter. Hence by their paper currency, and by their wealth of precious metals, the United States have been tempted on into ways and into obligations which must for some time yet exercise a retardant influence upon the country. At this present time all industry except that of agriculture and the mining of gold and silver may be said to suffer from the consequences of an inflation and over-rapid forestalling of the future which came to a head in the autumn of 1873. Up to the middle of September of that year everything had been going on almost as usual, barring one or two rather heavy failures which passed with little remark. Commerce was apparently sound, and railway and other undertakings holding their own. A comparatively slight event sufficed, however, to upset the entire credit system of the nation and reveal the fact that this prosperity was hollow, and that the trade of the Union was literally hanging over a great abyss. The mushroom speculative banking firm of Messrs. Jay Cooke & Co. suspended on September 18, and its suspension was followed immediately by that of a number of other banks and speculative as well as trading houses. An immediate crisis supervened, aggravated by the drained state of banking-tills and by the paper currency, which, being a hard, inelastic quantity, that no raising of discount rates would bring into larger supply, could not be used to sustain sinking credit in any efficient way. It aggravated the troubles, therefore, and for a short period general bankruptcy seemed impending. Gold rose in value compared with the greenback and other paper currency, and the more it rose the more impossible did it become to use it as a means of calming the excitement. Ultimately, in part through the banks extemporising a sort of credit currency of their own, the terror subsided, and those who weathered the storm gathered courage to go on again. Some of the banks that had suspended resumed, and by various means the acute form of the crisis was got over. But the stagnation of business which followed it has lasted till this day. The four years that have followed must have been for many persons a long-drawn-out agony, and failures have been more numerous every year since the crisis than at the time, spreading their disastrous effects further and further over the lower ranks of traders all through the Union. The breakdown revealed the fact that all kinds of business enterprise and credit had been pushed too far. Private traders, municipalities, and above all railways and joint-stock ventures of all kinds, had gone on piling debt upon debt till the business credit of the nation had become inflated with mere wind. Banking houses and private firms had so deeply pledged their resources to extravagant undertakings that the collapse of these ramified everywhere and crippled almost everybody. When the nation came to itself again, therefore, and the business of life went on in its old channels, aims had to be greatly narrowed, industries of all kinds to be curtailed, and the task has even then continually proved too much for multitudes who have since gone to the wall. The mere shrinkage in prices due to a stagnant state of business and to the slow approach of the paper currency to the level of metallic value were themselves sufficient to drain away the property of tens of thousands all over the land. Some particulars of trade movements and figures since 1873 will convey the situation, as far as it concerns us, more clearly to the reader. For example, the exports from this country to the United States have fallen off since 1873, when they came to nearly 37,000,000*l*., a lower figure than that for 1872, till last year they reached only 20,226,000*l*., and the latest returns which have been received since show that they continue still to decline.[1]

[1] The following figures published by the United States Bureau of Statistics will enable the reader to see at a glance what the effect of the panic has been. They contain the specie as well as merchandise imports and exports, as the two cannot fairly be separated. The contrast between the ante-panic and post-panic periods is thus all the more striking. It must not be forgotten that these figures are, so far as exports of merchandise are concerned, somewhat delusive, owing to the fact that

These facts and figures clearly indicate that, up to 1873, the country had been buying much beyond its strength. While saddled with a very heavy debt-charge, and with the interest due on speculative domestic undertakings which, but for European, and especially English, assistance could never have been set on foot or carried out in the time, the country continued to buy more than it sold, and to get, therefore, year by year, deeper into debt.

The panic reversed this state of affairs, while at the same time the comparative cessation of foreign supplies of floating capital, and the continued necessities laid upon the country by the demands of the foreign creditor combined to compel the Union to push

most of the values are 'currency' values, whereas the imports are all entered at 'specie' values. Hence, according as the paper dollar is at a large or a small discount as against gold, the nominal values of the exports will be heightened or lowered. It may thus happen that the export account looks favourable when it is not really so. For purposes of generalisation, however, the following figures are sufficiently near the truth to be useful enough:—

Ante-Panic Period.

	Imports	Exports	Excess of Imports
1870-1	$541,500,000	$541,500,000	—
1871-2	640,000,000	523,900,000	$116,100,000
1872-3	663,600,000	542,600,000	121,000,000
Average	615,000,000	536,000,000	79,000,000

Post-Panic Period.

	Imports	Exports	Excess of Exports
1873-4	$595,800,000	$653,000,000	$57,200,000
1874-5	553,900,000	605,500,000	51,600,000
1875-6	476,500,000	596,500,000	120,000,000
1876-7	491,150,000	658,395,000	167,239,000
Average	529,300,000	628,300,000	98,000,000

her export trade as a means of meeting engagements. The economic effect of this change of position has therefore been practically to throw the country back upon its more primitive and natural articles of commerce; and in consequence to embarrass still further those more artificial industries, so to say, which owed their existence to the inflation of credit and inpour of foreign capital previous to 1873 and to the tariff. Hence we find that almost nothing except Nevada mining and agriculture has thriven lately in the States. The farmers and cotton-planters have done well, as a rule, all over the continent, but the manufacturers have fared very badly, as we shall presently see, and in spite of their much increased exports.

But it will be said, 'If the States have thus come round to a more healthy and natural trade position, the panic must have done them great good, and the gloomy predictions as to the future must therefore be belied.' That has indeed been said these three years past at least, and it would be true were the revolution altogether a natural one. The decline in American demand for English goods so much complained of would then be a thing to be endured cheerfully till better times came, and we should all look forward hopefully to a speedy revival of business so soon as the States had rounded off some of their heavier obligations, and strengthened their position, say, by bringing home a considerable part of their outstanding debts, corporate and national. Unhappily, the stagnation of British exports, and of all exports to the States, is not quite the natural outcome of the crisis in the strictest sense of that term, but is due largely to the artificial influence of the trade tariff to which we have already referred. As long as that tariff continues in force there is no possibility of a revival of our export trade to the States. Not only that, but before long I believe our import trade from thence will be seriously affected by its reflex action. Indeed, the latest figures given in the note above indicate instability here also, although the totals for 1876–7 are a considerable improvement on those of the two previous years, from influences which I am disposed to think exceptional.

Hitherto the great expansiveness of the export trade of the United States has afforded an illustration of the truth I have contended for—that the true policy of the country is to develope first of all its crude resources, so to say—to make the land, which is the cheapest commodity it possesses, and the most easily worked, yield its utmost. The United States could distance almost all the world in providing endless varieties of raw produce and food grains if the people were so inclined, and that they have continued producing as they have done in the face of a prohibitory customs tariff, is proof of this. But I do not think, if the tariff continues in force on its present footing, that this predominance can go on. Nay, I do not think it could have lasted so markedly up to now had other countries not been, in their several ways, tied up against more effectual competition, and any material lowering of the price of corn in Europe through one or two good harvests would produce serious results in the States, even under present conditions.

We must understand this customs tariff a little if we are to get at a true view of the trade position of the Union whether as regards imports or exports. I say a little, because I do not believe that anyone can understand it except in a limited and general way; the framers of it did not, it is evident, themselves understand it fully. It was framed on a combination of mistaken economic principles and clamorous private interests which offer a singular commentary on the equality secured to men by democracy. I have already stated the general ideas underlying its inception, and may now, by way of diversion, give the reader some of its detailed peculiarities before proceeding to discuss the consequences which it is producing. For example, we find throughout the tariff, which comprises altogether some two thousand articles, a determined effort made to shut out foreign competition in all kinds of articles which were either attempted to be produced at home, or which Americans thought they might be able to produce. Thus, a crude or raw article will be admitted at a low duty, or perhaps free, but let that article bear the least indication of manufacture, of labour spent upon it, and a duty more or less heavy is instantly imposed. Hence we find this sort of thing occurring constantly: 'Unmanufactured agates,' duty free; 'ditto, cut for bookbinders,' 20 per cent. duty. Amethysts, 'not set,' 10 per cent.; ditto 'set,' 25 per cent. Crude ammonia is admitted free, but the various preparations of it pay duty, according to an arbitrary scale, of from 10 to 40 per cent. Grasses and the pulp of grasses for the manufacture of paper are admitted free, but every variety of manufactured paper pays duty—curl paper and paper balloons 50 per cent., cigarette papers 75 per cent., and most other sorts 20 to 35, chiefly 35, per cent. Nearly all kinds of smokers' articles, except clay pipes, pay 75 per cent. duty, and so forth. I might fill a dozen pages of this book with the enumeration of those articles, large and petty, which are subject to the demands of this far-reaching tariff. Throughout the whole of it the one idea runs of making anything manufactured pay severely, and to such an outrageous and unreasoning extent has the theory been carried, that, after a rather minute study of the tariff, I should say that I am within the mark in estimating that there must be about 1,000 articles at least on which the total annual yield of the duty cannot, on the average, pay for collection and trouble. That was notoriously the case with our own old tariff, and it never could be compared for rigour and weight to that of the United States, which is in hundreds of instances not protective merely but prohibitory.

For if all small articles are hunted down and made to pay heavy duties, it is merely because the larger, the staple articles of trade, are treated with the severest measures of all. The framers of the tariff have laid it down as a basis of their action that the foreigner must be fined in order that native manufactures might flourish; and therefore any fabric containing silk, wool, iron, flax, cotton, copper, &c., had to be treated with especial severity. Hence it is that we find nearly every article which is made wholly or in part of silk charged 60 per cent. duty, any article of cotton or woollen materials charged 35 to 45, and even 50 per cent.; nearly all iron manufactures charged about 35 per cent., nearly all steel articles 45 and 50 per cent. And these duties do not always represent the real incidence; many of them are taken not merely *ad valorem*, but by weight, measure, or in bulk as well; and thus it not seldom happens that a duty of 35 or 40 per cent. comes really to be a duty of 80, 100, and at times as much as 200 per cent. on the prime cost of the articles, before they reach the hands of the American dealer. Take, for example, woollen goods of nearly every description. We find that they pay an *ad valorem* duty of 35 per cent. in most cases, and of 40 per cent. in some; but that is not all. Woollen dress goods pay an additional duty of 3*d.* per square yard, woollen cloths one of 2*s*. 1*d*. per lb.; flannels of a certain value a duty of 10*d*., and of higher values 1*s*. 3*d*., 1*s*. 8*d*., and 2*s*. 1*d*., and so on throughout the whole woollen tariff. A complication of this kind makes it almost impossible for an importer to know what the duty will really be; it may be 60 per cent. on the value of his goods, or it may be 150 per cent. This, too, is only a small sample. All through the tariff the same sort of double duties are constantly put on, the intention being distinctly to prohibit imports, not to obtain revenue, so that on mere fiscal grounds the tariff is a singular monument of the ingenuity of human folly. This style of fining industrial products breeds an endless amount of confusion, loss, and annoyance, and certainly acts as a most effective check on the development of foreign competition in the States. Taken over all, the duties levied according to this tariff represent, it is computed, a fine of about 34 per cent., but taken according to the real incidence, they represent one of at least 50 per cent., and probably of 60 per cent. Can we wonder, after thinking a little and realising what this means, that the import trade of the United States is steadily declining? The wonder rather is that it has stood out so well, and, no doubt, without the abundant private borrowing of the past few years, and the remarkable fertility of the soil and low prime cost of the raw products which the States export, it would not have kept up. As things stand, year by year it is shrinking, and it will continue to shrink as the Union grows poorer and its fostered unhealthy native industries more extensive.

We have not yet told all the story, however. In order to realise what the States are doing to choke up the channels of their international trade, we must see also the curious restrictions and impediments which their fiscal legislation has put upon foreign merchants in their own countries. There are a series of rules to be conformed to, and of fees to be paid at ports of shipment, which add both an additional tax and an additional vexation to the already heavy burden of the unhappy trader. Naturally, a tariff so onerous as this gives an impetus to the trade of smuggling, and compels stringent measures to be taken for its suppression and for the protection of the revenue or of the home producer. That these are not always effectual is proved by the cases of prosecution which, my readers may remember, took place some three years ago in New York, against prominent merchants there, who were accused of falsifying invoices for the purpose of defrauding the revenue. The consular rules I speak of are designed as a check on such frauds, and we find a very useful account of them in Mr. Trendell's introduction to the Tariff Appendix of the Catalogue of the British Section in the Philadelphia Exhibition. According to this, an English merchant who has goods to export to the States must first of all make three invoices, stating the quantities in weight, measure, and number of his goods. These the merchant or his authorised agent must take to the American Consulate, and there swear to their accuracy according to a prescribed and very stringent form. The consul thereupon signs a sort of warrant, endorsing the merchant's declaration, and the latter has to pay a fee of 10s. 4d. and a commission of 2s. 6d. for getting the business done. This makes a charge of 12s. 10d. on each consignment of goods beyond the value of, I believe, 20l. Of the three invoices, one is retained by the consul, another sent direct by him to the collector of customs at the port of destination, and the third returned to the shipper, authenticated by the consular certificate, who can then forward it to the consignee. If the consul is not satisfied that true values are given, he can place his own estimate on the invoice and allow the consignee to fight the matter out with the customs authorities when the goods arrive. Consuls can retain invoices 'a reasonable time' for inquiry, if they are not satisfied, or they may demand samples of the merchandise to be left with them. The inconvenience and loss of time, as well as irritating cost, which regulations of this kind entail, are in themselves no small hindrance to trade.

I have said enough, perhaps, to give the reader a general idea of the elaborate enactments which the law-makers of the United States Congress have passed for the purpose of shutting out foreign manufactures; but those who want to have a stronger notion of the minuteness of their labours will find in a note a list of a few of the lesser articles culled at random, all of which are condemned to bear prohibitory duties.[1] We

[1] Accordions, gallic acid, tannic acid, adzes, agate balls and hooks, alabaster ornaments, alcoholometers, almond paste as cosmetics, hartshorn, apples, apple sauce, silk aprons, argentine (German silver), architectural plans, artificial flowers, artists' colours, asthma cigarettes, augers, awls, axes, cotton bags and bagging; flax, jute, and gunny ditto; ballast, bagatelle and billiard balls, barytes (6 varieties), baskets of every description, bass mats, bassoons, bathbrick, oil of bay leaves, bead necklaces, bed-screws, bees and bees'-wax, bells, beltings, Berlin blue, Bibles, bindings of various kinds, biscuits, bladders, sword and knife blades, blank books and labels, Berlin-fig and Prussian blue, board nails, bodkins, bog-oak, boots, boot fronts and laces, bottles (cut and uncut), boxes (packing, wood, tin, shell, paper, musical, &c.), braces, brads, braids, bread, bread baskets, Bremen blue, bricks, bridles, Bristol boards, Britannia ware, brooms and brushes, building stones, bulbous roots, bull's-eyes (glass), bullrushes, bunion or corn plaster, bunting, buttons (11 varieties), card-cases, cards (blank, playing, picture, &c.), cassia, catsup, cauliflowers, caulking mallets, Cayenne pepper, celery seed, billiard chalk, chatelaines, chestnuts, children's rattles, chilli peppers, chimney pieces, chip bonnets, chloral hydrate, chlorine, cigars and cigarettes, cinnabar, china clay, clay pipes, clippings of brass, clocks and clock-cases, cloves, Cluny lace, codilla, cod-liver oil, extract of coffee, coffee mills, cold cream, combs, comfits, comforters, condensed milk, copperas, cut coral, coralline, cord, corsets, corundum ore, cotton-goods (over 70 varieties), court plaster, counting-house boxes, crackers (bread), crayons, crochet needles, crystals for watches, cucumbers (pickles), curbchains, cymbals, dandelion root, darning-needles, decalco-manie, dentifrices, decoctions of dyewoods, demijohns, dextrine, dice, dishes (metal), dolls, dominoes, draughts, draintiles, drawer-knobs, dressings for the hair, dressing cases, dress ornaments, dynamite, eavetroughs, effervescent preparations, elastic garters, emery cloth, emetic tartar, enamels, epaulets, Epsom salts, fans, felspar, feeding bottles, fiddles, fifes, figs, filberts, flat-irons, frizettes (hair), frying pans, fuller's earth, fusel oil, galloons, garden shears and seeds, gelatine, gig hames, ginger essence, grand marbles as toys, masks, matches, milk, milk of roses, miniature cases, mitts, mock jewellery, moon or poppy seed, mouse traps, mules, mushrooms, music, neatsfoot oil, needle cases, newspapers, nutmegs, oatmeal, oilcloth, oilskin, onions, orange peel, paddy, paintings, paints,

have now to try and realise what the effect of this trade policy and tariff has been, and is likely to be, both on the development of the industrial wealth of the Union and on its own export business.

First as regards the home industries of the States. Superficially there cannot be any question that the barrier imposed by the customs tariff has been the means of inducing a great expansion and some prosperity in the home manufacturing interests. A great many iron foundries have, for instance, been started

panoramic views, paper, paraffine, parasols, parian ware, parsley seeds, paving stones, paving tiles, pearl barley, pearl beads, peas as seed, peat, peterines, pencils, pens, penknives, peppers, percussion caps, photographs, pills, pincushions, pipes, pipe cases, pipe clay, pitch, plasters, plumes, plush, polishing powders, pork, portmanteaus, potatoes, poultry, powdered acorns, prisms, putty, quadrants, quill toothpicks, quinine, rabbits, ragstones, raisins, rape seed, rapiers, rattles, razors, reaping hooks, reindeer tongues, rifles, gloves, grates, grease, grindstones, gridirons, groats, guava jelly, guitars, gunbarrels, blocks, locks, &c., gunpowder, hackles, hair cloth, human hair, hair oils, hair pencils, hair pins, hair restoratives, hair guards, hammers, handbills, handkerchiefs, head nets, Hervey's magnesia, hobby horses, honey, horse-shoe nails, hour glasses, hyacinth bulbs, hydrometers, hypo-sulphate of soda, India-rubber balls, India-rubber imitation jewellery, India-rubber setons, ink, ink powder, salts of iodine Japan wax, jellies, jet beads, kaleidoscopes, kerosine oil, watch keys, brass kettles, knitting needles, kreosote, lamp black, lanterns, lard, lasts, laudanum, lavender flower, lavender water, licorice juice-paste or rolls, Liebig's extract of meat, limestone, liniments, linseed meal and oil, lint, lotions, lozenges, maccaroni, mace, mackerel, magnesia, malt, marmalade, Rimmel's extract, ringlets, rings, rivets, Robinson's patent groats, Rochelle salts, rosaries, rosin, rouge, rules, saleratus, salt, saltpetre, sand, sealing wax, seal oil, sewing needles, sextants, shale, sheep, shingles, shirt fronts, shoddy, shoebinding, shot bags, show bills, shuttlecocks, sieves, sinews, slates, sleeve buttons, slipper patterns, snuff, snuffers, soap, soda, soy, spectacles, sponges, spurs, stilettos, stomach pumps, surplice pins, tacks, tannin, tapers, tar, tares, tassels, teapots, thimbles, thread, tinfoil, tooth brushes, tooth paste, toys, truffles, twine, twist, Vichy lozenges, violins, walking-sticks, wash balls, wax flowers, whiting, wigs, willows, &c. &c.

and kept going for years, and with them has come a rapid extension of coal-mining, and of machinery and engine-making, as will be seen from the note at foot.[1]

[1] American statistics substantially confirm English figures as to the remarkable decline which has occurred in the demand for European iron among the Americans. Thus we learn from some American returns that while 247,528 tons of pig were imported into the United States in 1872, the corresponding imports in 1875 sunk to 53,748 tons; and even as regards this reduced total it should be observed that a considerable proportion of it was spiegeleisen, to be used in the manufacture of steel. Even spiegeleisen, again, begins to be produced in the United States, so that as regards the great Transatlantic Republic its exportation will soon cease to be a source of profit to Germany. Thus it was computed that last year the United States produced nearly 8,000 tons of excellent spiegeleisen; and this year this total is expected to be nearly doubled. It may be interesting to note the cost of producing a ton of pig-iron in the United States. Taking a general view of matters as they stood in 1875, the cost price of each ton of American pig-iron was estimated as follows: Minerals, $10·82: fuel, $7·20; casting, $1·03; labour, $2·57; interest on capital, $1·62; general expenses, $1·86; making a total of $25·11 currency, or nearly 4*l*. 10*s*. per ton in English money—say, 4*l*. 9*s*. 6*d*. per ton. This total was somewhat above the corresponding average of the 35 years ending with 1875 inclusive, but it was much below the corresponding cost price of 1873. During the quarter of a century ending with 1875 inclusive, American pig-iron was made with the greatest cheapness in 1851, and under the least favourable conditions as regards price in 1873. Taking the average cost price of 1875 as the basis of calculations upon the subject, it would not appear, however, that pig-iron was produced at a very decided profit in the United States in 1875. On the other hand, the heavy import duty imposed upon European pig entering the United States—a duty of no less than 1*l*. 8*s*. per ton—deprived European shippers last year of any possibility of realising any profit, more especially as European pig imported for consumption by the Americans has to sustain expenses for transport, brokerage, commission, &c. Of the pig produced in the United States last year Pennsylvania made 42½ per cent.: Ohio, 18½ per cent.; New York, 11¾ per cent.; Michigan, 5 per cent.; while no other State attained a total of 3 per cent. The production of pig in the United States has exhibited a very great— in fact, an enormous—increase during the last few years. In 1810 only 54,000 tons of pig were made by the Americans; in 1830, the total had grown to 165,000 tons, and in 1840 to 315,000 tons. Since 1840 the production has grown in an accelerated ratio. In 1850 it had risen to

The home production of pig-iron in the United States has been rapidly and steadily on the increase, till last year it was almost quite up to the level of the diminished consumption. This has, of course, occurred in spite of the much higher cost of production in the States. But for the duty Scotch pig-iron might have been sold in America cheaper than the home-made during the highest period of the inflated prices that prevailed till 1873, and it is probable that the cost of production is still considerably lower here than in America, notwithstanding the heavy fall in wages there. The same has been the case with cotton manufactures. Between 1868 and 1876 the consumption of cotton in mills situated within the United States has increased by some

664,755 tons, and in 1860 it had further expanded to 919,770 tons. In 1870 an aggregate of 1,865,000 tons was attained. We have now arrived at quite modern times, even for this restless, rapid age; but it may be well to recapitulate the production and consumption of pig in the United States during the five years ending with 1875 inclusive. This information is afforded in the annexed table:

Year.	Production.	Consumption.
1871	Tons 1,911,608	Tons 2,154,813
1872	2,854,558	3,149,048
1873	2,868,278	3,012,883
1874	2,689,413	2,734,589
1875	2,266,581	2,324,300

The difference existing in 1875 between the production and the consumption of pig-iron in the United States was, in fact, so slight, that the Americans may now for all practical purposes be said to supply their own pig-iron requirements. At present, if the blast furnaces of the United States were fully employed, they could produce, according to a careful estimate made upon the subject, no less than 5,439,000 tons of pig annually.—*Mining Journal*, September 30, 1876.

32 per cent.,[1] but the cost of manufacture, quality for quality, is not much more than half in Lancashire what it is in the States, while Lancashire has the immense advantage of securing the cheapest raw cotton of all nations, which she can mix at will. We are thus able to produce a variety of low-priced fabrics which the States cannot touch now and will never touch while free intercourse with foreign countries is forbidden.

Almost the same thing may be said of the woollen industries. There is no use, however, in denying the plain fact that the States have succeeded by their high tariff policy in diverting a considerable part of the industrial energies of the community from the pursuits natural to and most profitable in a new country to the highly artificial, and, for America, mostly very expensive industries of long-settled and civilised nations. Were the sheltering tariff swept away, it is very questionable if any, save a few special manufactures of certain kinds of tools, machinery, railway cars and fancy goods, and a few of the cruder manufactures, could maintain their ground; and without that barrier there can hardly be a doubt that the natural forces bearing on the occupations of a country not above one-tenth part populated must seriously tend to destroy all that has been so elaborately built up.

I am aware that this conclusion is strongly com-

---

[1] Mr. Thomas Ellison's *Review of the Cotton Manufacturing Industries for* 1870.

bated by protectionist writers in the States, but the grounds of their contention are quite fallacious. It may, however, be worth while looking at the arguments adduced, and I know of no more clear and uncompromising statement of them than that contained in Mr. James Swank's report on the iron and coal trades of the Union for 1876. The prosperity of these trades is the most striking instance of the effects which protection has had on American industries, and, to my thinking, Mr. Swank's reasoning affords the best possible means of proving the illusory character of much of this prosperity. We shall, therefore, turn aside a little to discuss it.

There is much in his general statement of the case for protection which is irrelevant and a good deal that indicates imperfect acquaintance with the principles of free trade as developed in this country, and were I so disposed much amusement might be extracted from his blunders. But the main theses of the protectionist's argument are ably and boldly stated and deserve serious attention. Avoiding then the long discussion to which Mr. Swank treats himself on the industrial policy of England, in which, amid some very fair hits at our inconsistency, there is a mass of very confused arguments and illustrations, we will deal with his statement of the position of the United States. Mr. Swank affirms that protection tends to cheapen the prices of commodities and at the same time to raise the wages of labour and the value of agricultural products, and he gives numerous examples to prove that this is the case. Further, he insists that protection has increased very materially the exporting capacity of the Union, not in raw produce merely but in manufactures as well, and the statistics with which the assertion is supported are of a very striking kind. The facts he adduces in proof of these, his main contentions, are indeed all striking, and if there be no flaw in the arguments, we must admit that the case is proved. We find, for instance, that wages have been very high in the States compared with other countries, and that in not a few cases the establishment of home competition under the protection tariff has brought prices down very materially. This has been the case not in the iron trade alone but in nearly every branch of American manufacture. We also find that the exports of American manufactured and partially manufactured goods have steadily increased under the protection *régime* until, according to an interesting table which Mr. Swank gives and which I print in the Appendix (No. II.), they were more than double the value in 1874 which they stood at in 1862 when the last protection era began. These are strong facts, and I admit their force to the full, but I do not believe that they prove Mr. Swank's case, nay, some of them, by his own showing, prove the contrary.

Let us take the points *seriatim* and see what they

mean for ourselves. Wages, we are told, are raised by the institution of protection. It gives the chance to new industries to spring up and therefore creates more demand for labour, thereby raising its price. This is true, and nowhere more true than in the American Union, where labour, if left alone, would have gravitated towards the land. It was absolutely necessary that high wages should there be offered to begin with, else no industry of a highly artificial kind could have been started. But that is tantamount to saying that no industry could be started without large capital, and the natural inquiry therefore is—did protection furnish capital to pay these high wages? There is, I think, no disciple of the heresy in America bold enough to answer that question in the affirmative, and if protection did not furnish the capital to pay these high wages, where is the good it did? I fail to see it. The English money which had been poured into the States for the purpose of developing their mines and building their iron furnaces and factories would have done so in most cases better without protection than with it had men been forthcoming to do the work. As men were not forthcoming except when they were tempted away from more simple and more profitable labours, it may of course be asserted that protection provided the labour. It barred the ordinary roads to wealth which the States furnished, and turned men aside to dig in coal pits and to work in puddling furnaces. But what is that but another form of saying labour was scarce and therefore dear, and in order to secure it at all an artificial state of society had to be created from which certain capitalists almost alone derived any benefit? The high wages were not due to protection but to the paucity of men, and Mr. Swank's triumphant conclusion is based on a *non sequitur*. Events in the States are now proving it to be so. There are more men than there is work, and wages have fallen. The fallacy of the protectionist reasoning is, if possible, still more apparent on the question of prices. Without doubt these have been in some instances reduced by the artificial competition which has been set up in America, but the reduction is not therefore and necessarily the result of protection. It is an effect which follows competition however established, just as much as high prices follow on monopoly. The reasonable inference in this case therefore is, either that the reduction in price has not gone nearly so far in the States as it would have done had free trade prevailed, or that it has been pushed beyond the point which the resources of such an artificially protected trade would warrant. In the first part of the protective period the former was the true state of the case. Prices were inflated both here and in America, and competition there did not do more than moderate the competing power of English products. But since 1873 the later state of prices has supervened, and we now find that depressed prices, the result of unhealthily confined and artificially stimulated domestic competition, have either seriously trenched on the wages of the operatives or stopped them altogether. Mr. Swank's boast written early in 1876 is no longer a justifiable one. Trade has entered on the second stage of 'development' in America, and the true effects of protection now begin to reveal themselves. Foreign capital has ceased to flow in or has been partially withdrawn, and employment has partially stopped, prices are excessively low, wages have fallen to starvation point, and men by thousands are out of work altogether, and the Union can no longer taunt England with the exclusive possession of miserable pauper operatives. In its early history the effects of protection were such as we might fairly expect to flow from abundant foreign capital and dearer labour; in its later stage we have the effects which a long experience has brought us to look for in England—stagnant trade, starving people, immigration at an end and emigration begun, oppressed industries, and bloody riots. Before the logic of inexorable facts like these the vaunted benefits of protection vanish like a morning mist.

But what shall we say, then, of the increased exporting power which the States have undoubtedly displayed? Only this: that in no instance cited by Mr. Swank has this power been the direct effect of protection, and in only a few instances has it been the indirect effect. America exports cottons to China and Japan, because the quality is better than the shoddy goods sent in some cases from England; and therefore honesty, not protection, is the cause of success—honesty and perhaps better cotton. Let our manufacturers produce goods as fair in quality, and America cannot stand before us. Again, the States send tools and machinery abroad, because of their special ingenuity of construction—an ingenuity stimulated, if you will, by the oppressive burdens of protection—not because they are cheaper than foreign goods. It is here also quality, adaptability, ingenuity of device, not price, which regulates the demand, and free trade could, therefore, only expand business in such goods, because it would make them cheaper. A continuance of protection may, on the other hand, destroy the advantages of even superior ingenuity and workmanship—is in fact at present doing so. The exports of the United States are not at present progressive in manufactured articles any more than our own. On the contrary, if we deduct the higher values which were last year (the United States fiscal year runs from July to June) obtained for cereal crops, the extraordinary demand for munitions of war from Turkey, and the extra shipment of animal food, we shall find that the normal export trade of the United States is at present actually shrinking. This must be inevitable, in fact, while the present tariff lasts, for the effects of that tariff are in nothing more sure than this that they always in the long run restrict the exporting capacity of a country as surely as its importing. By extraordinary ingenuity, such as the people of America have undoubtedly displayed, in special articles and through certain channels, this inevitable result may be for a time apparently arrested, but it is the inevitable notwithstanding, and just as surely as wages have fallen in America and the whole tide of progress has been reversed will the power to hold any foreign market grow weaker.

If proof be wanted of the fact that the United States export trade in manufactures is in spite of these special exceptions not making progress, let the reader turn to Mr. Plunkett's report published in the Embassy and Legation papers for the present year (Part II.). He will there find a list of the articles which showed decrease in 1876 as against 1875, and amongst these will be found such things as agricultural implements, clocks and watches, copper manufactures, iron and steel manufactures, bar and pig iron, leather, &c.,—surely most significant items. In spite of trenchant reductions in the cost of production and of the severest economies at home, the surplus manufacturing energy of the States cannot command a market abroad with anything like certainty. What was true in 1876 is still more true in 1877, and must continue to be so.

So much, then, for the main arguments of Mr. Swank. They prove nothing in his favour and betray a singular capacity for misapprehending the force and drift of plain facts. We have had in the United States a prosperity indeed, but a prosperity attained under highly artificial and forced conditions, many of which have now disappeared. Not even the unspeakable boon of free land can enable the States to hold their own in fetters, great though the advantage may be that their land gives them over us. And even this advantage they have already partially flung away. I have already alluded to the reckless alienation made for the benefit of the jobbing railway proprietors, but this by no means represents all the mischief. So great is it that a sensible man and careful statistician like Mr. David A. Wells endorses the assertion that the spare land of the United States is already exhausted. In an able and interesting article which he publishes in the 'North American Review' for July and August 1877 called 'How shall the Nation regain Prosperity?' amongst other very interesting statements relating to the manner in which prohibitive duties and the invention of labour-saving machinery have told upon the wage-earning power and the labour field of the working classes, Mr. Wells makes the following:

Heretofore, owing to various circumstances, there has been no country in which a man, through industry and economy, could so rapidly and easily raise himself from the position of a labourer, dependent on others for employment, to the position of a capitalist, himself controlling employment, as in the United States. But the conditions for effecting such desirable social and economic changes are every year becoming less and less favourable. Labour-saving machinery, by the use of which alone can production be carried on to the best advantage, is expensive, and in general is not at the ready disposal of those whose only capital is their hands and their brains. The sharp competition in all exchanging (buying and selling) has also so reduced the rate of average profit that the transaction of large business is essential to the realization of any considerable gain. But the transaction of large business in most cases requires the use or control of large capital, which, in turn, represents previous accumulated labour. Note also the changes affecting the prospects of the American labourer without capital, growing out of the change in respect to the occupation and tillage of new lands. Formerly an enterprising man without capital could, as the result of a few years' service as a labourer at the West, acquire sufficient means to enable him to enter upon a tract of fertile government land, and put it, in all or part, under immediate cultivation. The result of the first year's crops not unfrequently reimbursed him for all his expenditures, and made him a capitalist, independent and with means sufficient for attaining larger results through greater production. But the opportunity for achieving such results, although perhaps not terminated, is rapidly drawing to a close. The quantity of fertile public land suitable for farm purposes which can now be obtained by pre-emption or at nominal prices is comparatively limited, if not nearly exhausted. According to Major Powell (in a communication recently made to the National Academy), 'all the good public lands fit for settlement are sold. There is not left unsold in the whole United States, of land which a poor man could turn into a farm, enough to make one average county in Wisconsin. The exception to this statement, if it is open to any, may perhaps be found in Texas or the Indian Territory, elsewhere it is true.' And in respect to the arid region of the plains, which, it is alleged, is eminently fitted for grazing, Major Powell further says: 'In this whole region, land as mere land is of no value; what is really valuable is the water privilege. Rich men and stock companies have appropriated all the streams, and they charge for the use of the water. Government sections of one hundred and sixty acres that do not contain water are practically, or at all events comparatively, worthless.' But whether these statements be fully warranted or not, there can be no question that the time draws near when the wave of population, which for so many years has uninterruptedly flowed westward from the Atlantic, will reach a natural limit; and that thereafter its tendency will be to stop, and possibly flow backwards. But when this change takes place, if it has not already commenced, the United States will have entered upon a new social order of things; an order of things similar to what exists in the more densely populated countries of the Old World, in which the tendency is for a man born a labourer, working for hire, to never be anything but a labourer.

Admitting that there are still splendid territories in the Far West unoccupied, and that great regions now squandered away to 'bloated corporations' may in time be liberated and available for the smaller settler, there is enough left in this picture to startle the most optimist advocate of protection out of his serenity. Is the net outcome of American progress, then, to be, not merely the subjection of the masses of the people to the landowners as in England, a kind of subjection that on the whole is mild and tempered with much of the milk of human kindness, but their slavery to the gigantic capitalists, the men who have no personal relations with their slaves at all, who treat them as a part of their machinery, as things to be bought in the cheapest market as one might buy bricks and mortar? If this is whither the fine theories of labour and capital, of protected industries, and stimulated production are tending in the States, they have indeed troublous times ahead, and the labour party now so lightly looked upon may grow strong enough to burst the entire federation in pieces.

Altogether the condition into which the American Union has fallen by the manner in which its resources have been worked for the benefit of a handful of moneyed people and wild borrowers, does not afford much scope for self-congratulation. Protection is, it is evident, a grasping paralysing force that may in time become a positively destructive one. Yet the progress of the American Union in domestic manufactures has excited a deal of genuine alarm in England, and merchants and manufactures here, disposed at present to take rather a gloomy view of everything, predict that the progress made at home will soon pass beyond the borders of the States, and enable them to enter into competition with English manufactures in other countries. Some few months ago quite an alarm was raised at the news that American goods were actually selling in the Manchester market. I think this reasoning quite fallacious, and the alarm altogether groundless. A moment's reflection must show anyone that while American manufacturing industries can do little more than exist under the shelter of a tariff which gives them a margin of 30, 40, or 50 per cent. and upwards in their competition with foreign goods, they cannot possibly produce at a price which will compete abroad with the old manufacturing nations. Judging by the tariffs, the United States manufacturers must either be now making profits of 40 to 100 per cent. beyond what is legitimately theirs, through the aid of the tariff, or the cost production must be from 30 to 50 per cent. at least higher with them than it is with us after all the drastic effects of dull times have been accounted for. I think there can be no doubt that the latter is now the fact, for, although they have spread themselves in extent, the United States manufacturing industries cannot be called prosperous. In a vast country like the States, too, where such great distances lie between the places whence the materials have to be brought together for, say, cotton and iron manufactures, the unavoidable cost of transport cannot but tell strongly in the direction of retarding profitable competition. A multitude of natural forces thus combine with want of population trained in manufacturing industries and willing to follow no other, as well as with want of free capital, to pull against the establishment of the highly artificial life which these industries really require and imply. Reasoning accords with the fact, therefore, in demonstrating that United States manufactures have not been very prosperous as a whole hitherto in spite of larger exports in special articles and great energy.

Since the panic there has been in many places severe suffering and great stagnation, and it has been found that protection from foreign competition could not prevent fellow-manufacturers from ruining each other at home, or save the people from having to buy bad articles very dear. It has been the old story : the man with no capital but with some bank accommodation has undone the man of means, to the misery of all concerned, and gradually trade of all kinds has fallen into the hands of a few giant monopolists who alone make profits by it and by whose folly and greed every industry in turn has had to suffer. Glutted markets, over-stocking, and unremunerative prices were the causes that brought the United States cotton goods here, not the prosperity of manufacturers there. In that view American cotton goods exported are often neither more nor less than consignments of bankrupts' stocks, sent abroad to be sold at any sacrifice for cash. Upon this point I may quote the testimony of a writer whom I have often found to be very well informed— the New York correspondent of the 'Bullionist.' In his letter dated September 16, 1876, alluding to this very subject, he says :

Our manufacturers, where they have had adequate command of capital, have, within the last twelve or fifteen years, made important progress, both in the quality of their product and the economy of production ; but I infer that this progress has not much surpassed what has been accomplished in other countries, from the fact that our improvements have been mostly imported, and, in many cases, the machinery also. Our friendly critics saw at Philadelphia only our best work; had they canvassed our markets, they would have learnt, what we too well know, that the curse of home manufacturers is the vast preponderating mass of mediocre and poor goods with which we are always flooded, and on which we cannot improve because so many of our manufacturers are too poor to better their facilities. The prices of our goods naturally appear to an exceptional advantage at present, for they were produced on a scale of prices for raw material and wages lower than has been known since 1860, while current prices for British products represent a scale relatively much higher, and higher probably than they will be when the present reaction in England has worked out all its results. If wages should decline in England as much as they have here, the comparative values of the goods of the two countries would probably appear very different from what they did to the eyes of your very candid manufacturers when at Philadelphia. So much in the interest of a fair judgment upon a very important question. Depend upon it, from the way in which the agricultural interest here has been lately extending as compared with the manufacturing, we shall still need to import a very liberal amount of foreign manufactures. Within the last three years most of our manufacturers have been crippled; many of them, with inferior advantages, have been ruined, and their comparatively worthless machinery will be little used again. Thousands of our factory hands have been driven to other employments; the vast army of workmen employed before the panic in railroad construction are now working in the field, and the constant increase of the traffic of the Western roads shows that our expansion is principally westward. All this implies a course of things on this side tending to an ultimate enlargement of our exchanges of products with foreign countries.

Still more striking testimony to the same effect is

given by the well-informed Philadelphia correspondent of the 'Times' in a letter dated April 13, 1877. Speaking of the possible help which a war between Turkey and Russia might give, he says:

That something is needed to stimulate business in the United States is universally admitted. Such branches of manufacturing industry as are producing any large amount of goods, like the cotton, woollen, and iron trades, are complaining that prices are unremunerative. In the iron trade it is generally believed that the rolling mills are either losing money or else losing reputation by making inferior iron. Several foundrymen at Pittsburgh declare that they cannot make iron except at a loss, and they prefer shutting down if prices do not get better. There seems a large enough demand for these products at present rates, but no one can make any profit. Coal-mining has begun in several sections with some vigour, but there is the same complaint of unremunerative prices. Wages are cut down so low, that it is becoming a problem how some of the operatives live, yet there are constant efforts to cut down wages still lower. The very few strikes that now occur are against reductions, and their usual end is against the working men. The tendency of everything seems downward—prices, values, wages, and profits. The nation is practising an enforced economy of the most rigid character.

Now, if an European war can change all this, sad as it may be for you, what a benefit it will be to us. You may deprecate, but can pardon our anticipations of the advantages such a conflict will bring the United States. If it restores prosperity here, the reflex benefit to England with so large a capital invested in America will be great. We expect the war to quicken the demand and advance the prices of breadstuffs, provisions, and naval stores, and advance ocean freights and give our vessels increased employment. This will move our crops and thus enlarge the traffic and earnings of the railways. While the downward tendency of the Stock market will be suddenly turned upward, the farmers, who are four-fifths of the population, will be paid for their corn, and can then buy manufactured goods. Thus the whole fabric of American commercial prosperity will be given renewed vigour by the firing of a gun on the Danube, and in this way it is expected that the most serious, protracted, and widespread depression that has yet visited the United States will be removed.

These writers express very fairly the facts as to the nature of the manufacturing progress of the States. It has been very hectic, and it has cost the nation infinitely more than it is worth. It has stopped the expansion of the nation, and may presently seriously reduce the purchasing capacity of the countries who now buy United States raw produce. If we can no longer export our manufactures to the States; if wages are here thereby reduced, it stands to reason that we shall soon come to buy both less raw material and less food from the Union. Not only so, but other competing countries will soon be able to beat it in all but a few special products. Misery will thus tend to increase in America; land will fail to pay the farmer as well as mines and mills the capitalist, and we shall find not one or two shiploads of people leaving the country for more favoured lands, but a rush of emigration. Not a dozen wars in Europe can prevent this consummation, and the short-sighted folly of building hopes of prosperity on the ruin of other nations must soon become apparent. A comparatively moderate tariff, such as ours was forty years ago, had an aggravating effect on the social distresses which from time to time fell on the country; and there can be no question that the United States tariff has had an influence on the distress which has there followed the crisis of 1873, which is not yet over, though the labour rebellion in the cities may be quelled. What a ghastly commentary on the progress of the Union under protection tariffs this rebellion was! Hundreds of men slain in the streets, the representatives of tens of thousands almost dying of starvation with a fertile continent open before them.

Could any more complete refutation of the whole false doctrine of the benefits of protection be found than the present state of labour in the Union affords? It is useless to cry out about over-speculation, excessive railway building, and so forth; these are bad, but they have been bad with us, and we have overcome the evil, although our natural advantages were in many respects neutralised by our antiquated social order. The plain truth is, that the Union has been punishing itself in its foolish endeavour to make other people bear its burdens. It has legislated for the pockets of the few in trying to make other nations pay its war bill. Nothing can well be more absurd than to suppose that a country can drag a tax or fine out of a foreign merchant who sends his goods to it for sale. If the merchant finds that the tax stops his profits, he ceases to send his goods; but if he continues to send at profit to himself, then the importing community simply pay their government 30, 40, 50, or 100 per cent. by way of tax, beyond what the goods need have cost them. One plain result of such a tariff as this of the States, therefore, is to heighten directly the price of every one of the multitude of imported articles, and so to increase the cost of living, or, failing that, to compel the people to buy home-made substitutes very much dearer than they could be supplied elsewhere. The tariff must affect wages in the States, for example, much more than it can affect foreign prices. It raises the cost of every material worn, of every luxury, of every piece of machinery needed by the manufacturer, the farmer, the cotton or tobacco grower, and the artisan, so that the difficulty of living becomes many degrees greater. But for the prodigious natural resources of the States, but for the good credit they enjoy, and for the borrowings of her large railway and city corporations, the reactionary course would have commenced sooner and have been more marked and disastrous than it has yet been. These influences in the case of the productiveness of the land may continue partially in force, but so far as the borrowings are concerned are almost at an end. The great railways of the United States cannot hope to obtain much more money in this country, after the suspicions which have lately been cast on them, for some time to come, and the absence of that money is not unlikely to bring one or two of them into serious difficulties, which must still further retard the speedy recuperation of the nation. The fiscal outcome of it all is this:—the country enjoying protection pays a higher price for its manufactures than it need do with free trade and loses its foreign customers into the bargain. Those who think these results good are welcome to their opinion. The truth is, the best friends and strongest upholders of the high customs tariff in the States cannot prove that any good has come of it. Industries that could not otherwise have taken root have no doubt become established, but the cost of them has been already much more than the gain. There is backwardness now, instead of progress, and many industries struggle on with difficulty, while not a few individuals go to ruin. Such a state of things need never terrify people here about the dangers of American competition.

It may be urged, however, that by this policy the States have taken the right course to prevent the balance of debt obligations and trade together from going against them, to the serious embarrassment of the national finances. Up till a few years ago that danger could not be said, however, to have been averted by the tariff. The States imported more than they exported in spite of it, and they did so because of the large sums of money which they raised abroad. It is a natural and obvious inference, therefore, that if the States had not gone ahead so fast, but kept well within their resources, hastening slowly, the natural course of trade might have been kept undisturbed even had there been no prohibitory tariff at all. The nation would then have spent only what it could spare, and, free from debt contracted to force on 'progress,' would not have had the heavy debit balance hanging over it which now renders a large excess of exports an absolute necessity if the country is to avoid ultimate inability to meet its fixed corporate and State debt obligations. Supposing all the millions of borrowed money honestly paid back, we therefore fear that the only definable result and ultimate outcome of the tariff in the long run has been to make all railway and manufacturing materials imported cost the companies in the States from 30 to 60 per cent. more than they otherwise might have done, and to increase by so much the amount which they needed to borrow. The tariff has thus been a loss to the nation in all ways. All in the end recoils on the community imposing the taxes, not on those which supplied the goods, unless—and that has happened often enough to lead to doubts whether it may not happen again—the borrowers become bankrupt, when of course the lenders will suffer.

Left to its natural course, it is not improbable,

therefore, that, had United States trade been free, the balance would have been just as well kept as it is now. Less money would have been borrowed, less goods bought, and more goods exported. A revenue to pay the debt could have been collected by internal taxes, which would in themselves have had probably the salutary effect of forcing on a resumption of specie payments, while at the same time they would have burdened the people infinitely less, because they would have been only taxes not taxes and inflated profits together. It can hardly, on the other hand, be denied that if the manufactured products of the States are practically shut out of foreign markets in all save isolated articles and instances by the high tariff, the general trade of the nation is also hindered. Between nation and nation trade is in the long run always pure barter, however disguised, and if the States take less cotton goods from us they will soon of course sell us less cotton. At present the United States have the corn supply of Europe to a great extent in their own hands, but competition threatens to become every year more effective, for our far-distant Australian colonies find it possible to enter our markets and sell against American corn, and Hungary, France, Spain, and Russia, burdened as they are, by no means find our market shut against them. Even heavily weighted India sends year by year greater quantities of wheat to Europe at a price with which the States cannot hope to compete. But for special causes, indeed, which hinder European competition, such as the troubles of Eastern Europe, the debt burdens of Russia and Austria, and the anarchy of Spain, the States must have felt the force of competition from many quarters more severely before now. As it is, it is only territories in the States which are either near the sea, like California, or which have command of an easy access to the sea, like the Mississippi, Ohio, and Missouri Valleys and the shores of the lakes, which can at present benefit highly by the corn trade. It is hampered even there, and the agriculturist is kept in the hands of rings and speculators much more than need be were the millstone of the tariff not round everyone's neck; hence the 'Granger' combinations and the war of railway rates with their looming bankruptcies. On the most general survey, then, I believe that it must be concluded that this modern republican engine of oppression is seriously affecting for the worse United States prosperity and trade on the export as well as on the import side.

I have dwelt at length on the tariff question in this chapter, because I wish to combat the fallacies of protectionists once for all and on their chosen ground. We shall often come across protective tariffs in the course of this inquiry, and it will save much time if the arguments here set forth are to some extent taken once for all. I have also insisted on this topic because it is at present the supreme one in the Union; the life of the nation may almost be said to hang on it. Its interest to ourselves is also by no means small, though I cannot think that it is vital. Nothing that I have said can be expected to change this foolish policy; the Union will only give it up when loss and suffering have brought its mischief home to every man's understanding. Only self-interest will force remedies, as it bred the mischief, but the subject is none the less worth reiterated illustration and study. We, for example, see that, although it cannot be said that the tariff will make the States our competitors in other markets, but just the opposite, it may for long effectually shut us out from their own. While these causes exist, I do not, then, look hopefully for a revival of trade, either within the States themselves or between this country and theirs; and it would be useless to disguise the fact, that disappointment of such a revival means to England a very great deal. Our total exports this year to the States will probably be about 30,000,000*l.* less than in 1872; and although we may in time find other markets able to take all the difference, that does not lessen the aggravation which the loss causes now, or the despondency which a prospect of still further decline engenders.

Before closing this subject it may be well to revert to two branches of United States finance which have so far only been touched on incidentally in this paper. I mean the interest-bearing debt of the Union, and the paper currency. Anything like a complete investigation of the influence of these important factors on the prosperity of the nation is out of the question, but a general observation on them may be of some value. And, first of all, the real debt of the United States is much greater than those who look at the funded loans and the 'Five Twenties' suppose. Every individual State almost has something of a debt, and multitudes of corporations and townships, all over the Union, are more or less steeped in it. A great deal of this debt, national, State, municipal, and joint-stock, has been contracted abroad—how much I find it impossible to say exactly, but, including the railway debt, I should say at least 400,000,000*l.*[1]—and the consequence of this is that the Union must always have against it a very large debit balance for interest. This acts, as I have shown in the case of India, directly as a retardant on the purchasing power of the community, and, added to the tariff restrictions, cannot but most seriously affect its course of trade. It is all-important that the States should sell a great deal more than they buy; and if they are hindered by any cause from doing so, the consequences will be disastrous. At present there is no

[1] The exact amount of the Federal debt held abroad is not to be ascertained, the holding fluctuates according to the state of trade in America and from other causes. I believe, however, that considerably more than half is so held, and if we add to this the debts contracted abroad by various States of the Union, by the larger cities in it, and on behalf of the leading corporations, the estimate I have given will seem moderate. This is assuming that 260,000,000*l.* Federal debt is held abroad. I confess, however, that my figures are only an estimate, and it is impossible to make them anything else.

cause whatever for apprehension, so far as the national bonds are concerned, but that is nearly all one can say. Outside the limits of them the uncertainty is very considerable, and the burden of even these becomes much more obvious as the period of wild inflation passes away. Under this burden the separate States may yet grow restive to the imperilment of the Federation, while the present fiscal policy, so easily imposed, will be made excessively difficult to abandon by reason of the obstructive force of the rights which some of these States are more and more disposed to assert. The United States have therefore by no means done with the troubles of their debt, which fiscally and politically may yet cost them many a dangerous hour. The common vaunt we are accustomed to hear about the wonders which have already been accomplished in its redemption and refunding is in great part an empty vaunt. Ten years hence the boasting will be more subdued, for then the true weight and extent of the debt of America will be better understood. Debt prevails everywhere and is almost grinding the life out of many a promising outgrowth of national progress.

The paper money opens another set of problems; it affects trade in another way. As we have seen, when the crisis came on in September 1873, the country was found apparently not to have enough currency to relieve the public apprehension of a general collapse, and the distress was aggravated because, while itself insufficient, it, by being at a discount, shut out gold, the only possible substitute. Ever since then a party in the States have clamoured, on mistaken inferences from this scarcity, for an extension of the paper circulation. Want of currency is, they say, the cause of all the stagnation and distress. There could be no greater fallacy. A fresh flood of paper might, no doubt, produce a hectic flush of seeming prosperity, because means would be found to float new adventures, and prices would rise all round by the mere lessening of value which the currency would thus undergo; but it would all end in greater disaster than ever, because, when the balance came to be struck between real values, the currency would have to be left out of count, unless it also had a solid value at the back of it. A State's promise to pay cannot be considered such a value, simply because outside the limits of that State nobody will take the promise. Were the United States to lock their doors altogether against a foreign trade, and not permit a single pennyworth of goods to enter their ports, the paper money inflation would still be a mistake and the precursor of disaster, because ultimately the same balance would have to be struck between the State and its creditors, the people; and if they had nothing to give it in payment of its own taxes but paper, the State would be powerless to pay the paper off. It could not redeem its pledges, and must fall into bankruptcy, to the enormous loss of the people.

We have not to do with this aspect of the subject, however, so much as with the consequences of the non-redemption of the present paper currency on foreign trade. And these are very simple. For a time paper produced inflation, apparent prosperity, great profits; but afterwards there was reaction, loss, and uncertainty. The dealer who has to do work with a currency of a fluctuating value always in the long run works at a disadvantage. At first he buys cheap and sells apparently dear, but after the effects of the inflation have permeated all departments of trade he may often buy dear and sell cheap, and especially in all foreign business is this kind of see-saw disastrous. The trader may buy goods at a certain price in gold abroad which he calculates to sell at home for depreciated paper currency at a profit. But by the time it arrives he may find that the depreciation is a little less, and he has to sell at a level he did not calculate upon. He gets a lower value in 'greenbacks' for his goods than he expected. Yet when he comes to remit for these goods he may find that the relative values of gold and paper have again altered, and that the depreciation in the latter has again increased, or, in other words, that gold has become dearer, so that while getting a lower value in 'greenbacks' for his goods he may have to give a higher for the gold he has to pay them with. And even when relative values are comparatively steady, the foreign trade has always to work under the disadvantage of apparent high prices according to these values. The paper currency of the Union has unquestionably exercised a severely retardant effect on trade in this way, and the more such currency is inflated the more is it sure to play havoc with all sound business. And obviously also a see-saw of this kind compels the merchant to protect himself by putting as high a price on his goods as he can possibly obtain. He must allow in fixing that price a margin for fluctuations. Therefore the direct effect of an inconvertible paper currency is to increase the cost of goods to the consumer beyond the legitimate level which, in Adam Smith's phrase, ' the higgling of the market ' would fix. The time preceding a resumption of specie payments is, if possible, even worse for the trader, because then the value of the paper is likely to be approximating to that of gold. The values of all articles in relation to the paper are therefore falling, and in a time of falling values many men must succumb. This, probably, helps to explain the enormous number of comparatively small failures which have of late taken place in the States—this and the general poverty, the lack of work, or starvation wages.

At present the Cabinet of Mr. Hayes is seriously bent on carrying resumption through, and the discount on the greenback currency is lessening, although I doubt the wisdom of the methods by which its ' appreciation ' is being accomplished. There is always grave danger surrounding any contraction of the circulating medium of a country, and in this instance the danger may be aggravated by the difficulty which the States experience in retaining their gold. While so great a proportion of the funded debt of the country continues to be held abroad, and while the various industries of the nation continue to pay heavily for the necessary foreign capital, it will be extremely difficult for the States to establish their currency on a specie basis. At present, as is well known, the intention is to renew paying in coin on January 1, 1879, the date fixed by law, and already a large amount of the small note circulation has been called in, silver being substituted in its place. The most formidable difficulties remain, however, and there is about $360,000,000 of greenback currency still circulating which ought only to be paid in gold, and to meet these notes an indefinite amount of bullion must be provided within the next twelvemonths or so if the resumption is to be made effective. Some of the difficulty may perhaps be got over by the law which allows the national banks to issue a large amount of notes, convertible into coin as in England, in lieu of the 'greenbacks' or national currency retired; yet at best this plan is only the substitution of one danger for another. In order to make the note freely convertible the national banks of the Union, of which there are upwards of 2,000 in active operation, must keep a much larger coin reserve than they now do, and I doubt their ability to do this. Just now the reserve of these banks is practically held in New York, and it is a very small one; but when the 'greenbacks' are withdrawn, and national banknotes substituted, every bank throughout the country will have to keep a certain store of cash. How they are to get this is more than I can discover. As many of them now trade, without Government aid they would not find the means to hold 10 per cent. of coin against their notes. These considerations make it obvious that, however desirable the speedy resumption of specie payment may be, the path on which the Government has entered is a most difficult one.

The present Secretary of the Treasury, Mr. Sherman, apparently sees no difficulty. He has stopped the issue of $4\frac{1}{2}$ per cent. funding bonds and began to sell 4 per cents., and is confident that by this means he will not only redeem a large portion of the present 6 per cent. debt, but provide coin for resumption on January 1, 1879. If these 4 per cent. bonds are all taken up and held in the State, and the foreign creditors paid off, he may succeed; but this is not in the least likely. On the contrary, the 4 per cent. conversion will probably be a partial failure. While the debt is held abroad, however, there must always be serious difficulties in the way of accumulating large stores of bullion, difficulties which the high import duties, by their ruinous effect on the metallic revenue, seriously augment.

I am aware that great hopes are entertained that the exports of the Union will so continue to exceed the imports as to make the accumulation of gold easy. The harvest of 1877 has been a fine one in the States, and an indifferent one in England and France. The States are therefore experiencing a large demand for grain, and may be able to accumulate a deal of bullion. This may prove to be the case, and indeed in one sense the fact that we hold so much of the American debt makes it certain that we shall continue to resort to the Union for much of the food we need. But the results of one harvest or two will not bring the necessary gold into the Treasury or secure its permanent stay in the country. So long as any of the debt is held abroad, there will be a steady export of 'tribute' which must neutralise the gains to some extent. Not only so, but every year in which we are compelled to send a deal of money to the States for food, they buying nothing in return, impoverishes us. In effect we part with our bonds to the Union for food, and though that may go on for a little time, it must come to an end. We grow less able to buy, and the States, independent altogether of the effects of competition, find less and less market for their goods, more and more difficulty in getting the necessary surplus. Yet they must continue to make extensive exports while any considerable indebtedness abroad remains, else their store of gold falls off. There is therefore a dilemma in the situation which there is no getting over. The import tariff seriously reduces the gold revenue, and the one-sided trade impoverishes the customers of the Union.

I do not therefore believe that specie payment can be secured by 1879, or that if resumption be effected then, it can be maintained. The tariff in this case also bars the way in spite of the temporary advantages in exporting which European richness in United States bonds may give. Before the Union can make sure of maintaining a gold currency it must call home its foreign debt and substitute for its absurd customs tariff internal taxes payable in coin. But here again a fresh difficulty meets us. Granting that gold becomes plentiful so that such taxes could be gathered, how is the Union to impose them? It has little power to make internal taxes of any kind owing to the pernicious effects of the separate States system, a system that is at the root of two-thirds of the political mischiefs under which the Confederation now labours. The sums now yielded to the Federal treasury by such fairly taxable articles as spirits and tobacco are quite insignificant, and they are almost all the articles that the Government can tax. Land it cannot touch, and it is doubtful whether it could impose an income tax. People in this country, so-called democrats or republicans in particular, are never tired of descanting on the cheapness of the government of the Union, but they might just as well boast of the smallness of the budget of the German Empire. The duality which exists all over the Union and between State and imperial interests is in truth a source of incalculable waste and extravagance, and suffices to make the country perhaps the most expensively governed in the world, and in some respects one of the worst governed. It is often the perfection of no government bought at a ruinous expenditure of money, political agitation, and chicanery, and the time is perhaps not far distant when the Union will either have to control the separate States system, which lies at the root of the evil, or be itself condemned to extinction.

The imposition of fresh internal taxes by the Union is therefore a very ticklish affair, and I do not at present see how it is to be carried out, although a new source of metallic revenue is absolutely necessary to safe resumption. If, then, the national bank-note plan is not likely to secure easy convertibility, if the foreign debt cannot be brought home, or if new taxes or even existing internal taxes cannot be raised, and payment of them secured in gold, I do not see how resumption is to be accomplished at the date fixed or at any proximate date. Something is no doubt gained by the reduction in the interest of the funded debt, and by its exchange for corn sent to us; but that barely counterbalances, if it does counterbalance, the falling off in revenue. Something has also been gained through the stoppage of excessive imports; but that is a gain which cannot be counted on as permanent, since the present tariff will reduce exports in time as well, and since the proceeds of a fine harvest may again make America extravagant. Hence I am not sanguine about this resumption policy. It is being undertaken as both the Union and its customers are growing poorer, and may not unlikely result in serious financial difficulties. After all, as the late Secretary Morrill said in his Treasury report for 1876, the note circulation of the States is a debt, and as a debt it has got to be paid in coin, and where the coin is to come from to meet it all or half of it in the next year no one can say. The 'Bonanza' people see the dilemma of the Government and press silver on its attention as a cheaper metal, more easily retained in the country, and advocate at least the institution of what is called a double standard—gold and silver of equal legal value; but though this would undoubtedly ease the pressure incident to resumption, it is a plan which cannot be adopted because the States are in some ways solemnly pledged to a gold standard. In no other could they pay honestly the interest on their foreign debt.

Not to weary the reader further with this dry discussion, I repeat, in conclusion, that I do not believe in the ability of the Union to resume specie payments effectually and permanently without a modification of its trade policy. Hitherto since the stoppage of lavish expenditure on borrowed money, the effects of this tariff have been felt principally on the import trade, but it will not touch that alone. It will also tend more and more to choke the export capacity of the Union, and unless that is well kept up to the level of the requirements of the community on its foreign debt obligations, the mere resumption of specie payments by a supreme effort at a given time would do little good. Specie would be again, before long, drained from the country, and paper credits of some kind substituted in order to maintain these debt payments, and distrust and mercantile distress and derangement would prevail as before.

In the meantime, whatever the fate of Senator Sherman's efforts, this currency must be taken as one of the hindrances to a revival of the trade of Great Britain with the United States. It is a secondary one compared with the tariff, but it exists, and with the other, renders any likelihood of a revival of business in that quarter very remote. Things must, on the average, I think, grow worse instead of better both for the States and for us; and in time, if no change comes, the imports which we draw now from the Union will fall away, as our exports to that country have already done. They will do so, if for no other reason than that as regards the States we will be poorer—we will have less of their debt and stronger interest in other directions, where our money is more largely invested. Our poverty, too, will compel us to grow more corn at home, to eat less bread and meat, and so bring our spending again within our means. This is, I know, a gloomy conclusion, and in coming to it I lay myself open to the charge of pessimism. But who can fight against facts and plain common-sense? Everything tends to choke up the channels of trade between this country and the United States, and it is only because the same factitious influences have been at work there as in other countries that the force of the inevitable has not been sooner felt. We have lent to the States untold amounts of capital, and by these trade has been kept going in spite of every barrier. Cease that lending, and collapse is sure to come, revival almost impossible—both sides of the trade account being sooner or later taken with decay.

While I say this, however, I must not be misunderstood. The hindrances to trade with the United States are artificial altogether, and not natural. Left to itself, the reciprocal business between England and the American Union would grow beyond anything that it has ever reached. The two countries could be the means of giving innumerable benefits to each other—we with our hoards of surplus wealth and our old deep-rooted manufacturing capabilities, and the New World with its boundless resources for furnishing raw materials.

In one of the lectures which Professor Huxley delivered in the States in the autumn of 1876 he predicted that, by the time America held its second centenary celebration, if it managed as a Union to weather the dangers which will beset it for generations yet, it would probably have a population of 200,000,000, instead of, as now, 40,000,000. This prediction is but a moderate one, if the Union will but open its gates again and let the tide of immigration flow in as freely as natural forces impel it to do; if the population is not forced into artificial employments, which ebb and flow behind the wall of the prohibitory tariff, to the profit of some and the loss of many, now causing a dearth of men, and again such a dearth of work that thousands so forced into unnatural currents are threatened with starvation, and, driven desperate, rise in blind rebellion. And if the States do surmount all these difficulties, economic and other, so as to go forward united in their path of national development, could we set bounds to the reciprocal good which the new country can do the old and the old the new? I trow not. As the years passed we should find trade between the two changing in character no doubt, but also ever expanding in volume. I could not frame a supposition as to when this mutual interchange of the fruits of labour might stop; and, however dull the immediate future may be, I cannot but persuade myself that when certain accidental barriers are removed, the business transacted between the two countries must again enter on a new career of prosperity and advancement.

That happy change is not yet come, and it may not come for years—not until the States have learnt that selfishness and exclusion in business are as unproductive a policy in the economy of nations as they are unlovely and unprofitable in private affairs. But some day it will come, and until it does business men in this country must bear their deprivations as best they can, resting assured of this one thing, that whatever shuts them out of the benefits of trade with the Union must also shut the Union out of all effective competition with them in the other markets which they now command or monopolise.

The conclusion of the matter therefore is that I can see no sign of immediate recovery in our trade with America. All forces are against it, and as far as that branch of our foreign business is concerned the present stagnation must increase year by year. It should be no satisfaction to us that the troubles of the Union may also increase till political disruption may again be threatened as a means whereby South and West could throw off effectually and for ever the industry crushing trade laws of the triumphant Republicans of the North.

Disruption is perhaps a dangerous cure, but the last Presidential struggle, the late labour war, the agitation of the 'Grangers,' and the determined endeavour of the South to free themselves from the dominance of the Yankee, suggest many reflections. The political machine of the States, which it was the cant formula to adore till Abraham Lincoln became President, manifestly creaks with age and hard usage, and some day will go to pieces, to give place, let us hope, to a better. It would be most interesting to speculate on the probabilities of when and how this may take place, but I forbear. All that I can now do is to reiterate that the fiscal policy of the party which still through the unscrupulous use of legal means controls the Union, breeds misery, and therefore tends to bring all kinds of disorder in its train, to render the most necessary reforms almost impossible. Dark days are coming for the American Union, not in trade matters only, although a mistaken trade policy is having much to do in bringing them nearer.

CHAPTER V.

RUSSIAN PROGRESS.

To go at once from the progressive Continent of the West, with its popular institutions, its enterprise, and its high civilisation, to the most autocratic empire, except China and the moribund Turkish horde, which exists in the old world, seems rather a questionable step. I can, however, produce abundant justification for it, I think, apart altogether from the political agitations which now centre round the designs and future of this empire. The simplest of all reasons, from my point of view, offers all the excuse needed. Next to the United States of America, Russia is the one strictly foreign country in the world which is deepest in our debt, and which, by consequence, has done most in recent years to give a factitious prosperity to certain departments of British industry. Because this is the situation of Russia, I think we shall do well to examine into the nature of her prosperity now, irrespective of the war or of the political situation as regards Turkey. That, indeed, we must look at in estimating the future, but, so far as the past is concerned, it should be rigorously dismissed from the mind.

After all, when we come to look at Russia a little more closely, we find other points of resemblance between her and the United States than that they are both heavily our debtors. Both countries own vast territories; including her Asiatic conquests, Russia has more than double the area of the United States; both are sparsely peopled in many parts, and contain within their borders fragments of many races.[1] So far as regards Russia in Europe, it, like the States, is to a considerable degree dependent upon its waterways for the conduct of its internal commerce; and both countries are compelled to a similar suspension of traffic on these arteries during the winter months. With differences which we need not detail, both the Republic and the Empire have a certain similarity of climate, and distinct though the character and extent

[1] The population of Russia looks large when stated in round figures to be 83,000,000 odd, but the magnitude is much diminished when we call to mind also that this population inhabits a country nearly 8½ million square miles in extent, or nearly five times larger than the area of all other European countries put together. Germany is not an over-peopled empire, and yet, with only some 212,000 English square miles of territory, Germany has a population of some 42,000,000. To be sure we must deduct Siberia with its dreary wastes, in which there is practically no inhabitants at all; but when that is done, and we confine our attention to Russia in Europe alone, we find the population as a rule sparsely dotted over the country. Great portions of northern Russia could not sustain a large population, and in the south the barbarousness of the people proves a considerable check on their natural fecundity, as do also the patriarchal institutions of the Commune and the gross immoralities to which they conduce.

of their civilisation may be, each has to work out the most momentous social and economic revolutions before it can hope to reach the calm solidity of internal peace and unity.

The parallel might be drawn out further, but the further we went the more glaring would the divergences appear; for, after all, these resemblances are only superficial. In the States we have communities, richly endowed with the inheritance of ancient civilisations, taking root anew, and spreading in luxuriant growth towards results of which men little dream; but in Russia we are at once face to face with a crude barbarism, with a people who, fifty years ago, did not know what was meant by a 'constitution,'[1] who barely fifteen years ago were the majority of them slaves, and few of whom can now read or write. In Russia we find dense ignorance, strong but childish passions, a press born of yesterday, and still shackled by the supreme authority of the autocrat who, in the midst of

[1] It is related by Schnitzler, in his *Secret History of the Court and Government of Russia under the Emperors Alexander I. and Nicholas*, that during the turmoil which attended the accession of the latter, certain ardent reformers endeavoured to raise the cry 'Hurrah for the Constitution!' amongst the disaffected troops. These troops had been induced to revolt, under the idea that Nicholas's elder brother Constantine was the true heir to the throne, whom Nicholas was trying to subvert, and along with a motley crowd were shouting in the streets of St. Petersburg, 'Hurrah for Constantine!' So ignorant was the populace of what it meant that, when they heard in Russian the word 'constitoutzia' (i.e. constitution) shouted by the revolutionary enthusiasts who were leading the rabble, they thought it referred to Constantine's wife. 'The word *republic*,' Schnitzler adds, 'had it been pronounced, would not have been better understood.' Such was the enlightenment of Russia fifty years ago.

all changes, and through his very concessions, has sought to maintain at least the form of his autocracy intact. In the States we find few signs of a military despotism except where here and there the iron-thewed Yankee may have put his heel down on the subjugated South; but in Russia militarism dominates even the emperor, and nearly one half of the net revenues of the Empire goes towards the maintenance of the army and navy. Both countries possess a venal and contemptible bureaucracy; but, in the one, the corruption is merely tolerated by the people, who can cure it if they please, and, in the other, it is imposed upon the people from above—is, I might almost say, the bone and marrow of Russian despotism. Finally, to crown all, from our point of view, both countries are steeped in debt; but the debt of the United States is one that she can bear unless legislative folly drive the country towards insolvency, and that of Russia is—well, we shall see.

Leaving, then, this drawing of parallels and contrasts, which, however amusing and suggestive even, do not much advance our knowledge of the actual state of the Russian Empire, I must now, as usual, ask the forbearing reader to go back with me over a few recent events in the social and economic history of the country. It is not necessary for our purpose to go beyond the close of the reign of Nicholas; for, from his death, modern Russian progress—such as it is—

undoubtedly begins; so new is the civilisation and wealth-veneer of this mighty empire, the thought of which has for the past year and a half made our statesmen vacillating and a section of our journalists hoarse with the reiteration of their jealousy and dread. Russia has sat on our imaginations like a hideous nightmare, till one cannot help asking, What is she, this terrible monster, that haunts our dreams, at whose name so many among us quake or howl, forgetting alike the dictates of prudence and the common feelings of humanity?

Only some twenty years ago Russia was an empire almost on the verge of dissolution. Up to the end of the reign of Nicholas the whole land was held down in a grip of steel. That narrow-minded, dubiously-respectable, and self-adoring ruler had resolved that his country should remain as much as possible barred against the progressive, and as he believed revolutionary, inventions and ideas of the West. Russia was to him one huge parade ground, and no man in it dare call his eyes his own. It was with difficulty, for instance, that Nicholas could be brought to allow such dangerous levellers as railways to be introduced within his borders, and there is reason to believe that before his death he doubted whether in giving a reluctant consent to the construction of one or two lines he had not done wrong. Certainly, little was done in his lifetime, only the small line to Zarskoe-Selo and the Nicholas Railway from St. Petersburg to Moscow having been built, with a portion of the line from Warsaw to connect with the Austrian Ferdinand-North-Railway. Nicholas dreaded above all things the possibility of anything within the bounds of his empire that he could not control; and no stranger even was allowed to enter its borders without a special permit from himself, and the payment of 500 roubles. The life of the community was stifled, its literature an unhealthy plant growing in darkness; on all the land lay the impenetrable shadow of a cold, capricious, terror-inspiring military and police despotism. Everyone has read stories, droll and pathetic, of the petty things to which such an Emperor of all the Russias has been wont to direct his attention, and one instance will be enough to refresh the memory. A reprimand was once conveyed to the censor of the 'Northern Bee,' a leading Russian newspaper, as newspapers then were, because a complaint had been permitted to appear in it about the uncomfortableness of some seats in the park of Zarskoe-Selo. It appeared that these seats were designed by the Emperor Nicholas, and nothing that he did could possibly be considered wrong.[1] While Nicholas lived, Russia's life was, in consequence of a rule of this kind, the stagnation of a sleep which, had the Emperor had his way, would never have been troubled by silly dreams

---

[1] Dr. Eckardt's *Modern Russia*, p. 9.

of freedom and progress, and the joys of individual rights.

There was life of a sort in Russia though, and the sleep had dreams which the stern waking of the disasters in the Crimea made a few advanced spirits among the people wild to realise. How utterly must Nicholas have regretted the blindness which kept him from carrying his railway south of Moscow towards the Crimea! For it was not the Allies who beat the Russians so much as their own folly—the bigoted self-adulation of the emperor, and the venality which it bred. The defeats in the field were something, but without the other defeats on the march and in the camp they might never have occurred; or having occurred, would not have sufficed to break down so utterly the autocratic system of Nicholas. It was this break-down which lent the popular agitation more than half its force.

With Nicholas's death and the speedy cessation of the Crimean struggle, a new day dawned upon Russia. His system had crumbled to pieces—was, in fact, dead before him; and the new monarch had to find a new foundation for his despotism, or see it slip away in the turmoil of a social revolution that might have split the empire to pieces. Indiscretion at that critical period might have ended the Russian Empire for ever, to the great disgust, I have no doubt, of those amongst us who cannot live without a 'bogie,' and to whom

Russian aggression is the one thing left in the world capable of exciting the old 'fighting fever,' with which the English have ever been inconveniently troubled at intermittent seasons. Russia came out of the Crimean War not merely with her military system demoralised, but bankrupt. Unable to raise loans in Western Europe to carry on that war with, the empire had resorted to the expedient which appears to commend itself alike to despot and democrat, and flooded the country with fresh issues of paper-roubles, so that at the accession of Alexander II. the amount of these floating about, absolutely without any solid backing, was computed at over 100,000,000*l.* No wonder that chaos rose threatening destruction, for the miseries that this paper alone imposed on the people must have been incalculable. But Alexander was prudent, and had been besides warned in some degree by the experiences of his father of the dangers before him. He therefore adroitly identified himself, to some extent, with popular aspirations, and while retaining the semblance of an iron repression of everything revolutionary or hostile to the old *régime*, allowed the popular enthusiasm to effervesce in the discussion of socialist theories and in projects of freedom, hoping always to step in and control them when they seemed going too far. Almost at once he ameliorated considerably the grievances of the old imperial rule, suffered journals to be established, and habits to be adopted that in his father's time could not have faced the daylight for an hour. Above all, he set himself to the task of bringing Russia into closer administrative accord with the progressive civilisation of Western Europe, inaugurated improvements, and encouraged the building of railways. The administration of justice was nominally reformed, education was encouraged, and in 1861 the serfs were set free. Russia had fairly embarked in the quest of wealth, and soon emulated her Western neighbours in both the rapidity of her political and national development and the amount of her debt. At first the material improvements progressed slowly. It took time to get the nation into order after the war was over, and a few years passed before the money markets of Europe could be successfully appealed to for money to aid Russia in her schemes of development. And then, when the foundations had been fairly laid, the Polish insurrection intervened, to produce anew disorganisation and a pause in the execution of public works, so that not till 1868 could Russia be said to come fully under the influence of Western railway fanaticism. The fever of lending money for that kind of public works has since then reached its most extreme development everywhere abroad, and Russia has had her full share. Some 8,000 out of a total of about 12,000 miles of railway have been built in Russia between then and now. Her railway system is the newest thing she has got —except her 'Popoffkas,' those tubs of war about which Mr. E. J. Reed was some time ago so cruel as to frighten people here—and it is not yet nearly completed. It consists of a few main trunks and innumerable spurs leading as yet nowhere. There is a certain allowance to be made for this newness, and it would be unwise to assert that Russia cannot reap great good from her railways in the future because she has not done so in the past. All that can be fairly said is that Russia has so outrun her resources in her feverish haste that the chance of future benefit from her enormous expenditure in this direction is much more remote than wise administrators would like it to be.

Of that, at least, I think there can be no doubt. The public works carried out by Russia do not pay as a whole directly, and the majority of them do not pay indirectly. In the budget estimates for 1876 the charge put down for the service of the railway debt is 4,600,000*l.* (or 32,457,000 roubles) of which the Government has to find fully 2,000,000*l.* out of the general taxation. The amount of the deficit has, I believe, on the whole increased with the increase of railway mileage, and naturally enough, when each new branch built away from the main roads involved an additional loss. In 1870 the Government had only to find 932,000*l.*, but in 1872 its net payments on railway account had risen to 1,785,000*l.*, and in 1875 the amount was about 1,500,000*l.*, having been less the previous year by about a fourth of that sum. For the year 1876, whose accounts are not yet known, the deficit payments have probably proved much larger than the estimate, as the gross receipts of the lines open were less than in 1875, while the expenses were probably more. The war has of course disorganised everything, and in 1877 the charge on account of the railways falling on the national exchequer may be double that of 1874. How heavy the burden of these instruments of trade and civilisation is upon a poor country may be in short inferred from the fact that the total net return is not in ordinary years more than $2\frac{1}{2}$ per cent. on the capital spent, if so much. One or two of the smaller lines do not pay their working expenses, only some eight or nine companies earn a respectable net revenue,[1] and the rest involve a more or less heavy loss to the Government. The total of this loss up to

[1] Amongst these we may enumerate the St. Petersburg-Moscow (Nicholas) Railway, the Moscow-Nijni-Novgorod, the Warsaw-Vienna, the Koursk-Kiew and Kiew-Brest, the Moscow-Riazan, and Moscow-Korusk. The Riazan-Kozlow also yields a good net income, but all the rest of the forty-six companies are either struggling behindhand or not yielding any net income at all. If, therefore, we were to add the heavy deficits of each year on to the capital cost of the Russian railways, we should find that very soon they will prove to be the most costly undertakings of the kind in the world. Originally the cost of some of them would not appear to have been enormous; only from 10,000*l.* to 15,000*l.* per mile; and, taken all over, the outlay represents a cost of only some 22,000*l.* a mile; but year by year renewals, maintenance, additions, and repairs have, I fear, to be taken out of capital in not a few instances, and when the cost of these is added to the interest deficits, we can hardly place a limit to the ultimate capital outlay on this hurriedly-developed, often ill-constructed system.

the end of 1877 cannot be less than 20,000,000*l.*, and may through the war be nearer to 22,000,000*l.*

True though it be, therefore, that Russia possesses the main portions of a useful network of railways, and that her trade has been in some ways immensely benefited thereby, I cannot see that the progress has been altogether of a sound character. With all her increased trade, with her banking institutions for trade purposes and for advancing on real estate mortgage, so as to aid agricultural development, I doubt whether Russia has progressed at all in proportion to the extent usually supposed—whether the forcing process of the new *régime* has not made her poorer, and less able to bear up under any sudden strain. Nay, I will go further. It seems to me that the influx of new wealth and ways upon the dull, stereotyped barbarism of the Russian people has had a considerably deteriorating effect. They have got more put upon them than they are ripe for, and suffer to some extent in consequence. This statement may look paradoxical in face of the evidence which Russian trade figures give of the development of the country under Alexander II., but I think a little consideration of the circumstances will show it to be really reasonable enough. The newness of everything counts, no doubt, for much, and the progress in gross which has been actually made for something, but, when these admissions are made, enough remains to make us doubt seriously whether

Russia is not now economically weaker than she was eight or ten years ago. Her heavy debts are a huge mortgage on the national estate, and the very increase of the trade of the country is an evidence to a certain extent of the impoverishing effects of this mortgage. All countries who borrow abroad to enormous amounts run the greatest possible risks of impoverishment, unless their population possess energy enough to assimilate the good that may be extractable from foreign wealth. I doubt whether the Russian populations have this energy, and, more than that, I doubt whether their position is not too barbaric, too poverty-stricken to suffer them, however energetic, to profit by this wealth. I must ask the reader to revert again to the situation out of which the superimposed progress in material wealth has come in order to make my assertion seem just.

The first point to which I wish to draw attention is the one already incidentally mentioned, viz. that at the close of the Crimean War, Russia had at least 100,000,000*l.* of paper-roubles in circulation, as an almost purely fiduciary currency.[1] Her coffers were

[1] The course of Russian paper money issues during the earlier portion of the third quarter of the present century is given very clearly in the late M. Wolowski's pamphlet on the Finances of Russia, published in 1864. He says that in 1849 the paper-rouble circulation exceeded 300,000,000 roubles. The Crimean War brought a perfect avalanche of fresh notes into circulation, however, and the attempt made at first to maintain a certain metallic reserve was abandoned. By 1857 the rouble circulation had risen to 735,000,000 roubles, and the exchange against specie had to be suspended. For either the wealth or population of the

exhausted, the land was impoverished, and trade nearly at a standstill. In the exercise of ordinary prudence such a country should have rested for at least half a generation before launching into further debt, and, above all, foreign debt. All the more was this a necessity in the case of Russia, a country suffering under deficits which had been chronic almost since the time of Peter the Great, and whose paper-roubles had never been redeemed since Catherine II. gorged the land with them. This paper money formed so serious an obstacle to the growth of national wealth, and hence to the formation of credit companies, that again and again efforts were made to accomplish the impossible, either to raise the value of the rouble by issuing other interest-bearing credit documents for its redemption, or to fix by decree its exchange value against gold or silver. As late as 1863 a combination of these two measures was tried with a view to check a panic similar to that which terrified speculators all over Europe in the middle of October 1876. The Polish insurrection and its costly ruthless repression had necessitated the issue of more paper, until the Imperial Bank was unable to keep up the exchanges and the

---

country such a circulation was altogether excessive, and all sorts of miseries and derangements inevitably followed. Efforts made from time to time to redeem this heavy inconvertible State debt by means of internal and external interest-bearing loans have proved unavailing, and Russia finds herself just as heavily laden with this ruinous kind of debt as ever, with a desperate all-absorbing war on her hands.

Government itself hardly able at enormous sacrifices to provide the means of paying interest on its then small foreign debt. A loan was therefore raised, and part of it applied as a temporary backing to the rouble notes, the exchangeable value of which was fixed at a graduated scale as against silver over a series of months, in the foolish hope that par would then be reached and maintained. As soon as the borrowed money was exhausted in this ridiculous operation of course the whole artificial fabric crumbled to pieces, and the notes were once more a drag on trade, and a source of loss to the Government.

This is but a sample of what has been natural to Russia for a century and a half, and yet it was on such an internal credit foundation as this that Russia began to pile up her modern foreign debt, to become a great improver, a far-reaching conqueror and trader. Is it not an astonishing thing that she could have pursued this course almost for twenty years and still be apparently strong, still trusted; that all through there should have been no visible hitch, and that now with this war on her hands she should go on paying apparently as quietly as ever? Several things have favoured the longevity of this airy credit, however, which lessen our wonder. In the first place Western Europe, and especially we in England, have been very superstitious about Russian wealth. It has been a sort of fatalistic creed among the monied classes here that

Russia would go on paying always, simply because she did not default upon her foreign debt in the time of the Crimean War. It was of no use reminding these people that whereas she had then only a little over 500,000*l.* a year to pay, she has now nearly 10,000,000*l.* on her foreign debt alone, and that the total charge for interest, internal and external, has been growing year by year, until it was estimated at 15,500,000*l.* for the year 1876. Including paper-roubles, interest-bearing Treasury bonds, internal debt, foreign debt, railway and Land Bank bonds, the total debt of Russia cannot be much less than 500,000,000*l.*, of which some 240,000,000*l.* to 250,000,000*l.* is foreign interest-bearing debt, distributed in England, France, Holland, and Germany. This estimate, which I had arrived at independently, exceeds that made in an elaborate analysis of the debt of Russia given in the 'Economist' of December 9, 1876, where the total is placed at 413,063,000*l.* The difference arises, in part, from the different values given to the rouble in making the calculations. I have taken the rouble roughly at seven to the pound throughout, and the 'Economist' has converted all the internal loans at an exchange of 29*d.* per rouble. This plan has always seemed to me an objectionable one, inasmuch as it makes the debt totals fluctuate with the rates of exchange. At present the home debt would, for example, be 25 per cent. less than the 'Economist' has made it last year. Debt is debt, and if Russia ever pays in full, she will have to give for her rouble 3*s.* 1*d.* or so in metal; and I think therefore that her internal debt should be returned according to something like its nominal amount whatever the exchange.

An additional great help to faith, as regards England in particular, has been afforded to Russia by our belief in the all-prevailing power of railways. We went mad about them, and in our madness were willing to trust anybody to any extent who would only let us build them. Long ago any other superstition would have given out with us, but this has lasted almost till to-day. Russia did not want money for fortresses, for ironclads, for conquests; no, she wanted to build honest, world-transforming railways, and therefore she could have English money as fast as she asked for it.[1]

These were external aids, and the money then given has been used in part to build the railways, in part in supplying gratifications to Russian official corruption, and in part to keep up the fiction of Russian wealth and solvency. But internally Russia has possessed all along the enormous advantage, as against solvent nations, of never being compelled to pay any debts except with paper promises. These always became

---

[1] The present amount of the Russian bonds quoted on the London Stock Exchange is about 150,500,000*l.* including the Land Bank bonds; but, besides this, there are several Dutch loans, of the oldest of which— that issued between 1788 and 1815—some 2,000,000*l.* is still outstanding, and large portions of the railway debt.

supreme at a pinch as they are now, and Russia could thus be internally bankrupt in 1856 and 1863 while paying her foreign obligations most punctually. Again, she has a certain resource in gold and platina mines which, under the paper-rouble system, and in the earlier stages of her loan raising, has helped to provide the necessary interest funds; and she had till late years a trade balance in her favour, which was also a powerful help, preventing her from having to buy so much bullion. All these latter aids to keeping up appearances would not long have availed anything, however, but for the credulity first mentioned, on which Russia up to 1875 made large and increasingly frequent drafts— borrowing then 15,000,000*l.* at $4\frac{1}{2}$ per cent. nominal with as much coolness and assurance as France, or the United States, or our Government could possibly assume. Since then her credit has been shaken by criticism and by events in Eastern Europe, and for the present she is thrown back on herself, with the result that the gold in store was rapidly leaving the country, till the drain was stopped by a new loan from foreign capitalists. In spite of that loan the exchange has fallen, panic has overtaken the community, and the paper-roubles are becoming a source of greater loss than ever as a medium of internal exchange by reason of their depreciation. The Government in vain attempted for a time to stem the tide by exporting gold at any cost instead of produce to draw against. Eastern

Question or not, had the foreign supplies of money stopped sooner, Russian credit must have collapsed in this fashion any time these half-dozen years. Russia has herself probably been deluded by the plentiful showers of gold thrown into her, and had these stopped earlier, would earlier have been brought face to face with empty coffers, depressed exchanges, and the summary necessity for drastic retrenchment. For want of a loan during 1876 Russia had to maintain her foreign payments by withdrawing more than 12,000,000*l.* of her bullion reserve, held as a sort of guarantee of the rouble note; and unless the balance of her ordinary trading account remains steadily in her favour long after peace has been restored, this drain of bullion must be resumed and go on until there is not a stiver in the country to pay a creditor with. The vaunted progress of the last twenty years has brought her no further than this, then, and the bulk of her great public works are directly and indirectly a burden to her, which neither the increased wealth of the country nor its available resources can stand up under unaided for any length of time. It is mockery indeed to talk of wealth while the usual signs and results of wealth are absent from the land, while rather the foreign gold has helped to augment the general poverty by raising the cost of living without giving compensating advantages. In plain terms, it must be said that the path which Russia has lately followed has been mistaken in many ways.

She has built strategic lines of railway when she ought to have been content with good roads or with canals and her great natural water-ways. Through the best part of Southern Russia these water-ways now compete against the railways, and from the nature of the produce carried must have the best of it. The Volga for Asiatic trade, and the Dnciper—navigable far into the heart of Russia—for the corn trade with Europe, these are the true commercial arteries of the country; and with them a large canal network easily made and maintained, and good roads, Russia ought to have been long for the most part content.[1] As it is she has got military lines that have a non-paying traffic one way only, and numerous spurs of railways that shoot off into country districts, where there are no towns and where thoroughly good roads would be much more to the purpose. A whim has been gratified, a mistaken ambition ostensibly realised, and the land remains grovelling in a wretched poverty.

The usual answer to criticism such as this is, however, the plea of 'indirect benefit.' 'The State has

---

[1] Herr Theodor von Lengenfeldt, in his admirable compilation *Russland im neunzehnten Jahrhundert*, published last year, states that Russia in Europe possessed 42,551 versts of water-ways, including the inland canals, and that all over the empire there were about 90,000 versts of post and other roads. The verst is roughly two-thirds of a mile, so that for so rude a country Russia was not badly provided had she had no railways, were the roads passable instead of being to a large extent mud tracks which are often nearly impassable and without trustworthy bridges. *Vide* the opening chapters of Mr. Mackenzie Wallace's graphic book on Russia.

gained enormously, we are told, as evidenced by its trade, by the growth of its general revenues,' and so forth. And at first sight this argument appears to have almost more force in the case of Russia than in that of any other country I know. The revenues of Russia have developed, and the trade has developed to what appears to be an enormous extent in the few years for which we have figures. I admit this fully and without reserve, but for all that I decline to yield upon the larger question of the wastefulness of the heavy outlay undertaken for public works since the accession of Alexander II., or to forego my doubts as to the real extent of Russian prosperity. The reason for this apparent obstinacy is that I set down both the growth of revenue and the larger part of the growth of trade to the direct action of the foreign money which the country obtained on loans, not to the works which were the chief product of that money—a most important distinction. I therefore believe that when this money stops pouring in both revenue and trade will shrink, because the money at best was used merely as an unhealthy stimulant and without regard to the true capacity of the people for absorbing and utilising capital. As far as the meagre figures can enable us to judge, the borrowings of recent years have quite reversed the sound trade position absolutely essential to the well-being of a nation heavily in debt to foreign money-lenders. Certainly up to within the last ten years Russia was always a larger exporter than importer, but of late the balance has been changed, and a poor country, possessed of no exchange medium except raw produce and printed paper of no value outside its own borders, has been steadily buying more than it sold. The actual adverse balance may not be so much as it appears because the Russian export figures are very inaccurate, but it exists and is abnormal. Its direct effect has been to increase the yield of the customs duties, and so to swell the revenue, and at the same time to increase the poverty of the masses of the community. Russia is a country which believes in a protective tariff with all the fervour of Pan-slavonic arrogance and ambition, and this in itself explains the rise of nearly 20,000,000 roubles in the budget estimate of customs receipts for 1876 over the actual yield of 1870, this increased revenue being entirely due to foreign borrowing. There cannot be a doubt either that with the stoppage of the foreign loans this growth will also stop, so that I should not be surprised to find that within a year or two the customs revenue had fallen off a full half. Nay, if the extreme protectionist views which have obtained the ascendency since Russia determined on going to war continue, they will cause her regular imports to cease almost entirely, and in time once more make Russia a land apart, buying from nobody and selling to nobody. The people could not have paid their customs dues in the past but for the stimulant of foreign money, and now when over-borne by debt—when poverty-struck, and as a nation bankrupt, it is little likely that they will bear the still more maddening burden which the folly of Russian financiers has imposed; a burden, not of prohibitive taxes merely, but of home bounties and prohibitory restrictions. But the ordinary customs alone do not form all the additions to a revenue which was estimated for the past year at 535,000,000 roubles, or 55,000,000 roubles more than the yield of 1870. There is a special salt tax, a tobacco tax, and a sugar tax, all levied on imports which have been swollen by the influx of foreign money.

For it must not be forgotten that the spending power of a certain portion of the Russian people has been for a time enormously increased by the heavy specie importations on account of loans, and that therefore the revenue drawn from both external and internal sources has been favourably affected by this cause. The Russian lower orders are, for example, great drinkers of spirits, if not drunkards, so that in the past year the Government expected to draw no less than 191,800,000 roubles from that source alone. Excise on brandy and other ardent spirits, and on beer, and the various customs duties, are almost alone amongst important sources of income estimated at increases in last year's budget; and it is these which have been most decidedly affected by the influx of foreign capital, and by the expenditure of the small wealthy class on the numerous schemes of improvement started of late years, chiefly on the spur of this inflation. About 226,000,000*l.* nominal, or say 200,000,000*l.* effectual, has been spent on the railways of the empire, almost a third of which has probably been directly distributed as wages and plunder, so that over many parts of Russia there has been freer spending than its acquired wealth warranted. To this free spending we must, in part at least, set down the augmented excise income. Putting these various considerations together, and bearing in mind also that heavy borrowing has gone on all round from prince to peasant, privately and by Government sanction, I think it must be admitted that the progress of Russia may well prove to be more apparent than real. It would at all events be very unwise to draw any inference from the augmented yield of the taxes as to the extent of the development of her material wealth.[1]

Making all these deductions, however, it must still be admitted that the general export trade of Russia has, according to official figures, doubled itself in about ten years, and that the new wealth has, therefore, stimulated this half of the national trade also, and for the time being. Her exports of cereals, of flax, of

[1] According to a recent return there were over 6,000,000 gallons of brandy and 10,600,000 gallons of beer consumed last year in St. Petersburg alone. This is at the rate of nearly nine gallons of brandy and fifteen gallons of beer per head of the population—an enormous consumption, even when we allow for the drinking of the multitudes who come and go as mere visitors to the capital.

hides, tallow, and wood, are all very much larger than they were ten years ago; and the figures alone would here again seem quite to refute my statement that Russia has not been made materially or permanently richer by all that has been spent on her improvements. But on this point it is well to remember that, to no inconsiderable extent, these increased exports of Russia signify a process of exhaustion. Her timber is being exported, and the planting of fresh forests is not going on proportionately to the waste. Crop after crop of corn is taken off her southern plains, and little or no attention paid to replenishing the exhausted soil; the breeding and housing of her cattle have been so neglected that they suffer from chronic rinderpest in one form or other, so that the landowners are not maintaining, as they ought to do, the flocks which an over-rapid export of hides and tallow has tended, as much perhaps as disease, to reduce. Let this progress go on and we shall find Russia in a few years with little or nothing to export to Western Europe worth having. Already for several years in succession complaint has been rife that the South Russian harvest has been bad, as well as the quality of the grain, and the trade of Odessa has in consequence fallen away, till its merchants have been compelled to liquidate by hundreds, and till they have filled the land with their complaining. The profits of the over-stimulated export have been also often indifferent, so far as the farmer is concerned; the middlemen, the foreign merchants, and the banks pocketing most of it. Moreover, a portion of the increased export trade of European Russia is due to the extension of her conquests in Asia, by which she has now exclusive control of nearly all inland traffic north of the Tibetan, Affghan, and Persian mountain ranges. By these conquests Russian trade with the Caucasus, Persia, Bokhara, Khiva, Turkistan, Kashgar, and Western China has been much stimulated, whereas with Great Britain, say, the yearly export business of Russia cannot be said to have increased, on the average, more than some 5,000,000*l.* since 1860, although Great Britain is by far Russia's largest European foreign customer and creditor. That is all that the stimulant of our money has done for Russia in this direction, all that our constant demand for interest on our loans has practically spurred her traders to accomplish. As to the figures of her general trade account, I find that the official tables inserted in M. Vessélovsky's excellent 'Annuaire des Finances Russes' for 1876 exhibit a total merchandise trade in 1874 of 903,000,000 roubles, say, 127,000,000*l.*, of which 471,000,000 roubles are imports. These figures include Finland. The totals are only approximate, however, especially so far as the exports are concerned, and it seems likely that these are really of considerably higher value than the above totals would show. A real value estimate appended to the summary given by M. Vessélovsky makes the exports slightly higher than the imports. But supposing that the true state of the case, the situation of Russian trade is not sound, for the exports ought annually to exceed the imports not by a million or so but by many millions.

The truth of the matter is that we cannot measure justly the progress which Russia has made internally except we take into account the influences of her agrarian system. It is a peculiar one, and based on habits and sustained by aspirations quite out of the run of Western ideas. For a detailed account of it I must refer the reader to the valuable publication of Dr. Julius Eckardt already cited and to the recently published volumes of Mr. Wallace, but I will try to give the salient features here.

As everyone knows, until the spring of 1861 there were really but two classes of people in Russia, the nobles and the serfs or slaves. The latter were substantially the chattels of their masters, or, on crown lands, of the State, and attached for the most part to the land, with which they might be bought and sold. In terms of their serfdom the agrarian slaves were compelled to render labour for so many days in the year to their masters—to till their lands, in fact, and in return got, not wages, but a piece of ground held in common by the village community, of which each serf was a member, and which they were expected to till for their own maintenance. This common land was apportioned out to the individual villagers or separate families of villagers according to usages which I need not detail, but the portions so allotted did not go out of the control of the collective inhabitants. They were merely assigned by lot for the maintenance of a particular family and roughly according to the working capacity of that family for a given time, generally nine years, sometimes twelve, and at the end of that period they reverted to the community, to be again allotted, probably to quite different individuals. As a family increased its patches would be increased, but these additions were not necessarily, nor, I gather, often, contiguous to the previous allotments. They might be at the other end of the common land, and thus it not infrequently occurred that one family would have a number of different patches, dotted here and there, as the fortune of the lottery determined. Now this arrangement might be tolerable so long as the peasantry were pure slaves, but it will strike everyone as strange that such a system should subsist now that the peasant is free. Yet it does prevail almost throughout Russia. The free peasant lives on his allotted patches as before, and has no more individual property in the soil than he had when he legally formed but an adjunct of it. When the emperor freed the serf from his master he left him just as much shackled to the land as ever, and, as Dr. Eckardt points out,[1] only the Baltic provinces, part

[1] *Modern Russia*, p. 77.

of Russia Minor, and Russian Poland are exempt from this agrarian system.

The causes which led to the adoption of so strange a method of granting freedom were various. For one thing, a kind of patriarchal communism had been diligently preached in Russia for years before the emancipation of the serfs as the true foundation of Sclavonic progress, as the peculiar endowment of the race. It had been gilded with the tinsel of a false philosophy, and sanctified as the fulfilment of the highest ideal of Christianity. There was, therefore, a powerful popular force at the back of the Government pushing it in this direction, and, on the other hand, it seems probable that the nobles acquiesced in the arrangement, from an idea that their interests would be better served. They may have dreaded that no labourers would be got on any terms were the peasants set absolutely free as those of France have been. At best the compensation offered to them seemed small in return for even the personal freedom of their slaves, and many of them must have looked with repulsion upon the coming change, as the period which would mark their lapse into helpless poverty. A variety of forces determined the adoption of half measures, therefore, and the serf was only half liberated. For a time, in fact, his condition was not perceptibly changed at all, except that the right to dispose of his person was no longer vested in a master. The village communities were bound still to pay either a certain rent or to render a certain amount of service to the overlord of their manors. This of itself, wisely arranged, might have sufficed to prevent the landlords from being left in the lurch, but, as if to render the worst evils of communism more apparent, it was governed by a right of redemption, under which, either alone or with Government assistance, communities might deliver their land from all such obligations. Whatever the determining causes the communal system was maintained, and with it that curious family arrangement which attaches every man to his house—his village family, wherever he may go, whatever trade he may pursue. This is an arrangement which works most disastrously against the development of Russian industries, because it leads the artisan to forsake his work in winter and go home to his village where his wife and children are residing, perhaps under his father's roof. It also conduces to the most gross immorality.

But obviously from a merely agricultural point of view a want of individual property in land would do nothing so much as tend to check industry and enterprise. No peasant could be expected to overtax himself for the general good. He would work just as much as was necessary to keep his family alive, to raise his quota of taxation, to provide himself with plenty of cheap spirits, and, unless bound to render so much service to the overlord, he would do no more, because without adequate inducement to do more. The direct consequence of this social arrangement must, therefore, be to make the Russian peasant lazy, unenterprising, and a bad agriculturist, and all testimony goes to prove that this is what he has unquestionably more and more become as he has got free from all obligation to the former lords of his land and body. Henceforth he need only work for wages; and if the wages or the work do not suit him, and he has enough for his own wants on his allotted patches, he need not work for a master at all. From a recent return published in the 'Messager Officiel' early in 1877 it would appear that the peasants are rapidly emancipating themselves from all their remaining obligation to the overlords, and that independence without freedom is becoming almost universal. Out of the peasant population on the great seigneurial domains in thirty-seven governments, 72 per cent. have bought up the seigneurial rights still remaining over their land or service, partly by the aid of the Government, but mostly without it, and including the peasants of the nine provinces of the west, the number of the ancient serfs now released is 8,130,000 out of a total of little more than 10,000,000, or about 80 per cent. This might be called, so far, a sign of progress, but only so far; there is indeed a premium on indolence in this arrangement, and from all I can learn the peasants are not slow to avail themselves of it. I believe that one reason for the ease with which the United States is beating the Russian farmer in corn-growing is just this, that the latter finds more and more difficulty in getting regular labour at a price which will make it worth his while to send his crops to market. Complaints are almost universal of the scarcity of labour, not so much because men are scarce as because they will not work. The peasant is secure of subsistence whatever comes, and, as a peasant, he can be but little more unless he leaves the community and betakes himself to trade—so, why should he work? No wonder that motiveless free labour, such as this happy indifference breeds, should be, as Dr. Eckardt says, most unprofitable. 'No farmer,' he states, 'can be certain that on the following morning his workmen may not be up and away, without having fed the horses and oxen, or heated the stoves; and may have gone, indeed, not in consequence of a dispute, but because there is a holiday in the neighbouring village, and Vanka has said to Fedka, "Let us go, comrade; a little brandy has been imported; you ought to go and see." The labourers return after three or four days; but, meanwhile, the cattle have died, or, at any rate, necessary work has been neglected.'[1] That picture is, I believe, not overdrawn, and it throws not a little light on what Russian progress means. It is, socially at least, progress backwards.

Modern Russia, p. 189.

For this arrangement not only makes labour scarce, uncertain, and dear, but it permanently divides the empire into two classes still, and two only—the noble and the peasant—and keeps both poor. There is and can be no middle order, unless we regard the small number of burgesses, or the venal Russian bureaucracy as such; no bulwark either to the throne or to the laws that bind society, between the dominance of an oligarchy or a priesthood on the one hand, and an ignorant democracy on the other. Indeed, and this is a very tempting subject, on which I must only touch, this gap has, it is clear, exercised a most powerful influence on the form and character of Russian despotism in Alexander II.'s day. He has been driven to lean on the peasant rather than on the noble; and, at the present time, instead of controlling, finds himself, I fear, to some degree controlled by blind popular passions. The communistic enthusiasts openly preach autocracy, as the natural, nay, divine topstone of communism, and the policy of the emperor has, I cannot doubt, tended to use that doctrine, so as to seat his somewhat battered throne directly on the solid ground once more. Not only is the power of the emperor now based upon the democracy, instead of on the nobles, and through the democracy on the bureaucrats, who are in part sprung from the peasant or ignoble classes, and in part from the debased priests, but it is limited in several very important ways by this new source of power. Absolutism is a striking-looking thing in the abstract, but it has no real existence in Russia, any more than in India. There are dominating interests which act as controlling forces upon the individual will, and which ultimately compel obedience. The despotic caprices of the ruler of all the Russias may be indulged, as Prince Dolgoroukow finely says, against individuals, but the emperor cannot compel general obedience to a law which the bureaucrats do not like. No more can he resist popular impulses, however blind and ignorant they may be. The *residuum* in Russia has the ultimate voice, and the unlettered, rather brutish *residuum* there forms nearly nine-tenths of the population. Hence, probably, the vacillating course which ended in the present war with Turkey. Popular passions might not at first seek that war, but they were driving towards other ends more immediately dangerous to despots and their satellites, and it was thought wise to change the current. The popular drift going towards greater freedom compelled the emperor into a course tending to direct men's minds to new objects, and he encouraged panslavism. It was the old story of Napoleon III. and Germany over again. Popular forces, popular discontent, if you will, grew threatening, and to save his throne, and perhaps his life, the Emperor of Russia let loose the dogs of war. The motive was vile be the outcome of the war what it may, but it offers a curious glimpse of the shifting sand on which the throne of the semi-divine Czar rests.

Returning to our direct subject. I think it may be assumed that agricultural progress in the conditions I have sketched can never be a solid thing in Russia. The landowners—the old nobles and the State—have an enormous amount of land on their hands in the aggregate, which can neither be let to 'improving' tenants nor be farmed effectively by the owners. The landowner stumbles on, therefore, often deeply in debt, rarely or never able to rise above his surroundings and farm even as an Ohio or Texas squatter would. The Government has had to come to his aid by the establishment of a series of land banks in various provinces, whose business it is to make advances to the distressed proprietor under mortgage, and the money for which has been mostly found in England; but in the long run this help will only be another weight added to his burden. The banks and he are not at all unlikely to go to ruin together. I am told that the backwardness and poverty of resource manifested in Russia generally over agricultural matters is something quite beyond description, and it must remain so until the serf is emancipated from the commune as much as from his overlord. Only here and there in the South are proprietors found rich enough and enlightened enough to try to work their land on sound principles, but many of these have seemed to be more enlightened than they are. They have imported agricultural implements of the newest types freely from England, and make but indifferent use of them. I cannot then admit that the material benefits forced on Russia by the modern efforts at following in the ways of the West, governed as they have always been by a restless military ambition, have been of much use to the people; or that the empire can be said to be sensibly richer thereby. In spite of a flush of trade, which cannot be reckoned on long, there are signs of lethargy and exhaustion which indicate only too surely that the load is proving too much for the country. All these railways, and steamers, and many of the canals and banks, have been called into being on pure credit, and the empire cannot hope to be floated into a safe haven by that bladder alone.

Certain is it that after twenty years of 'progress,' the paper-rouble circulation of Russia is larger, without counting the enormous amounts issued since the war began, than it was at the close of the Crimean War, and not one whit better secured. It circulates in normal times at a discount of from five to ten per cent. as against silver, which is in turn at present a degenerated currency in the rest of Europe as against gold. How this affects Russian trade for the worse I need not stay to explain; but how it helps to drive the Government of Russia towards bankruptcy is seen in the significant fact that it took in 1876 so much of the bullion reserve to meet foreign interest payments, and keep up the foreign rate of exchange, and that as soon as a fear seized the mercantile community that this gold supply would be stopped, discount rates rose to eighteen and twenty per cent., and the rate of exchange fell at once nearly ten per cent. Since the war began the course of exchange has been more disastrous still, the rouble sinking to 23*d*.; and had the Government not been able to borrow abroad the interest on its foreign debt, it would probably have now been on the eve of default.

No doubt, as in the case of the United States, and of India, when foreign supplies of capital cease, the export trade of Russia will be partially stimulated and her imports diminished: but the forcing which the former will bear cannot be great, if what I have stated as to the agricultural condition of Russia, the poverty of her nobles, and the general exhaustion of the soil, is at all true. Russia, it must not be forgotten, has nothing but raw produce to offer the world. Her manufactures are almost utterly out of reckoning in any estimate of her European foreign trade. Some kinds of coarse cotton cloths are made in Russia, and there is a considerable home industry in linen and woollen goods; but hardly one of these could exist for a day against foreign competition but for the high customs tariff, and they are therefore powerless to compete abroad. The whole industrial population of Russia, including miners of all kinds, and metal and wood workers, probably does not exceed a million—Herr von Lengenfeldt places it at 919,000—and it is employed, almost entirely, in supplying home requirements and the Asiatic market. The cotton, woollen, linen, and hemp industries employ about 295,000 workpeople in all in European Russia, or 554,000 in the whole empire, including Poland; and, except food and drink-producing industries, there are no others which employ a quarter of a million people. The population employed in metal working of all kinds is under 140,000. In a population of upwards of 80,000,000 these numbers are quite insignificant, yet the half of them at least probably quit the factories during winter, and retire to wallow in their villages, whither their earnings have been sent and where their wives are. For her export trade Russia has therefore to depend on her raw products. These do not, of course, yield much directly as revenue, because taxes cannot be imposed on exports, and they do not greatly tend to enrich the country, because much of the profit on them must go as tribute to other nations—tribute or usury—it is the same thing when money has been borrowed and wanted. The buying power of Russia must, therefore, inevitably fall off to a large extent whenever foreign money ceases to pay for what she buys, unless the exports can be stimulated sufficiently to pay the debt interest and leave a large balance of surplus profit; and even then the Government must obtain the large revenue it requires by increased internal taxation. With a diminution of imports a falling off in customs revenue would at once ensue, and this process has, in fact, now begun. The import totals have fallen off with great rapidity since the middle of 1876, and neither England nor Germany is now sending much to Russia, partly because of the tariff, and partly because of the poverty of the people and the war. The exports, also, have decidedly not improved, notwithstanding the extreme necessity of the Government to find the means of remittance in the face of its heavy debts abroad. Wheat, barley, oats, flax, hemp, and seeds were all in 1876 decidedly below the export of 1875. Since then there has been a spasmodic increase in some staples due to the urgent need of money, but the general trade of Russia is dull and must continue dull for several reasons. It is easy to export all the goods you have, but if people abroad do not want to buy, your exporting power will do little to help you. Trade has been dull all over the world for nearly four years now, and Russia finds fewer customers for the crude articles she has to sell. That is one reason for the decline. Another is to be found in the history I have already recited. Russia is not producing so well nor so cheaply as she must do if she is not to see herself cut out of the market. The quality of her wheat is deteriorating rather than improving, just like that of her little neighbour Roumania, and in other respects she is getting beaten.

The decline in customs receipts alone must have last year involved a deficit of about 1,000,000*l.* on the estimated income of a budget which barely balanced. This will be all the more severe a strain on Russia at the present time when she is groaning under the weight of a series of large armies in the field, and when distress prevails sufficiently to hinder the peasant from being able to drink the Government out of its difficulties, even when aided in doing so by an augmented excise duty which makes a little liquor go further as a revenue-producing article than it did before. There is, indeed, only one way out of the dilemma which Russian progress has brought the country face to face with—a dilemma that may now end in a national collapse—and that is a rigorous and immediate reduction of expenditure; but that also must be most difficult. Between them the army and navy in a time of peace take 27,000,000*l.* to 30,000,000*l.*, or nearly half the ordinary net revenue, and in their degree other administrative departments— all except that of public instruction—are nearly as expensive. The Russian army is, it is stated, capable of being raised to 1,320,000 men, but normally consists on paper of 760,000 with 28,000 officers. These are ruinous figures enough, granting that a third of the soldiers never figure in the ranks at all, and, were these men abstracted from the working power of the nation, the weight of their maintenance would be itself sufficient to crush the industries of so poor a country, and to throw Russia out of the international race for wealth altogether. But I believe this is, as usual, only a paper enumeration in peace times, and that the real secret of the enormous money cost of the army is to be found in the venality with which it is surrounded, and in the heavy outlay rendered necessary to keep down or acquire the conquests in Asia and the Caucasus. There is little chance of the Government being able to remedy the first, although corruption has, more than all other causes put together, been the origin of the weakness of the army in its struggle with the Turks, and it would almost be worth more than the emperor's existence to draw back from the latter. And we may safely assume that economies will prove as difficult elsewhere. Something—in some respects much—has been done to purify the internal administration, but it is as yet quite out of comparison with those of Western Europe. The bureaucracies of France, Germany, and Austria are not models of uprightness, but I think no one will deny that they excel the officials who settle down all over Russia, and who flourish under the delegated despotism which Russian autocracy renders indispensable. What the blundering in the field or the gross commissariat frauds may do to stir the people up to fight the mischief, I cannot of course say; but whatever they do they must fail to purify an administration whose fountain is so corrupt.

Taking all these things into account, then, I should say that the progress of Russia during the reign of Alexander II. has been progress towards a catastrophe of which the first hint was given in the October panic of 1876, or rather perhaps in the Moscow panic, which signalised the collapse of that Cagliostro of financiers, Dr. Strousberg, three months before. And I can find in Russia few elements of a commercial prosperity capable of averting this catastrophe. No doubt here as elsewhere the result of the swollen credit upon which the empire has floated so long may ultimately be productive of good, but I have never been able to see that the process of a barbaric nation's growth can be much hastened by such means. There is always the recoil sure to follow, by which the nation may be carried for a time back farther than artificial pushing ever advanced it. The roots of a nation's progress must be in itself, and the impetus must come from within; it cannot be imposed from above. Money sown broadcast over a country does not necessarily fructify. It may blight, and in the case of Russia has blighted much. The wonderful way in which Russian credit has kept up, and Russian exports also during the campaign of 1877, goes for nothing. Peace and the attempt to pay her way without help will be the true test of Russian economic strength; and when these are applied I can see nothing to prevent the whole elaborate fabric of credit from tumbling to pieces. The rich financiers who back the country now may be strong, but even they cannot fill a bottomless pit with gold, and Russian needs have no end. Before the war began she had to raise an internal loan, she has needed two since, besides all the paper forced into the circulation and an external loan for 15,000,000*l.* which refuses to 'float.' The war over, paper and debt alone will remain for many a long day.

So much, then, for the position which Russia has placed herself in by the policy of progress—a policy which has been itself a species of fraud, for there was often no progress save a warlike progress south and east.

Like other countries in like circumstances, Russia has aggravated the mischief of her mistaken attempt to make the land prosperous by trying to tax the foreigner. I need not expatiate on the mischief of this policy after what has been said in the previous chapter, but it must be taken into account in estimating the chances of renewed English trade with Russia. Practically, I believe, we are now nearly shut out of her market as iron merchants, for even the Germans, who had a growing trade in iron and machinery with Russia, are for the time debarred. That is how Russia fines the foreigner. The Russian merchant is very jealous of foreign competition, and sets his face against it when he can; and to please him the Government put on prohibitory duties, which fluctuate in their degree of oppression with the rates of exchange, foolishly imagining that thereby it has both benefited the native producer and secured its own revenue.[1]

[1] The tariff of Russia is as difficult to estimate the true incidences of as that of the United States. Most of the articles pay so much duty by weight, or weight and fineness, and the manner of fixing the cash sums leads to many arbitrary results. For example, coarse cotton goods, up to the limit of 21 square feet or so to the lb. (8 square arshines to the funt) pay 5l. 10s. 4d. per cwt., but at and above about 80 square feet to the lb. the duty is 21l. 13s. 6d., with intermediate duties for intermediate qualities. Dyed cotton goods pay according to a different and higher scale, the highest being 23l. 12s. 11d. per cwt. The duty on lace is 59l. 2s. 3d. per cwt., apparently quite irrespective of quality. Ready-made clothes pay 35 per cent. *ad valorem*. Linen and hemp or jute goods pay in a similar way. Silk ribbons, velvet, handkerchiefs, and clothes, except printed goods, pay about 20l. per cwt. The duties on woollen clothes are about 23l. 13s. per cwt., and on flannels 7l. 17s. 8d., while shawls, scarfs, &c., pay 59l. 2s. 3d., and so on. On this class of English manufactures its duties may be considered on the average more prohibitory than those of the States; but in respect of yarns, hardware, and miscellaneous goods, the tariff of Russia is lighter. But what makes the tariff of Russia most dangerous to trade is not these figures: it is the new law which came in force at the beginning of the present year compelling all import duties to be paid in gold. This makes the duty on any particular article a fluctuating thing from day to day, and at the rates of exchange current prices the war has raised the increase of all duties by about 50 per cent. A more unwise law could hardly have been enacted, but it shows us what progress through the medium of foreign debt may drive a poor country to. The Government wants some 10,000,000l. a year in gold and the railway companies want several millions, what more easy than make the customs furnish it all? Words could not adequately describe the folly of such reasoning, or paint more clearly the dangers which surround Russian trade, Russian credit, and Russian finance. But this is not all. Not only is the foreigner to be fined, but the home industries must be fostered in order to prove how wealthy Russia can become, and this must be especially done with iron, for the reasons adduced in the text. Hence the following regulations, which also came into force at the commencement of 1877. I extract them from the late Mr. David Forbes's report on the iron and steel industries of foreign countries, published in the last number of the *Journal* of the Iron and Steel Institute for 1876. 'A heavy duty will be put on rails imported into Russia, and all railway companies in Russia,

Of course the tariff does enable the Russian trader to find a market—though a market ever becoming both now in existence and hereafter to be formed, will be compelled to employ one-half their rails of Russian manufacture. For a period of twelve years a premium will be allowed by the Government on all steel rails made or old rails re-worked in Russia, and during three years a premium will also be granted on all pig iron produced. With respect to the new Russian works in the district of Bakhmutski, the premium will only be allowed when the production exceeds 300,000 pouds per annum, when it will be at the rate of 50 copecks per poud. During the first eight years of the twelve before alluded to, the premium is fixed at 35 copecks per poud, in the ninth at 30 copecks, in the tenth at 25 copecks, and in the eleventh and twelfth at 20 copecks per poud; the premium to be paid upon a certificate being delivered to the inspector appointed by the Ministry of Ways and Communications containing a receipt for the rails signed by the company. These regulations apply both to works at present in operation, and to such as are erected within three years for the manufacture of steel rails, which will be entitled to order for rails for a period not exceeding five years, these orders to be decided by the Ministry of Finance, in conjunction with the Ministry of Ways and Communications, but the ultimate decision lies with the Council of Ministers. The quantity of steel rails to be manufactured and delivered to the Government is fixed as well for new railways as for the repair of those already in operation. Of the orders, which are to be given for a period of from three to five years, re-manufactured rails must not exceed one-third of the quantity, the rest being new iron or steel rails, and these orders are to be in the form of contracts, the price stated therein to include the premium. The manufacturers have, however, no deposit to pay, and if they do not comply with the terms of the contract, it is simply terminated without any penalty. The manufacturer, if he desires, can receive one-half the amount of one year's supply of rails in advance, giving his works as a guarantee, which guarantee, however, is in no case to exceed 75 per cent. of their estimated value. All further concessions to railway companies are to contain an engagement obliging them to accept a certain quantity of rails manufactured by order of the Government, and it is announced that the Ministry of Finance, in union with the Ministry of Ways and Communications, are now preparing a reduced tariff for the transport of rails, iron ore, fuel, &c.'

This needs no comment except that it is by no means an isolated example of the way Russia has of fostering trade. She has done even more than this with her beet-root sugar industry, and the only result that has come of all her coddling and bounties is that the growth of beet-root and the manufacture of native sugar appear to be threatened with extinction.

poorer—for his goods, which would otherwise, both from their quality and their price, be unsaleable; but prohibitory as it may be, the tariff could not shut us out entirely were it not for the trade tactics of the people. These are decidedly hostile to the foreigner, and, tariff or no tariff, an English or a German merchant finds little encouragement to do business in the interior of the country. Russian goods and Russian merchants secure a practical monopoly by refusing to let anybody trade but themselves. Hence all through the regions in Asia, where they have laid their grasp, English goods are now almost entirely shut out. For example, this country used formerly to do a large trade with Persia and Turkestan by way of the Black Sea and Tiflis in Georgia, but since the treaty expired by which we were allowed access to that city by Russia our trade has almost altogether stopped, or works along painfully against Turkish anarchy. The Russian Government has established cotton and woollen manufactories of its own at Tiflis, and supplies the people within its dominions without foreign help. The same policy has been displayed towards foreign iron. Although Russia possesses minerals of all kinds in considerable abundance, her appliances for winning them, and the capital available, have been hitherto extremely small, while labour has been difficult to procure at any price. In her great schemes of improvement Russia has therefore had to depend upon foreign iron-makers, and the process has been, of course, to borrow money from us with the one hand from the general public, and pay it back with the other to the big iron masters and railway contractors, who were, profitably to themselves, carrying out Russian projects. At the same time a certain amount of stimulus was given to native production, particularly during the periodical gusts of inflation to which iron speculation has subjected this country, and the native-won iron has increased in quantity in Russia till it reached in the beginning of 1874 about 960,000 tons a year. That it is still a feeble, ill-supplied industry is sufficiently proved by the fact that this was the out-turn of some 1,270 mines.[1] When the reaction began in Europe generally after the great inflation of 1872 and 1873, Russian iron miners and makers no doubt felt that their profits and chances were going. No duty which the Government could lay would be able to prevent foreign iron from entering, so long at any rate as foreign money was lent to pay for it. The emperor seems therefore to have been induced to come to the help of the home industry in the usual way, by decreeing that an arbitrary preference should be given to home-made iron and iron manufactures. In addition to a heavy duty to be levied upon foreign iron, its import is checked by a decree which compels all Russian

[1] *Annuaire de l'Economie politique et statistique.* Par M. Maurice Block. 1876.

railway companies to take half their rails from home makers. These makers are also, as will be seen from the extract given in a note above, to be stimulated by a premium on the pig-iron they produce. In the financial distress now prevalent all through Russia —with continued fresh issues of inconvertible paper, and all commerce disorganised — this foolish kind of assistance may not mean much for the native producer, and may be taken perhaps as a sort of revenge. But it may mean, permanently, a good deal for us, as the steady diminution of our iron exports to Russia proves. Our export trade to Russia has been unduly inflated by the proceeds of the loans in past years, and in spite of natural trade laws; and now we must either lend more money freely, and brave these laws a while longer, as well as the Russian tariff, or suffer this trade to all but collapse. If the latter course is pursued I should not be at all surprised to hear that in a few years' time some of the Russian railways were falling into decay, for with little or no traffic, without sufficient renewal of permanent way, with bad rolling stock, dilapidated locomotives, and no money, how can they do otherwise? The outlook for that unhappy country is therefore of the worst kind— these fostering and propping measures can only hasten the catastrophe.

There is yet another aspect in which this trade policy of Russia presents itself to us, when we think

of the probable extension of her influence over Asia
Minor and over the European provinces of the Turkish
Empire. Whatever bad qualities the Turk possesses
—and they are legion—he is not a prohibitionist in
trade, nor does his political economy comprehend
the bounty system as anything beyond backsheesh.
Rather he is a sort of free-trader—not given, that is,
to impose heavy customs duties, only to plunder the
unlucky subject who presumes to get rich by trading
as he pleases. As far as the utter misgovernment of
the Turk will allow, he has therefore been negatively
the friend of English business interests throughout his
dominions. If the people had the means to buy from
us the Turk would have no objection to let us sell,
and in former years, before the access of corruption
came over Turkey—in the guise also of modern progress
—we did a considerable business both in the European
and Asiatic provinces of the empire. So far as regards
Northern and Central Asia, all that has, as we have said,
long been changed. Russia has almost entirely ended
our trade with the Caucasus, Persia, and Turkestan.[1]

[1] Some interesting memoranda regarding the Russian trade with
Central Asia will be found in the collection of Travels translated by
Messrs. J. and R. Michell, and published in 1865. We are there told that
Russian cotton goods cannot compete with English either in quality or
cheapness, that consequently whenever the competition is free Russian
goods are driven out of the market. But for all that Russian trade with
Central Asia was rapidly expanding. 'Until very lately,' we read at pp.
459-460, 'cotton manufactures constituted little less than one-half of the
total goods exported (from Russia to Bokhara, Khiva, the Kirghiz Steppe,
and so on); in 1860 they had already exceeded that figure.' And ever

The same result follows wherever Russia gets a footing. As yet her trade in the newer regions conquered in Asia is insignificant, but she takes care that no one shares it. We have made strenuous and in my opinion most foolish efforts to lay hold of a Kashgar business; but when Russia puts her hand on that country, as, unless checked in her march eastward by reverses in Europe or by aggressions of the Chinese she is likely to do, there will be an end to all chance for English traders there, just as much as if our access to Kashgar had been as easy as formerly to Tiflis.

In connection with Russian conquests in Asia, I may observe here, we have heard frequently of the competition which her traders exercise against us for the trade of China. Russia is said to be pushing an overland business in her coarse manufactures, and to be in some instances cutting out English goods. I do not regard this competition as of any moment so long as this trade has to be conducted across the wastes of Siberia, or through the mountain passes and deserts of

since Russia has been doing her best to grasp the complete and exclusive control of Central Asiatic trade, hindered only by the utter poverty of the territory. Had Turkey a government this might still be prevented, and through Koordistan and Persia a considerable English business carried on; but all round the south shore of the Black Sea there is only anarchy and decay, about which English consuls dare not speak out under penalty of removal. But for that anarchy, the Russian business with Persia and its neighbouring communities might have lately been seriously diminished, the Poti-Tiflis Railway notwithstanding. *Vide* Commercial Report from H.M. Consuls, part iv. 1874, p. 1456; as also No. 4, 1873, (Erzeroum), and generally on Russian trade statistics Longenfeldt's volume, or Kolb's *Handbuch der Vergleichenden Statistik*, 1875.

Central Asia. The striking picture which Mr. T. T. Cooper gave in his 'Travels in Pigtail and Petticoats' of the coolie transport of brick tea over some of the passes of Western China should be studied by those disposed to take an alarmist view of Russian aggression in that quarter. But there is another way in which the Russian trader may become much more inimical to us—two ways in fact. In the first place, should the Slav dream of a conquest of China, or, as Tchernayeff put it modestly to a correspondent of the 'Times,' of the northern half of China, be realised, there cannot be a doubt that British manufactures would be entirely shut out of a large and populous region. Or if, on the other hand—and this is the most important point —Russian designs are successful in Europe, and a new Russian Empire or Protectorate should be set up upon the Bosphorus as a result of the anarchy, bloodshed, and iniquity now filling the fairest provinces of the old Eastern Empire, we cannot doubt that a more or less effective maritime competition, aided by the sword, will be set up against us. Portions of Asia hitherto almost entirely supplied with English goods will be snatched away, and especially in China and the far East will an effort be made by sea to wrest from us our trade supremacy. It may almost be taken as an axiom, that where the Russian gets a good foothold the English trader will have to give way sooner or later, and Tory politicians are theoretically right when they say that our true rivalry with Russia can only begin when she gets to the ocean. I am not writing now in an alarmist spirit, however, because I think Russia too feeble to compass her purposes fully, and have no sympathy whatever with the Russophobist cry which certain portions of the English press have set up as counterpoise to the just indignation excited by the horrible revelations of Mussulman anarchy and rapine, to which our present Government has been reluctantly compelled to give heed, so far as to prevent the country from perpetrating one more iniquitous war. If Russia is formidable at all, it is we ourselves who have made her so. Without English money she would still have been feeling, more or less heavily, the consequences of the terrible disaster of the Crimea. Nay, Russia might by now have been dismembered, the Polish insurrection of 1863 might have been successful, and conquests in Asia, long-accomplished facts, might never have been begun, but for our ready help. We gave Russia the means of doing more than half what she has done, and now cry out against a creature of our own making. Yet Russia is not really any better for all that has been done for her; the elements of a conflict within her vast borders are intensified rather than diminished; the Romanoffs, or rather the Holstein-Gottorp representatives of the Romanoffs who occupy her throne, are not stronger now than they were twenty years ago; and I am disposed to believe that the triumph of Russia in Turkey, almost as certainly as her defeat, would lead to the disruption of the empire, by the startling divisions which it would reveal among the Russian people. We, at least, have nothing directly and in a warlike sense to fear in Asia for generations, perhaps, from such a hollow fabric, and need not bemoan ourselves that we have not, in terrified haste to avert our doom, rushed in to support a creed which embodies the negation of all law, order, and justice, when it comes in contact with subject peoples. To side with the Turk in the present struggle would, in my humble view, only have aggravated the mischief, because we could not hold Turkey in Mussulman company, even if the Russians were beaten off, and we should only have been preparing a home for some better power than the North Slavonic Empire, whose competition might prove, indeed, effectual outside its own territory, or be compelled to take on us the burdens of fresh conquests. The only sound argument to be drawn from the commercial view of the Eastern Question is, therefore, that which Lord Derby thought the best a dozen years ago, when he was possessed of that independence of mind which comes of an irresponsible position. Our sympathies ought to be with the races struggling upwards towards daylight out of their centuries-long slavery and degradation; our hand should be held out to help the fragments of old races still lingering in Turkey to renew again the life of their youth, not for selfish reasons to uphold the oppressor. By doing this we should not only keep Russia out of Turkey, but might help to raise in that fair portion of Europe communities which should look to England with an affection greater, almost, than that of our own colonies, and whose trade with us might compensate in after days for the loss of much in other parts of the world. But our ruling statesmen do not see these things, and the nation appears still half disposed to let them lead it into whatever absurd position or political crime they please. Men joke on the miseries of the down-trodden subjects of Turkey, and applaud the vigour of the Turks, as if they were witnessing the mock atrocities of some licentious opera-bouffe. It will be strange, indeed, if the nation fails to suffer for this blindness. Come what may out of the present death-grapple of races, we shall have lost not a little merely as traders by giving our sympathy to the oppressors, to gratify our Russophobia. There are enough enemies of the Russians without us, and we could be best their enemy by being the friend of the down-trodden races of Turkey, also best the guardians of our mere trade interests. I am not writing in an alarmist sense, therefore, but merely pointing out the strongest illustrations that I can find as to the trade policy of the Russian Empire, as well as the best means of baulking it where inimical to ourselves, when I say that the true course for us to have pursued in order to avert the dreaded competition and hostility of a new Russian Empire on the Bosphorus would have been to protect the populations of Turkey, as our Crimean blunder gave us the right to do. We have now probably barred the way to trade extension in European Turkey, however the struggle may end, and we have certainly done nothing by our petty shilly-shallying to make more sure our road to that East which may yet prove our ruin. The terror which has influenced the English people against Russia all through this weary conflict is a striking sign alike of our ignorance and our impotence. A bankrupt semi-barbaric State will bar the road to India, forsooth, and prevent a few hungry speculators from perpetrating a profitable job in the Euphrates Valley railway, just as useful to us as a railway through the Sahara, and so we must hound it down, curse it for daring to act for itself, and hold the Turk up to the admiration of Europe as a chivalrous if somewhat rough-handed gentleman.

However, any success that Russia may get over Turkey cannot now save the empire from the financial consequences of the heedless career of the past twenty years. The first development of her success may indeed be bankruptcy. But that cannot alter the fact that our half-and-half policy as regards Turkey directly traverses our own interests. It is not the Turk who is our customer, but his oppressed subjects; and be Russia strong or weak in the future, broken or whole, we have successfully alienated the survivors among these, the true inheritors of the Turkish horde. Our trade with Russia must inevitably fall away for years, perhaps for ever, but we might have found compensation in the growing business of Constantinople and the freed European provinces of Turkey, in renewed trade possibly in Asia Minor, and in security for our Eastern Asiatic and Indian trade had we chosen to stand up for the oppressed. Generosity would here have proved the best selfishness; and on mere money-making grounds I cannot but regret that a great opportunity has been lost. Whatever power succeeds the Turk may now prove more or less a danger to us; and if the Russian succeeds ultimately in Europe, as I believe it will, although the empire may be bankrupt, although it may be dismembered and unable to cope with us on the seas, it will, unless a new spirit overtake its financiers, gradually make the conditions of our Asiatic business harder, as well as deprive us of what good business we have left in South-eastern Europe. But whatever the result to British trade from the aggrandisement of Russia in European Turkey, there can, I think, be no doubt that any conceivable gain to Russia cannot for many a long day make up to her the cost of the present horrible war. Already the strain of it has involved commercial Russia in bankruptcy, already the Government finds the means of the people exhausted and can do nothing to cover an expenditure which may reach 300,000,000*l.*, and which must already have cost fully half that sum, except print inconvertible notes. These notes have depreciated the value of the rouble by 10*d*. already, and with a disorganised mercantile credit, with the weight of a heavy foreign debt and the partial cessation of foreign trade, this generation can hardly see that value half recovered. Russian internal revenue is lowered in value nearly 30 per cent. by this depreciation alone, and new taxes to that amount must be imposed. It is more than probable also that Russian banking institutions may sink under the weight of accumulated financial troubles before this war is over, also because of the enormous inflation of the currency, and the whole artifical fabric of Russian banking is almost certain to go to pieces at its close. The cash and securities held by the banks must have suffered in the general depreciation, and they are cut off in a measure from remunerative operations through the disorganisation of all business. Long before the war began their cash balances were small, and ere the war is ended there will hardly be any cash in the country. What a banking panic or collapse may imply to Russia one can hardly predict, banking being so new there, so mixed up with mortgage business, and so little understood and trusted in by the general community ; but if it mean the loss of some 60,000,000*l*. of deposits, or a part of them, national ruin can hardly fail to follow. I regard this as a moderate estimate ; and their losses from depreciated securities no one can estimate at all. In short, I regard the general situation of Russian finance as at present well nigh desperate, and with it the situation of Russian trade. What Russia may gain in Turkey, therefore, she is more than likely to lose for a time elsewhere. The new markets which can now take her place in supplying other nations with her staples will probably retain a part of her old trade when she is again in a position to compete, for not even her debt held abroad can drive us and other nations back to her in the face of her fiscal policy and internal insolvency.

The position of Russia may therefore, in my opinion, be summed up briefly enough. Had she abstained from going to war, and had this country continued to lend her money, she would have held her head up for yet a few years, but for all that she was going towards ultimate bankruptcy. Once having plunged into a huge war, that bankruptcy is near and certain. No fiscal regulations can prevent it; they only bring out more clearly her incapacity to raise a large revenue. Her trade cannot avert it, for her trade is not large enough to enable her to recover even from her fearful losses at home, and bankruptcy therefore approaches apace. The truth of the matter is, as this brief and imperfect review must have shown, that the Government of Russia was practically bankrupt at home when it began the march of improvement on which it has spent so much. It was unable to make good its promises to pay to its own subjects, and had been so for generations.

Yet on this rickety foundation a huge foreign debt has been raised, a show of solvency maintained, and great public works executed. Russia has borrowed abroad what her own people were utterly incapable of supplying and has called it progress. She has in so doing impoverished still more her already poverty-struck peoples, and in mortgaging their wealth to the foreign creditor so freely that unless they can produce and export enough surplus to enable them gradually to bring this debt home, they have to see a heavy percentage of their annual profits disappear in foreign tribute. A country with a barbaric population very poor and ill-developed had no business whatever to get itself into this position. Borrowing on a mortgage is a luxury that should be practised only by nations that are rich, and it was almost as foolhardy for Russia to get some 250,000,000*l.* in debt to other nations as it would be for a private trader deeply insolvent to attempt to retrieve his position by borrowing at high usury from the Jews.

CHAPTER VI.

TURKEY AND EGYPT.

It is impossible to dismiss the Turkish Empire merely with the observations made in the preceding chapter, for there is more to be considered regarding it than the condition of Bulgaria. While the existence of the Turks as the dominant race among a hundred shreds of old nationalities trembles in the balance, it would be idle to try and forecast dogmatically the future of our trade with their empire as a whole, but we can at least point out the course of that trade in the past, and endeavour to take to heart some of the lessons with which our financial policy towards Turkey and Egypt is overcharged.

The most prominent thing in our connection with Turkey and its overweening vassal has been of course their marvellous borrowing. Future generations will cite the conduct of the English in regard to the Turks' constant demand for money as one of the most original examples of folly and perhaps of crime that the nineteenth century has to offer. The Turkish and Egyptian bonds are, more than any other, striking examples of adroit manipulation of the modern Progress superstition, of desire for the 'development of resources' run mad. They are also, and of course, by far the most remarkable instances of successful financial juggling on record. Year after year the ball was kept rolling, year after year the miseries of the population increased, and the ill-gotten wealth ministered only to the lusts and whims of a besotted Sultan and his court, or of the English, Greek, and Israelite financial operators who traded on the credulity of a silly public. In Turkey especially no public works were executed to speak of, except palaces for the Sultan, and in Egypt what works were executed afforded but additional pretexts for jobbery and extortion. Instead of improving the condition of the populations every fresh loan added to their miseries, until the reports of disinterested observers grew heart-sickening to read; but for all that the borrowing went on bravely, and might have been in full swing now but for the stupidity of the Sultan's advisers. Egypt has resumed payment and manages to struggle on, and doubtless those who rule her hope to have so demonstrated their honesty and solvency by the end of a year's exertions as to be entitled to come to us for a fresh loan in order to pay off those incurred now in keeping up the national credit. There was little reason against Turkey doing the same, and but for that unfortunate decree of repudiation in the latter part of 1875, we might have been lending her money now to enable her to carry on the war against Russia.

From first to last the history of the debts of Turkey and Egypt is full of disgraceful episodes, which it would be entirely foreign to my purpose to recount here; but there are disastrous consequences, commercial and other, flowing from our share in them which ought to get more than a passing notice. First of all, however, it may be well to correct a popular misconception regarding the actual gross amount which has been lost by the British investor in these swindles, especially as the correction affords opportunity for pointing out some of the indirect mischiefs which this kind of loan necessarily engenders. The estimate which follows I drew up as long ago as May 1876, but it will serve to give as fair an idea of the real state of the profit and loss account as any other I could make, and I therefore transcribe it here:—

'A balance-sheet as between Turkey and her creditors is an impossibility, if absolute exactness is sought; but an approximate estimate of what she has received and what has been returned may be obtained, and possesses considerable interest at the present time. Except the 5 per cent. debt, inscribed in the "Great Book" of Turkey's national obligations, and the Treasury Bonds of 1872, we believe all the loans raised have been in the form of terminable annuities sold. Turkey agreed to pay so much a year, for a given number of years, for so much money down. If we treat her debt in this way, and regard the interest and sinking fund as part and parcel of the annuity, that subdivision being made merely to produce a more alluring effect on the investor, we shall find the following as the result of the Turkish Funded Loans.

Date of Issue	Issue Price	Nominal Amount	Net Amount	Amount absorbed in Interest and Sinking Fund Annuity
		£	£	£
Guaranteed 4 p.c.	102⅝	5,000,000	5,121,250	5,000,000
1854, 6 per cent.[2]	80	3,000,000	2,400,000	4,410,000
1858, 6 ,,	85 & 62½	¹5,000,000	3,800,000	5,050,000
1860, 6 ,,	62½	2,000,000	1,250,000	2,000,000
1862, 6 ,,	68	8,000,000	5,440,000	8,800,000
1863, 6 ,,	72	8,000,000	5,760,000	8,320,000
1865, 6 ,,	65½	6,000,000	3,930,000	5,568,780
1869, 6 ,,	60½	22,222,220	14,444,430	10,111,110
1871, 6 ,,[2]	73	5,700,000	4,161,000	1,938,000
1873, 6 ,,	58½	27,777,780	16,269,954	4,861,111
		92,700,000	62,576,634	57,049,001

Here we find that the earlier annuitants have got back a great deal more than the capital they originally subscribed, supposing that they had all bought their bonds at the issue price merely; and in the rough it may be said that Turkey has received 62,600,000*l.* on these loans, and has paid back 57,000,000*l.* In point of fact, the account is more favourable than this to some bondholders, and less so to others; but the individual

---

[1] Of this loan part was issued at 85 and part at 62½, producing about 3,800,000*l.*, as shown in the next column.
[2] Guaranteed on the Egyptian Tribute.

fortunes of investors in these loans cannot possibly be taken into account, nor, indeed, traced. Of course it is to be said that so much of this money represents interest, and only a small part of it capital, but in dealing with the gross results to investors this cannot be dwelt much upon. We have here a bad piece of business to deal with from first to last, and our object is to see what net dead loss has been sustained by investors. If we find that, one way or another, they have got back the bulk of their money, all that can be said is that Turkish Loans have not proved so ruinous as hundreds of joint-stock adventures. Besides the above debt, there is the 5 per cent. debt of over 96,600,000*l.*, according to the computation of the Imperial Ottoman Bank, and the 11,126,000*l.* 9 per cent. Treasury Bonds of 1872, the payments upon both of which it is quite impossible to give any exact account. The 5 per cents., in particular, were issued at any odd times when they could be thrown on the Constantinople market, and were frequently bought up there by speculators at a low price, and brought over here to be disposed of as a matter of mere commercial speculation, and they, therefore, fetched all kinds of prices to the Turkish Government, from 15 per cent. upwards, and cost the investor corresponding amounts. Not a few people in this country hold Turkish 5 per cents., which they probably obtained originally years ago at 25 to 30 per cent. of their nominal value. Such investors cannot fairly be said to have lost anything by this bankrupt State. They have got 15 and 20 per cent. on their money for five, six, seven, or eight years, as the case may be, and might now burn their bonds and be satisfied. Not only have there been irregular issues of these permanent bonds, but 4,000,000*l.* odd of the 9 per cent. Treasury Bonds have been converted into them at the rate of 1,000*l.* worth nominal of 5 per cents. for each 550*l.* of Treasury Bonds, and we cannot, therefore, say what Turkey has refunded in the shape of interest on account of these two items of her debt. Considering the discounts at which much of it was issued, however, we cannot be greatly in error in assuming that about one-half of the sum received from foreigners on the 5 per cents., and one-third on the 9 per cents., have been paid back; and, if we take the average receipts on account of the 5 per cents. at 40 per cent. of their nominal value, which is a high average, and the 9 per cents. at their issue price, we shall have the following as the position of the Turkish Debt account:—

'Nominal amount of debt, exclusive of present floating debt, 200,426,000*l.*; amount received by Turkey at issue price, and by estimate as above, 112,176,000*l.*; amount paid back by Turkey, 80,000,000*l.*

'This would leave about 32,000,000*l.* as the balance to the good which Turkey might be assumed to have received out of all the loans she has raised, and which would represent the net loss of her funded debtholders, looking at their investments as a mere speculation, and, of course, not taking into account the loss of the interest which their capital would have produced if it had been invested in some safer way. We believe, however, this is a too favourable estimate for Turkey, and a too unfavourable one for the bondholders, partly because only the latter portion of the 5 per cent. debt was issued at a high price, and also because the whole of that debt was never held abroad. The Sultan and his Court, as well as the Galata Bourse speculators, retained among them a considerable amount of it. Certainly, Turkey has not netted anything like this amount of money out of these transactions on any view of the case. Let alone the millions which the financiers who raised her successive loans got out of them at the beginning by means of discounts, commissions, and by amounts " taken firm " at prices much below those at which the bonds were sold to the public, the mere yearly " service " of the debt has cost Turkey from first to last probably about a third of this balance. Exact figures cannot be given, of course, but the little that is known of the manner in which such business is managed warrants us in giving this as a far from extravagant estimate. As between Turkey and her creditors, therefore, the account is not so very ill-balanced as people might suppose. Those who invested in the last 5 per cent. issue, or in the more recent 6 and 9 per cent. loans, will have suffered severely; but the holders of the earlier loans have had, on the whole, a by no means small return of their money. Suppose we take all Turkish bonds now at 10 per cent. of their nominal value, which is below the level to which the entire debt has as yet sunk, the account might almost be taken as balanced, only that, if no solution of the Eastern Question comes, the huge mass of paper will not remain at a level even so high as that. The residue of the capital of the Turkish annuities represents as yet, however, the major part of what, on an outside estimate, the creditors of Turkey would have to get in order to have back, not what Turkey contracted to pay, to be sure, but the capital originally invested. In any case, it is therefore impossible to say that this country, as a country, has lost very heavily by the Turkish debt. There has been a great deal of shifting of money from the pockets of the many who are not rich to the few who are, but of absolute loss to the country there is very little. Turkey itself has been the one great loser. Its Government has been deluded by the golden shower into the indulgence of all manner of objectless extravagances; and, as the pressure of these and of the incontinent borrowings became greater, it has striven to shift its troubles on to the shoulders of the population. Taxes and extortion of all kinds have ground the population of Turkey to the dust, and by the misery thus caused have contributed not a little to foment and give pretexts for the rebellions which now threaten the empire with dissolution. It is not a pleasing picture, but this is, after all and in plain terms, the net result of the financing of banks and syndicates in Turkey for the last twenty years.

'As with Turkey, so with Egypt. According to the statement of Mr. Cave's Report, the Khedive has only netted some 45,000,000*l.* on all the existing loans, State and private, which have been floated for him; and out of that he has paid back, including the last April coupon, over 31,000,000*l.* Of the remainder, some 10,000,000*l.* went to defray costs connected with the Suez Canal and the unjust awards of Napoleon III. connected with it; so that but a minute sum remains which the Khedive could by any possibility have spent on improving his country. He can hardly have thus spent even that minute sum, because it would be needed for commissions, discounts, and market operations, and for the "service" of the debt. Therefore, we have the huge floating debt as the sort of lumber-room into which the costs of all his extravagances have been flung. That consideration alone ought to make it doubtful whether its true amount has been yet revealed. Be that as it may, the loss of the investor cannot be measured with any greater approach to accuracy here than is possible in the case of Turkey, for there is reason to believe that a large portion of the last two Egyptian loans never really reached the public; they have been held by cliques and syndicates. Whatever it be, it does not reach so much as 14,000,000*l.* On balance, therefore, and viewing the whole as a somewhat adventurous speculation, the loss cannot have been great, except to individual holders who have recently bought their bonds at high prices. The floating debts cannot reasonably be viewed as an investor's loss at all; and, excluding these as well as part of the Turkish fives, and of later funding loans of both Turkey and Egypt, we believe a sum of 20,000,000*l.* to 25,000,000*l.* may safely be taken as the outside dead loss of the investing public, not more than half of which would fall on this country, supposing the Turkish and Egyptian Governments to fail absolutely. As prices now range, it cannot be said that the loss is anything like even that amount.'

The figures, as regards Egypt, may now be considered an over-estimate of loss, since, through the exertions of Mr. G. J. Goschen, Egypt has temporarily resumed payments; but, accepting them as a *maximum* estimate of loss, the English public have not been so heavily punished in this traffic as might have at first sight appeared. Many shrewd stock speculators have made money. To be sure there are numberless individuals throughout the country who have been ruined, or nearly so, and their ruin has yet perhaps to manifest itself to the full. They have lived extravagantly, it may be, on the preposterous incomes which these loans afforded for a brief period, and in squandering thus both capital and interest have now nothing to fall back upon. But the most of the money has, for all that, come back somehow to the country, and is in some form diffused through it, in the pockets of the speculators perhaps, or in those of manufacturers, engineers, shipbuilders, and others who enjoyed the lucrative patronage of the Porte. We have, therefore, as a nation, suffered less than we deserve from a mere money point of view, though certain of our industries may be seriously affected by these collapses. But what a ruinous process this has been for the taxpayer in the unfortunate borrowing countries! The Khedive, it will be seen, only netted some 45,000,000*l*. by his various loans, and of that sum he had last year paid back some 31,000,000*l*.; yet his debt, as made up by Mr. Goschen, is now little below 80,000,000*l*., and on the various funded loans he owed more than 40,000,000*l*. at the time of his threatened collapse. Granting that his wretched subjects are able to continue the liquidation of this huge burden, composed in part of compound interest at 20 or even 30 per cent. —a possibility I do not believe in—it means keeping them down in the very dregs of poverty for several generations. And the direct effect of the debt of both Turkey and Egypt has been an increase in the poverty of their unfortunate inhabitants, and a consequent falling away in their producing and buying powers. The whole substance of the people has gone to one object, and one only, the aggrandisement of the fortunes of the palace cliques financial and administrative, and the gratification of personal ambition.

No time was allowed for the capital of the loans to do any good in the country, even had it been well laid out. The annuity system on which most of the debt was contracted, involved the repayment of both capital and interest every half year according to a certain ratio, and hence the mischiefs which fell upon the people were intensified manifold. The rulers spent the money on wasteful objects or for military vanities, and the population were called upon to find the means of satisfying the national creditors, without having received one iota of benefit from the loans. The whole good, if it be a good, which now results from them is to be found in the strenuous resistance which the Turk has been able to make against the encroachments of Russia. By the money which we lent Turkey has been able to arm its savage troops with the finest weapons for modern wholesale murder, and as a consequence Europe has been since May last compelled to witness horrors such as it hardly expected to find mankind again capable of committing.

All the money we have lent Turkey and Egypt has, therefore, done but one thing for the peoples of these unhappy countries. It has made them poorer and more oppressed than they were before; it has given a significance to the old proverb, 'The grass never grows in the footsteps of a Turk,' such as, till England played the Shylock, it never had or could have.

No wonder therefore that the export trade of this country with Turkey has been steadily declining for several years past, and that our total trade with Egypt is also sinking fast. The loans were directly an instrument for the extinction of all trade.[1] At the present time the trade of European Turkey is, of course, in a measure destroyed, and it would be unfair to draw too severe an inference from the dulness of the past two years in any part of the empire, but the fact that the

---

[1] The total trade between England and Turkey was about 14,000,000*l*. in 1876, of which 7,144,000*l*. was imports from Turkey, and 6,380,000*l*. exports thereto. The exports have fallen to this figure from upwards of 8,000,000*l*. in 1872, and the total trade of the Turkish Empire with England, in spite of the stimulus given to Turkish imports by the country's bitter necessities, has not permanently increased 2,000,000*l*. per annum within the last fifteen years, although during that period more than 100,000,000*l*. of capital has been found for the Government. Our trade with Egypt is more difficult to determine, owing to its position as a transit country, but our exports thither have, according to our own customs figures, fallen from 7,300,000*l*. in 1872, the highest point reached, to 2,790,000*l*. last year; and deducting from the first-named year and the 3,100,000*l*. said to be goods in transit, this shows a most serious falling off. The import side of the account is not much more flourishing, as it has fallen in the same time from 16,400,000*l*. to 10,900,000*l*. in 1875, and to 11,500,000*l*. in 1876. These figures include, of course, a certain amount of transit business, but in such articles as Egyptian corn and cotton we find no substantial progress made. In spite of all that the Khedive has lavished in improving his property his profits obviously do not increase. The total export trade of his dominions does not hold its own.

trade of Asia Minor remains stationary is, after every allowance has been made, full of significance. The suspension of payment on the debt has brought no relief to the oppressed people, and when this war is over and peace restored, the consequences of the fleecing, induced first by the debt and then by the war, will make the trade of Asia Minor little worth wishing for these many years, whether Russia takes possession of Armenia or not.

It would be unfair in one sense to lay the blame of the stationary character of Turkish trade entirely on its loans, so much being due to the tithe-farming and the fiscal no-system of the Turkish administrators who go to the provinces for purposes of plunder and these only. But then, on the other hand, the evils of this system were all aggravated and brought into full play by the stimulating influence of these loan demands. The Turk is utterly incapable of executing any kind of work or of marching with events. He can only slay and steal, and consequently when the money came to him for purposes of improvement, he wasted it and then stole the goods of his subjects for the purpose of paying his creditors. No real good was done by any money ever sent to Turkey. Roads were here and there built in a slovenly slipshod way, and fell into decay as soon as built. A railway or two slowly came into being, for the most part by means of foreign enterprise independent of the Government loans, and straightway became a new burden on the country. Nothing could exceed the fairness of the Turkish promises of good works except the meagreness of their performance. Hence it is after all just to say, that the debt which the Sultan contracted has been the main cause of the desolation of modern Turkey. In former days the Turks oppressed of course and stole freely, but their wants were not exhaustless as they became under the 'development' fanaticism, with its glorious thirty per cent. to the usurers; and barring occasional massacres and ordinary cruelties, the lot of beings subjected to a horde of brutal and indolent savages, existence was not in many parts of Turkey intolerable. For the last fifteen years at least it has been intolerable, more especially in Asia and the outlying districts, where there were few people to observe and report upon what was going on.

There is no material difference in the case of Egypt unless it be that the oppression of the Turkish charlatans and such speculators who rule there has been more systematic and refined than that of the Sultan. The fellaheen of Egypt have been reduced to the most abject poverty by the schemes of the Khedive, and at the present time gangs of them are working at his sugar factories and on his Soudan railway—under English mastership too—as slaves have seldom been compelled to work. The negro and Circassian slaves in Egypt are probably far better off than the fellaheen, who dare not call a date-tree their own untaxed, who find almost all the produce of their labour swept away by the rapacious tax collectors, and whose lives are usually one long ceaseless round of toil more hopeless than that of the blackest felon who chafes within a prison. All testimony worth citing concurs in this, that the oppression of the lower orders of Egypt is terrible to behold. Yet a man professing to be a Liberal English statesman of philanthropic tendencies and a sound political economist went out last winter and strove deliberately to rivet the chains of bondage on these wretched creatures' necks. Like Shylock, his attitude was firm for the fulfilment of the bond, and we may find as a result of this firmness that tens of thousands of Egyptians will die of starvation before another year is over. Even if there were no failure of food through a low Nile, the margin of existence is so narrow for the mass of the people, that the effort to carry out the Goschen scheme will itself probably be sufficient to cause many to die of starvation. That is a truly horrible thing to contemplate, but a long study of Egyptian affairs has satisfied me that this is only a mild way of stating what we may expect. People in this country have been misled about Turkey and Egypt just as they are about India, and cannot divest themselves of the idea that these lands are full of stores of mysterious wealth. Their minds have besides been diligently prepared to expect much by a succession of fraudulent misstatements of revenue, until many people imagine that if Turkey and Egypt do not pay, it is because they do not choose.

Hence people talk about the riches of the soil in many a fair province, the oil and the wine, the tropical fruits, and the 'attar of roses,' and we hear of Egypt as the 'granary of the Old World,' and so forth. This is all nonsense, so far as the present condition of these countries is concerned. Under better government, and after the rest of half a generation from oppression, Egypt and many parts of Turkey might become wealthy and capable of sparing incalculable amounts of produce, but not as they are now. The exports of Turkey and Egypt fluctuate most seriously with the varying seasons, and there is no margin of wealth amongst the masses of the people, except perhaps in now desolate Bulgaria, to equalise the operations of trade based on this ebb and flow. The imports of the whole empire are hence dwindling and must dwindle because of the poverty into which the people have sunk, and because, in Egypt especially, there is no means left to the people to pay for anything. All the surplus cash goes either to the rapacious, extravagant Court or to the creditors of the State; some of whom actually got a bonus on their debt over the old bondholders. under the Goschen-Joubert scheme, although their situation was nothing more than that of reckless gamblers who deserved no consideration whatever.

Had people known anything of the true resources

of Turkey and Egypt in past years, they would no doubt have hesitated to trust their money to the financial adventurers who worked the loan business as Kurr worked the turf frauds; but they lent under the influence of a skilfully induced mental glamour, and deserved to be deceived alike because of their folly and their greed. Probably the actual revenues of Turkey reaching the Imperial treasury at Constantinople were never more than 20,000,000*l*., likely enough not really so much, but we have no means of knowing.[1] I doubt if the Turkish authorities themselves knew. This was, perhaps, about half the amount collected from

---

[1] The Turkish budgets have repeatedly given higher estimates of revenue than that I have adverted to in the text, but there is no reason in the world for believing them. They put out an estimate of about 22,000,000*l*. Turkish for the year of the default, and subsequent events showed it to be quite delusive. Their last effort at budget-making is not a whit more promising. A revenue of nearly 20,000,000*l*. Turkish is expected, although some of the richest portions of the empire have been deliberately given up to rapine, and although the estimate of revenue put out two years ago was notoriously never realised. The fact probably is that more is squeezed out of some districts by the supreme Government now than before the war; but so little is left anywhere to squeeze, that the improbability of such windfalls making up the general deficiency is very small. Now, however, Turkey can get on very nearly without money for a very long time. The Government pays only for powder and shot, and ignores all other creditors, home and foreign. It does not even feed its army, and hardly clothes it. The troops live on what they can steal, or what the Government has stolen for them, with but small exception, and they get no pay. Allowing for the necessities of the Court, Turkey might fight a long time on this policy with a resource of twelve or fourteen millions a year. That is, I should say, probably a full estimate of the amount which she can raise, and in the meantime the deficiency is eked out by plentiful issues of paper money, and by the sale of everything in the shape of coin which the officials can lay hands on. A large quantity of debased Turkish coins was lately on sale in London as old metal.

the entire empire by the provincial governors and their tax-farmers, the balance being used for local purposes or deliberately stolen. Yet on this slender basis Turkey ventured to raise a debt of over 200,000,000*l.* all told, involving before the default an annual charge of some 15,000,000*l.*, or nearly three-fourths of the net revenue. Could any reasonable being suppose that such a state of things meant solvency, or the possibility of paying any interest at all after borrowings ceased?

The folly or worse of the public in regard to Egypt has been almost equally short-sighted, and in spite of the spurt which has been made in 1877 default and the ruin of many is as certain to ensue there as in Turkey. Egyptian budgets have been equally delusive with the others—that to which Mr. Goschen has so unfortunately pinned his faith not less so than the others. When Egypt was at the height of her prosperity during the American war, her revenue was confessedly not half the amount now claimed; and how is the additional sum to be wrung out of the people when their produce is less profitable, when their misery is greater, and the cost of living more to most of them, while wages have not increased? With imports diminishing and exports stationary or falling away, how is it possible to make Egypt pay a revenue of 10,000,000*l.* when the country was poor with paying one of less than 5,000,000*l.* in 1864? The question does not need asking. Egyptian budget-figures have always proved false hitherto, and they are doing so now. By borrowing, by letting every kind of debt accumulate at home, and in other questionable ways, a struggle is now being made to pay the heavy charges laid on the country under the Goschen-Joubert scheme; but the effort cannot long be kept up. There will come before long a collapse in Egyptian finances such as I should not like to have a hand in bringing about.

At the same time there were certain merits in the efforts which Mr. Goschen made to secure a better administration for Egypt, and had he been rational or fair-dealing in his demands, or had there been any external force to back his elaborate system of control, it might have done good. To have had the taxes levied by Europeans who would not steal as Asiatics do, or to have had all the spending departments regulated on the same honourable basis, would have been an immense gain for Egypt. Unfortunately the plan has already shown the weakness of its origin. Its only real basis was a fraud, the fraud of the Egyptian debt, and the controlling force of this fraud has not proved sufficient to make Ismail Khedive depart from his ancient ways. The wants of the Egyptian treasury are as imperious now as they were before the controllers went out. Bondholders get periodical statements of the accounts handed over to the debt commission, but no account of Egyptian revenue or expenditure; and there is every sign that the state of Egyptian finances under this so-called control will be no better than under the low Arab mushroom Ismail Sadyk, who got sent to his long home probably to keep him from telling tales. The controllers have been appointed as a cloak—nothing more. It was hoped that they would restore confidence and pave the way for either a fresh loan or for the sale of the masses of bonds still in the hands of the Imperialist French speculators to English investors. That was in the Egyptian financier's point of view their sole use. If anything, therefore, the history of the Egyptian debt has been more disgraceful than that of the Turkish.

I must not wander further into this theme, however strong though the temptations to do so may be, strong also as are my convictions. Those who wish further to pursue the subject of the Egyptian debt will find in the Appendix an extract from an article of mine dealing with Mr. Stephen Cave's report, and published in *Fraser* for June 1876 (see Appendix IV.). In the meantime it may be profitable, before leaving the subject of Turkey and Egypt, to say a word as to the possible course of their future, and of our trade with them. The ultimate end of the present struggle in Europe must, I think, be the expulsion of the Turk; and if he is expelled from the Bosphorus he will never hold up his head in Asia Minor as a strong ruler. But his marauding powers may find further scope there, and our already weakened trade in that region may thereby be seriously lessened. It must not be forgotten, however, that we possess in the Greeks allies of some value, and that in their hands the trade of the Levant and of Syria and the Euphrates Valley is not unlikely to revive in the event of Asia Minor and Syria becoming free. Provided the peace is kept and no inimical trading power like Russia grasps at the Asiatic empire of Turkey, we ought by-and-by to find there some compensation for the loss of trade in Europe. And I do not think that Russia, at all events, will do much this generation to hinder anybody outside her present borders and Armenia from trading as they please; but it is just possible that her weakness may lead to other complications in that quarter which we do not yet look for. In regard to Egypt especially, the collapse of Turkey, or even the collapse of Egyptian finances, might seriously increase English responsibilities. At one time I leant to the opinion that these responsibilities would be best fulfilled by our taking the government of Egypt upon our own shoulders; but I hold that opinion no longer. Apart from the jealousies which such a step would excite in France, and perhaps in Germany and Italy, it would, in my opinion, be highly injudicious for England to mix herself up in Egyptian affairs more than she can help. There would, for one thing, be a constant clamour by interested parties and financial *chevaliers d'industrie* that we should assume some kind of responsibility for the debt, and if we did so we should be bound to oppress the people or to pay the money out of the English taxpayer's pocket. Not only so, but we should be compelled to take up the government of Central Africa, and to follow out some, at all events, of the Khedive's ambitious projects there. This would be a most dangerous task for the English race to take up while its energies are occupied to the full elsewhere. Our colonising task lies in the south of Africa, not in its centre, and we have already there and in India more subject races under our sway than we can well manage or than is good for us. Not only so, but the seizure of Egypt would in no degree secure our trade route to India in a manner that our fleets cannot now do. If we are not able to keep the Suez Canal neutral by our naval supremacy and our fair-dealing, we cannot do so by making Egypt a military station. A mere garrison at one or two points on the Canal would do little or no good, and we could not keep an army there. Therefore, I think an English absorption of Egypt fraught with more dangers than advantages.

But there might be no harm in a kind of international overlooking of that country and its Turkish rulers, such as the institution of the mixed tribunals for the administration of justice shadows forth. If no effort were made to interfere in internal affairs, and if the limits of the territory held by the representatives of the Maritime Powers were strictly defined, as in China, such a step might perhaps be productive of good. It is a question, however, that cannot be rashly answered, and on the whole the less that any country mixes itself up in Egyptian affairs at present the better. The world is too inflammable to make the occupation of that debatable ground safe for any Power. Least of all is it safe for England. We shall best secure the neutrality of the Canal by repudiating all sinister designs on the country. Let the one folly of the purchase of the Suez Canal shares satisfy us.

As to our trade with Egypt, in any event I believe it must continue for a long time to be very restricted, so far at all events as our exports thither are concerned. And our imports thence will not steadily increase under the present tyrannical *régime*. Not even the opening of the Soudan railway and the subjugation of Central Africa by Colonel Gordon will do much to extend the producing capacity of the Khedive's territory for a considerable time. As the days pass, and if the struggle to maintain the payments on the debt is prolonged, all Egyptian trade may become paralysed. It may seem cruel to say so, but it is strictly within the facts, that the best thing that could happen to Egypt, and the best thing for our future trade with Egypt, would be the cessation of all payment on the debt, and of all responsibility for it. If the Egyptian public understood their rights and would assert them, no doubt that is the course they would pursue. They have no more responsibility for the contraction of that debt than I have, except so far as their passivity has put power in a tyrant's hands.

All the course of our connections with Turkey and Egypt, trade and other, illustrate the difficulty of forecasting anything regarding the course of events there, and hence I had better refrain from further conjectures now. We deal there with civilisations and a barbarism of which nothing can be predicted beyond the fact that the civilisations stagnate where they were many centuries ago, and the barbarism drifts ever nearer absolute ruin. Whether the negative resistance of the old civilisations or the more active barbarism will now gain the day in these countries is more than any man can say, but I fear the barbarism, and should not be surprised to see it break out in active destruction even in Egypt, where we are told to look at it as tamed and 'quite civilised,'—in proof whereof behold the Khedive's receptions à la Louis Napoleon, his dinners, his carriages, his opera with its bevies of brazen-faced beauties, and his æsthetic tastes.

Let us even hope that those who believe in the good that all these things may do may never be deceived. Let us conceive an Egypt and Turkey purified and delivered from their barbarism, it will still be long before they can recover from the stripping to which we Englishmen—priests and people—have so largely contributed. And when they do recover, their trade may not be ours as it once was and might have continued to be. Other nations may have taken our place.

CHAPTER VII.

AUSTRO-HUNGARY AND GERMANY.

THE trade relations between this country and those regions of Central Europe dominated by German rulers are not so decidedly determined by the debt factor as others that we have already passed in review. Directly neither Austria nor Germany can be said as empires to have built up their recent trade and their expansion of civilising agencies through borrowing English money, and Hungary alone stands forth as a rapid borrower here on State credit. We have, therefore, to approach the question of the soundness, present and prospective, of our trade with the German and German-ruled countries from a somewhat new standpoint. The task is not, unfortunately, much simplified because of this alteration. On the contrary, there are few subjects more difficult to determine than the situation, say, of Austria or of Hungary; and even the new German empire is filled with perplexing issues, social, political, and economic, to the solution of which one might not unprofitably devote a volume. Here I propose to crowd the more salient features of the mere trade portion of the subject in all three countries into one short essay, and I can therefore but allude to the general political situation.

Speaking in a general way, the commercial prospects of all these countries are, of course, much affected by this political situation, which is itself most difficult to define. The very newness of the conditions under which all the territories involved in the two empires and the Hungarian kingdom abide makes it hard to say what may be the result of conflicts now raging, or but momentarily at an end, and what the overmastering policy of the rulers may do either to help or to hinder the advancement of their various countries in the arts of peace, on which all true trade progress must rest. Germany, from her newness and on account of the envy, hate, and jealousy that exist in various quarters against her, thinks it necessary to devote a great, if not a preponderating, portion of her national energies to the maintenance of a colossal military organisation, which must directly lessen her power to compete in the struggle for trade with less hampered nations. She is an armed camp, the dread of Europe in some senses, and living to no small degree in dread of her neighbours. No one can tell through what bloody ways Germany may have to travel before her peoples can settle down peacefully to pursue those conquests which advance the material well-being of mankind. Nor is she free from domestic troubles—religious bitterness, and internal political confusion—all hurtful to material prosperity. In the glitter of military success these sources of division almost vanished out of sight; but the very peace which that success has temporarily secured, must lay the foundations of a struggle for freedom among the people who, if they are worthy to be free, will grow more and more restive under the severe discipline of a military *régime*. Peace will also afford sects the opportunity for marshalling their forces against each other, to the imminent danger of social harmony and German unity; and while Germany remains in this condition, we can hardly look to see her directly ousting us from our old trade position. How her internal prosperity may develop, in spite of her dead weight and religious and social troubles, we shall by-and-by examine.

In Austria and Hungary the situation is, in many respects, different, and in not a few aspects much worse. The territories ruled over by the descendants of the Hapsburg Emperors of Germany are as a house divided against itself, and tend more and more to fall asunder. In 1867 Hungary obtained practical autonomy, and at present the separatist principles are being pushed further towards complete independence. Francis-Joseph is King of Hungary by much the same tenure as our first Georges were Kings of Hanover. He has inherited a crown that came into his family originally by marriage, and his Hungarian subjects refuse to permit him to do much more than retain the empty honour. To all intents and purposes, Hungary stands aloof, and she wants to stand alone. True, the military and diplomatic organisations of the Empire are theoretically united, but the race antipathies and divergent aims make the unity of little use to the Emperor-King. The difficulties of Austria over the present Eastern Question singularly illustrate this. Nearly half the entire population of the empire is Slavonic, and the sympathy of the German portion is, probably, to a predominating extent, against Turkey in the dispute. Yet the Emperor dare not throw himself boldly into the scale for the Slavs. He cannot attempt to carve out for himself a new empire eastward, by espousing the cause of liberty and helping to achieve the deliverance of the Christian population of Turkey, because were he to do so the ruling race in Hungary would, most probably, refuse to follow him, and by seceding from his authority, at once cripple his attempts. Not only so, but the different Slav elements to be found in the other parts of the empire—the Czechs of Bohemia and the Poles of Galicia—might each move to throw off allegiance to him, while the nine to ten millions of Germans in Austria Proper might be drawn away towards the progressive and more glorious empire of the North. Checked and tied down at every step, the Emperor of Austria is powerless to battle with his fate, and may live to see his inheritance split in pieces and its fragments divided with little regard to his paramount claims. When a political agitator and pro-Turkish fanatic of the thin maudlin enthusiast type of General Klapka condescends to tell his *claque* that he moderates his tone out of respect for the difficulties of the Imperial Government, the humiliation of poor Franz-Joseph may be considered almost complete. Should he need this moderation for his safety as Hungarian King, and I believe he does, his weakness is as great as his humiliation.

I allude to these elements of trouble on the political side of the subject with a view to make it clear that questions of trade progress in regard to the Austro-Hungarian empire cannot be arbitrarily settled by a mere glance at what has been already accomplished, even although the disturbing element of huge foreign borrowings may not have played so openly prominent a part there as elsewhere. The political impotence of the ruling powers may any day induce troubles which would upset all our calculations. And yet we must not build too much on these either, nor speculate on their occurrence; and in judging of the wealth and producing capacity of Austria and Hungary we must endeavour to confine the attention to points within the range of political economy.

Taking Hungary first because Hungary is weakest, it will be found that her situation ostensibly approximates more nearly to that of the big borrowers we have already dealt with than that of the other half of the empire. No sooner had she attained to political individuality than she set to work to pile up a foreign debt, and by the end of 1874 had succeeded in nominally placing upon the English market bonds to the amount of about 32,000,000*l.* At present, I believe, her debt is, in round figures, about 50,000,000*l.*, all told—tolerably quick work in eight or nine years. Yet this is not a large sum compared to some borrowings; and, were Hungary filled with a homogeneous and prosperous community, it would not be large in her case. But this is just what Hungary is not. To all intents and purposes, her fifteen and a half millions of people are composed of the oppressors and the oppressed, the Turks and their slaves, and only a few of the former are rich. Political power and social status belong to the Magyar or Hun conquerors of the kingdom; and in all that appertains to civilisation the general population is most backward. Benefits have no doubt accrued to a very considerable extent from the expenditure of the money thus borrowed, but the State labours under chronic deficits. Not only are State payments in arrear, but the floating debt is considerably increased by what is owing to the Austrian Government under the treaty of 1867, and there is good ground for believing that the houses which have 'financed' Hungary into her present difficulties are at present pretty heavily committed to advances that the lately issued loan will hardly cover. Herr von Tisza, the Finance Minister, is sanguine that by 1880 he will be able to show a balanced budget; but in the meantime the deficits of the three years, 1875-76-77, alone are likely to aggregate some 5,000,000*l.*, and the projected fresh issues of Rents necessary to cover this and to redeem Treasury bonds falling due in 1878 have not so far been successful. An effort has been made to prepare the market for such issues by well-known Stock Exchange methods, but hitherto the success of this effort has not been encouraging. Hungarian bonds excite considerable distrust, in England at all events, and the wonder is that they do not excite more.

A comparatively small portion of the population of Hungary is engaged in manufactures and mining operations, and the principal staples of her exportable wealth are agricultural products. A bad harvest has, therefore, a most serious influence on the tax-paying power of the people, who have comparatively little realised wealth. Her gold and silver mines yield a small amount annually, say, about 250,000*l.*; she is tolerably rich in other minerals, such as copper, coal, iron; and, if kept in internal peace, the country might struggle on and gradually emerge into a position whence she could command foreign markets with some effect. But at present it is decidedly otherwise. Hungary has mortgaged her buying capacity to a heavy extent, and has thereby crippled her selling power as well; so that, unless we can see our way to lend her further large sums of money, we can hardly expect to do any appreciable trade with her, as sellers, for years. Default on her debt is by no means an improbable event whether she keeps the peace or not. She may tide over a few more years if the financial houses implicated in her debt choose to risk their own ruin in maintaining her; but she can hardly do more unless by a radical change in her financial administration. The stoppage of the Danube trade will this winter have a most ruinous effect on her commerce.

The position of the Austrian half of the empire is different to some extent. In respect of its being an older and, in some ways, more civilised State, Austria has made much more progress in manufacturing industries, and her population is also decidedly, as a whole, more wealthy. Her cloth manufactures alone give employment to 800,000 people, and she possesses cotton spinning mills employing nearly 1,600,000 spindles,[1] besides weaving factories importing considerable quantities of cotton yarn. Her woollen tissues manufacture is also considerable, leading to a fair consumption of foreign-made yarn as well as imports on balance of raw wool. For example, according to a Return furnished to the Foreign Office by Mr. Mounsey, Second Legation Secretary at Vienna,[2] Austria imported in 1875, on balance, 208,000 cwt. of cotton yarn, in addition to

[1] Ellison's *Annual Review of the Cotton Trade*.
[2] *Commercial Reports*, No. 18 (1875).

1,042,000 cwt. of raw cotton, also 60,000 cwt. of raw wool, besides 44,000 cwt. of woollen yarns. And in Mr. Ellison's report, previously cited, it is stated that Austria consumed last year 104,185,000 lbs. of raw cotton. In addition to a considerable weaving industry, Austria has a large sugar-producing organisation, and is also endeavouring to produce and manufacture sufficient iron for her railway and manufacturing necessities, her out-turn of pig-iron in 1874 being 332,157 tons.

In spite of these and other advantages, Austria labours under enormous difficulties, which must make the further growth of her foreign trade slow under the very best conditions. She has for one thing a very heavy debt, which, although not held so largely abroad as to make it a direct mortgage on her purchasing capacity, acts from the form of a part of it as a more severe retardant at home than most other home-held debts do. It amounts in various kinds of interest-bearing securities alone to about 280,000,000*l.*, besides which there is the large paper currency always circulating at a depreciation which is seldom less than 10 per cent. As this paper currency is based on silver, it is easy to see how terrible the pressure of adverse exchanges must have lately been when an Austrian merchant had to find the means of paying in London in gold through an exchange of depreciated paper that itself represented a depreciated metal. The natural consequence of such a heavy tax upon the paying capacity of an Austrian trader ought of course to be a quickening of the export of Austrian produce so as to avoid the necessity of having to pay in coin for what has been bought; and if by any means the trader manages for a time to avoid this natural result we shall find evidence of the danger and folly of his so doing in trade disorganisation and industrial distress. I think Austria does give us abundant evidence that this mistake has been made, that the export trade has, save in one or two special articles, such as sugar, been ill-developed; but in order to show this I must abandon considerations relating to the separate portions of the empire, and treat Austria and Hungary as commercially one country. These observations have so far indeed been made chiefly with a view to show that the two halves of the empire have different internal capacities and difficulties, but their general trade positions are essentially similar.

Viewed as one, then, the broad features of Austro-Hungarian trade are these. For many generations the country was almost self-contained. Up to 1865 it may be said that the commercial intercourse between England and Austria was quite inappreciable. Her tariff, though modified ten years before, was still nearly prohibitory, and her internal condition so far behindhand that there was literally no room for trade. In 1866, however, a new trade treaty came into operation between this country and Austria, in virtue of which very considerable reductions were made in the tariff, and by which it was provided that from the 1st January, 1870, to the 31st December, 1876, English goods should in no case be charged duty exceeding 20 per cent. of their value at the place of production. Quite recently it has been decided to continue this tariff to the end of 1877, although there is a strong party clamouring for the imposition of higher duties upon English goods. From 1866, therefore, we find a decided increase in the volume of business passing between this country and Austria. At the best the business is still small—indeed insignificant—but it is greater than it was ten years ago, and probably greater also than the official figures make it appear, because no inconsiderable portion of the Austrian trade passes through Germany and some of it even through Italy, and comes to be included in the totals set against these countries. Looking at the figures from the point of view of Austria, we find that her total imports have increased from 21,000,000*l.* in 1866 to 59,000,000*l.* in 1872. Since then the amount of the imports has fallen off till they were only some 56,000,000*l.* in 1873, the year of the crisis, and they have continued to fall off ever since. Our share at the best of times was but small, and of late it has dwindled considerably. This diminution is significant, and leads us to consider the causes which brought about the commercial crisis of 1873 from the effects of which the

Austrian Empire is still suffering, and is likely for some time to suffer.

In the early part of the period beginning with 1865 the exports largely exceeded the imports, and there was therefore always an important margin of indebtedness in favour of Austria in the general trade account. In 1870, however, this state of things became completely reversed—not, as Austrian protectionists sometimes maintain, because the customs tariff had been reduced generally as regards all 'most favoured' countries, and specially as regards England, but because the people of Austria as well as the State itself had then launched upon a career of speculation which led to all sorts of commitments beyond their means. The disorganisation of Germany and France through the war may have had something to do with this, but I am disposed to look upon it rather as part of a general wave of commercial excitement which we find affecting nearly all civilised countries. This inflation continued throughout 1871, 1872, and part of 1873, and during that period all manner of financial undertakings were started, heavy amounts of railway obligations floated with or without Government guarantee, and banks and financial houses brought into being—Anglo-Hungarian, Anglo-Austrian, and their French and native imitations. Austria was bent on being developed and rich forthwith, and to outsiders she seemed to be making most successful progress, till in June of 1873 the bubble burst, and the country had to relapse into a long and painful struggle with her natural and accumulated artificial disadvantages. It is surprising that such a crash did not seem inevitable to the calm onlooker long before it came. That a country possessed of no great available store of exchangeable wealth, with nothing except her land to mortgage, one may say, and burdened by a heavily depreciated paper currency, should suddenly be able to stand forth as a leading buyer in the markets of the world, and go on acting this part with impunity, was simply impossible. The private and public loans raised abroad or at home only added to the mischief and the delusion, and when the day came for the solid backing to reveal itself for the support of the numerous credits that had been opened, it was nowhere to be found in sufficient abundance.

Inflation was thus the true cause of the temporary reversal of the trade account of the empire, and not any increased pressure on native industries by a reduced tariff, still less an increase in the buying power of Austrian trade wealth over the markets of other countries. Since 1873, therefore, Austria has been fighting against adverse fortune born of her own folly, and to some extent it is to be regretted that the duality of the empire enabled Hungary to go on with her separate borrowing after the financial collapse had warned her to stop. The trade of the empire has not again adjusted itself to the true level of its capacity and credit, partly because of this borrowing, and of the heavy sums which such corporations as the South Austrian Railway Company—the old Lombardo-Venetian lines—contrived to raise outside the empire, on grounds which events are proving to have been utterly hollow. In a national sense, too, the paper circulation, and the facilities with which temporary debts could be contracted by the State, through the usurers eager to lend, have had a very injurious effect. At present the floating debt of the Austrian half of the empire exceeds 45,000,000*l.*, including the State paper currency. This continual flooding of the country with fresh paper has had a most deleterious effect on commercial stability, an effect heightened by the separate note-issuing power of the National Bank, which, although protected by a bullion reserve of about 48 per cent., is none the less a means of inflating the already overblown fiduciary currency. So great is this inflation that during the worst period of the silver panic in 1876, that metal always commanded a premium. The premium on gold sometimes rises to 25 per cent.[1] This swollen currency had of course the usual influence on the course of business while the period of apparent prosperity lasted. Promises to pay, even if accepted at

[1] The paper circulation of the Austrian State Bank runs from 28,000,000*l.* to 32,000,000*l.* or 33,000,000*l.*, and the reserve of coin and bullion has for some time been about 13,500,000*l.*

some discount, are always easier given than actual cash or its equivalent in real value, and the ease with which Austria could expand its paper circulation of all kinds enabled the country to prolong trading on a mere credit basis, and to expend—at a ruinous loss certainly, but still to expend or mortgage—an unsafe proportion of its wealth in foreign purchases. All internal credit thus becomes based on a fiction or on future chances. The savings of the people are a fluctuating quantity, because represented by an unstable monetary instrument. Trade is uncertain in its result, and subject to recurring fits of depression. In years of great agricultural prosperity the country will seem to flourish, and trade will revive, so that it will look as if so many of the paper mortgages had been overtaken; but let a few bad harvests come, as they have done lately in Hungary, and there is immediate collapse. Revenues fall short, the cost of the debt increases, as well as its amount, and amid deficits, public and private, the nation stumbles on as best it can. This picture is no exaggeration. The Austro-Hungarian empire is thus struggling now, and the crisis of 1873 is not yet at an end; nor is it likely that it can ever come to an end while external and uncontrollable influences press on the resources of the empire to its injury, and while both halves of it contemplate a deeper plunge into debt. Gradually, however, the trade account is getting nearer a safe level. The great drop in the foreign exchange in 1876, owing to the fall in silver, has stimulated the export trade, it being cheaper to sell anything that could be sold at almost any price, than to get only eighteenpence or so for the two shillings, when remitting here, or to Germany and France, to pay debts in gold. An opportune shortening in the beet crop of France, with expected shortness in the West Indian sugar-cane crop, also helped Austria, and her exports of sugar alone materially strengthened the weak side of the trade account for that year. At the same time the imports have diminished several millions sterling in 1877, in part through force of circumstances, so that in some respects the country is not so badly off as it was. There is evidence also that, on the whole, the people in Austria Proper are growing wealthier. The deposits in the Austrian savings banks are now nearly 60,000,000*l*., or about double what they were in 1870. Trade discounts, and, above all, loans on mortgages of all kinds, have, however, shrunk very considerably since the pre-panic period, and continue to be injuriously affected by the chaos of the East.[1] For all that,

---

[1] The exact figures of the growth of Austrian Savings Banks deposits, as given in an official return quoted by the Vienna correspondent of the *Economist*, are these :—In 1860 the deposits were only 106,500,000 gulden, by 1870 they had risen to 258,700,000 gulden, and last year they reached 580,300,000 gulden, showing a very rapid growth since 1870, which must fairly be attributed to the extensive participation that the working classes have in the advantages of the industrial development. The fluctuations of the bank discounts and advances, as given by the same authority, were as follows: In 1871 the discounts were 399,000,000 gulden ; they rose to 481,000,000 gulden in 1873, and from that point shrank gradually to

I fear there is still room for business to shrink before Austria can be said to stand on firm ground.

The prolongation of the present trade tariff with England is, however, from our point of view, a very favourable feature. Had it been rescinded, as was expected, at the beginning of 1877, English goods would have had to bear duties higher by from 12 to 100 per cent., and whether Austria had been hampered by internal and external troubles or not, that would have for a time been enough to shut us out of her markets.

There are two attitudes in which we may look at Austro-Hungary if we limit the view to our own trade interests. We may take the empire either as a customer of England or as a competitor against her. As regards the first position, I should say that the facts I have summarised do not afford much hope of any immediate business expansion. On the contrary, trade may even grow worse and probably will do so. But it is quite possible that, in the east and south of Europe, her immediate neighbourhood, we shall find Austria a stronger rival than formerly, unless her ordinary Continental tariff destroys her force. It does not seem to

444,000,000 last year. The loans on mortgage have fluctuated much more significantly, having fallen from 854,000,000 gulden in 1874 to 238,000,000 in 1875. Previous to 1874 they had advanced for years. These mortgages were of course really, for the most part, pledged or pawned securities of the numerous industrial or credit undertakings started on mere wind, and their sudden shrinkage gives us some measure of the losses which the liquidation of the past three years has compelled banks and finance companies, and through them the incautious public, to accept. The gulden may be taken at 2s., or ten to the pound.

me that Austria can, under any circumstances, and for a long time to come, buy increasing quantities of British produce, because she cannot pay for more. Her paper credits cannot swell indefinitely, nor will they help her much further abroad if they could. Not only on that account is our trade with the empire likely to continue small, but also because the course of events does not lead to the conclusion that we are to be larger buyers of her produce than we have been. There is not much that she can send us except corn, wine, and oil seeds, and the harvests are so fluctuating that other countries are pushing her out of the field for these articles. Our direct imports from Austria are much smaller now than the highest points they touched in 1868 and 1869, remaining on the average of years much what they were in the period between 1861 and 1867. This can hardly be otherwise, when, to take a handy example, we find the oil-seed crop of Hungary fluctuating in the period between 1852 and 1872 in yearly differences between 150,000 pecks and 2,150,000 pecks.[1] So uncertain a yield as this could hardly be other than destructive of a steady business. Hungary Proper is, at the best, placed at a disadvantage in the average yield of the land in corn and seed crops as compared with other countries. Bad tillage has probably much to do with this; but whatever the cause, when the

---

[1] Consul-General Monson's report on the trade and commerce of Hungary for 1872 (*Consular Reports*, No. 4, 1873).

average yield of wheat per acre in Hungary is only from eight to nine bushels, against twenty-eight in Great Britain and over twelve in the United States, it is easy to believe that competition must be difficult, except in the immediate vicinity of the frontiers, where the tillage of neighbours may yield worse results than even that, or where corn is less cultivated. In spite of the increased railway facilities and the endeavours of Hungary to open up an independent trade for herself at the port of Fiume, an endeavour as yet nearly futile for want of a complete railway system, I must therefore doubt whether there is much likelihood of a greatly increased buying or selling between this country and the Austro-Hungarian empire in the near future. At all events it is certain that the value of goods carried in British bottoms entering the port of Trieste is steadily on the decline. In the five years 1871–75 it amounts to a drop of over 2,000,000*l*., or nearly a half. This is to be accounted for partly of course by the decrease in the total value of the imports, and to some extent by the larger number of vessels of other nations (particularly Italian) employed in the carrying trade.[1] A large part of the decrease of the exports of

[1] Report of Acting-Consul Brock on the trade and commerce of Trieste for the year 1875 (*Consular Reports*, Part V., 1876). The *Pesti Naplo*, a leading organ of the Deak party, gives the following gloomy picture of the state of Hungary. I am inclined to think it over-coloured, but it is not without truth:—'We are very poor. The value of the soil decreases; its yield is lessening; our agriculturists are deep in debt; our forests and mines give us no profits; every day merchants and manu-

the United Kingdom to Austria is due to the lesser demand for our iron and machinery, caused by the partial cessation of railway building and other manifestations of the development mania, and by the stoppage of supplies of borrowed capital. Austria is now endeavouring to make all that she requires for herself, and an empty purse here also compels greater thrift at the same time that it drives the nation towards foolish attempts at building an enormous dyke round Austrian industries, to keep them at an artificial level of profit and prosperity. At present, notwithstanding the duties and the advantage which a freight of 20s. a ton on iron shipped from British ports to Trieste gives to Austrian iron-makers, they find it hard enough to hold their own. Or rather, perhaps, it may be said that the severe depression to which they have had to submit has so far told only a little more severely upon them than on the English producer. He certainly has suffered severely, but his plight is not so bad yet as that of the few Austrian iron-makers seems to be, if we may believe their outcry; and if the adverse tariff does harm to English

facturers are declared bankrupt; and daily the want of confidence increases. The taxes on all articles of consumption bring in less, and the rate of interest rises. The taxes increase, and must do so, as the very existence of the State is threatened by its financial difficulties, and there is no resource but in the pockets of the taxpayers. Government, Parliament, and chambers of commerce do nothing and are silent. It seems that the country of autonomy is ripe for Cæsarism. The time may come when posterity will view with pity the efforts of an impotent people, and applaud their neighbours (the German Austrians), who conquered this nation (the Magyars) by work, understanding, morality, and perseverance.'

iron we have at least this consolation that, in the best of times, Austrian imports of English iron were not very heavy. They have fallen off since 1873, such as they were, and the import of all kinds, which was 73,340 tons in 1874, was only 12,173 tons in 1875, as near as can be traced. The Austrian iron industry has suffered in the past from other causes than the credit collapse, too, though these are partially at least removed. I refer to the obtuse trade laws which prevailed till two years ago, and under which it was often difficult to establish a business. These have been modified and repealed, but still contain some regulations of a doubtful kind.[1] Mining is an ancient industry in Austria, but it is rather a crudely organised one,

---

[1] An admirable account of the new trade laws of Austria will be found in the *Legation Reports* for 1875, at page 315 *et seq*. In this Mr. Ffrench gives a *résumé* of the proposed changes introduced by the new trade code, most of which have, I believe, been since adopted by the Reichsrath. This code regulates not labour merely, but such things as mining industries and concessions, copyrights in literature and art, domestic service, professions, banks, insurance, railways, and in fact all departments of human employment and business. Perhaps the most interesting and valuable portion of Mr. Ffrench's essay consists in the details as to the regulations of labour. They are, perhaps, rather too much of a paternal character, but in intention they are enlightened and often admirable. For example, men are allowed to make any contract they please as to the hours of work, and the same will be binding, but children under twelve must not be taken to regular employment, and up to fourteen they can only be employed for six hours a day, and on condition that the employer binds himself to see that the school duties are fulfilled. Up to sixteen the hours of work must not exceed ten per diem, and girls or women must never be allowed to work beyond that time, and so on. The whole essay is worth attention, and most people will re-echo the hope of Mr. Ffrench, so far at least as this section is concerned, that the new law may be more rigorously enforced than the old was.

and ore-smelters are besides hampered by the difficulty of finding coking coal in the vicinity of their ores. Add to these considerations the enormously heavy taxes which all industries lie under, and it is easy to believe that the iron trade of Austria has its hardships. Perhaps the best illustration of its position which I can give is a contract cited by the able and well-informed Vienna correspondent of the *Economist*.[1] He says that the Teplitz Ironworks obtained a contract for rails from the German Anhalt Railway over the heads of all the best German ironworks of Westphalia, the Rhine Provinces, and Silesia. In addition to the price at which they took the contract, this company promised to deliver the rails free at Berlin, and to guarantee them for ten years. It is hardly necessary to explain, after that, that the contract was taken 'to keep skilled hands going,' and not for profit. No wonder, either, that Austrian iron-masters clamour for protection, forgetful of what protection ultimately means.

The cotton and woollen industries of the country are, however, almost equally hampered, and the manufacturers are loudly crying out for more rigorous protection to these also. Should the two parts of the empire ultimately fail to agree over the fiscal questions which are still unsettled, or over the division of burdens, and decide to separate their general customs policy, it

[1] *Economist*, August 12, 1876.

is not improbable that a considerable increase in the Austrian tariff for the protection of all classes of home-made goods may take place in answer to this clamour. The difficulties of making headway against foreign competition are especially on the increase as regards the woollen trade, owing to the decrease in the number of sheep in Hungary through the ravages of disease and the greater attention paid to the cultivation of cereals. All these influences added to the general poverty of speculators and leaders of industrial developments produce a strong current against foreign goods, especially English, and may issue in measures which would effectually prevent a revival of trade with Austria whatever her buying or selling capacity might become. Even left to itself and unhampered, we cannot hope for an appreciable increase in our trade with Austria for some time to come; but with increased tariffs it is sure to decline, and our trade in iron with the empire is probably destined to become for a time almost extinct, if not through the growth of native industry, at all events through the greater effectiveness of German competition.

On the other side of the question—the increase of a certain kind of trade competition on the part of Austria—I think there are fair grounds for estimating that here also we may expect in some quarters to be at a disadvantage. This will be the case, for instance, should the ultimate pacification of the European provinces of Turkey take place largely through Austrian help or concurrence; and indeed, unless the empire quarrel and go to pieces over this and other matters which the German, Magyar, and Slav races look on from different points of view, I think it will be so in any event. Possessed of the magnificent trade highway of the Danube for a considerable portion of its length, Austro-Hungary can command against the world the trade of its banks, and, should it be possible to agree with Russia, the trade beyond its banks into all the ports of the Black Sea. If the Slav element gets the upper hand in the empire, and Francis Joseph goes, as he should go, eastward and southward in his political sympathies and endeavours, we may expect England to be, at least for a time, practically shut out of Central and Eastern Europe, almost as much as if the whole territory fell into the hands of Russia. True, these are 'ifs' which cannot be taken for granted; the world may shape itself altogether differently there, and empires may vanish in anarchy and social revolution; but I cannot well take these contingencies into account in dealing with trade tendencies. What is certain at present is that such trade as the Slav populations surrounding Austria may possess gravitates now to a great extent towards Hungary, and in the natural order of things peace and prosperity must increase that gravitation. Roumania, Bulgaria, Bosnia, and Servia, with adjacent districts, though not nearly all Slav, have all a major part of their outland trade with Austria and Hungary, or more or less in Austrian control, and a glance at the map must convince anyone that they should so have it. Between taxes and freights, growing antipathies, and the overshadowing influence of Austria and Russia, we are handicapped to a very serious extent in the future so far as these regions are concerned, whatever their fate politically may be when the present fiendish war is over.

Elsewhere Austria possibly may not, and if she adopts a retrograde trade policy, certainly cannot interfere with us to a large extent; yet her contiguity to Italy and Greece has not been without effect, and she has contrived to establish a considerable traffic with Egypt. The Austrian Lloyd's mail steamers trading to Bombay and the East have not done anything material to aid home commerce there, and cannot do so under the present conditions and burdens of Austrian industries and productions; but nearer home they are establishing a rivalry which can be felt.[1] These remoter contingencies need not be dwelt upon. All that I can say, in

[1] The shipping returns of the port of Trieste, almost the sole seat of the Austrian export and import trade, appear to indicate that the British shipping entered and cleared increases, but the Italian is increasing faster, and is rapidly coming up to it, while the native Austrian far exceeds either. Moreover, the tonnage gives but a very imperfect index to the real course of the trade, actual imports in British bottoms having, as I have shown above, fallen off very seriously in value during the past four years, while the imports in Austrian and Italian vessels have fully maintained, or rather increased, their value, notwithstanding the dull times. *Vide* Acting-Consul Brock's Report, already cited.

summing up this discussion so far as Austria is concerned, is, that as matters now stand there is a probability of a decrease in the near future in the interchange of products with this country, and of increased competition against us by Austria in regions within her immediate neighbourhood, should the empire-kingdom be able to keep quiet and to husband its scanty resources against the return of peace. She has erred much, and paid heavily for her errors; her financial distresses may grow greater before they are diminished; but for all that, when peace once more comes to Eastern Europe, if Austro-Hungary is in existence and free from war losses and new war burdens, she will reap a more direct advantage from it than we may be speedily able to do. Her own direct trade with us we can afford to lose without much sorrow—it was always insignificant—but it is not without twinges that the other eventuality can be contemplated.

I must now take the reader north-westward, to Berlin and the new German Empire, of which I said at the outset of this chapter so much might be written. But I am not now going to write much. Though the trade of Germany with this country is far more important than that of Austria—though the competition of Germany is a far more vigorous thing, and the questions involved in that competition much more vital, I can only view them at present as they are strictly and closely connected with the position and prospect of German business development.

In the first place, we may as well dismiss altogether the subject of debt in dealing with the economics of Germany. Her individual States have internal debts, but the empire has none to speak of—is indeed too new to have any—and these secondary debts no more affect us than the municipal debts of the United States may do.[1] Again, we may fairly lay aside political and social questions. They are not so all-prominent at this moment as to demand consideration in treating of the trade capacity of Germany, however much they may involve the fate of the empire in the future. Military considerations are not so distinctly out of count, as the pressure of the Prussian system on industry

---

[1] In Kolb's *Handbuch der vergleichenden Statistik*—quite the fullest and most accurate compendium of international finance and statistics which is published—the debts of the various component states of the German Empire are fully set forth. That of Prussia, according to the last edition of this manual, stood at the end of 1872 at about 65,000,000*l.* in interest-bearing securities, besides the floating debt; but a considerable portion of this has since been redeemed by Prussia's share in the French indemnity, and by the end of 1873 the debt total stood at about 52,500,000*l.*, of which 30,000,000*l.* was due to railway obligations. Since then the debt has been increased by a few millions on account of further railway building, but for all that it forms comparatively an insignificant burden. Saxony had a debt of about 17,000,000*l.* after the close of the Austro-Prussian war of 1866; Hamburg a debt of 6,300,000*l.* in 1872; and the other free cities, with their territory, had also small debts. The total debt of Bavaria at the beginning of 1874 was 46,000,000*l.*, 23,500,000*l.* of that being due to railways. The debts of Baden, Würtemberg, and other smaller states are all small, and need not be enumerated. There is also, of course, a certain amount of municipal and provincial debt, but none of that affects materially the question we have to discuss.

must be estimated, but they need not occupy us long. We are, therefore, at once brought down to the matter-of-fact subjects of barter, production, and the general trade prosperity of the empire.

According to our own 'Statistical Abstract,' the reciprocal trade of this country with Germany has been of a uniform, and, on the whole, progressive character for a number of years. Moreover, Germany has always bought more from us than we have bought from her. Between 1871 and 1875 inclusive, the gross balance against Germany in her dealings with England has been about 87,000,000*l*., or an average adverse balance of over 17,000,000*l*. per annum. It was greatest in 1872, and smallest in 1875, so that the figures correspond with the fluctuations in German prosperity pretty closely. And this fairly represents the general course of German trade of late years. Some considerable amount of the business done is no doubt transit business—goods destined for Russia, Austria, or Switzerland—but apart from that, of which we have no accurate account, the course of business indicates on the whole prosperity, and, allowing for inflations now and then, also steady growth in the exporting capacity of the new empire. But a trade in which an adverse balance or margin is left, against which a country has little set off of foreign investments, nothing to barter except credit or cash, is always liable to produce a dangerous periodical or continuous strain, and I think we shall find that the German trade has done so. We may to some extent trace its effects in the inflation which followed the war of 1870–71, with its succeeding panic, and in the depression which, since that burst, has continued till to-day. A great deal of astonishment has been expressed in many quarters that Germany should have apparently to suffer most of the ill consequences of that war in an economic sense, while France got off to all appearance scot free. I shall have something to say about the secrets of French prosperity in another chapter; but in the meantime, as regards Germany, it is not difficult to prove that the whole of the moralisings and puzzlings over this seeming anomaly were to a great extent founded upon an imperfect view of the situation.

First of all, we must remember, in dealing with this matter, that the mass of the German people are, and have for generations been, excessively poor, judged by an English standard. They stagnated in their little kingdoms and principalities, or lived hard lives scattered over dreary territory, and had neither the enterprise nor the outlet for great endeavours. The available wealth of the nation was gathered towards a few cities and ports, and what the people possessed was more the real estate, the flocks and herds of an agricultural population, than any abundance of floating capital. When the nation rushed together with a joy-shout at the time of the Franco German war, this was substantially their condition; and when they came out of that war victorious there is no doubt that they forgot this, and lost their heads in a wild whirligig of speculative dashes at sudden wealth. All at once the trade ambition of Germany expanded with her success, and her people rushed into thousands of industrial endeavours for which they had not sufficient available means, however good these schemes might have been. There could be but one end to this course. Wealth can never be created out of nothing, and no matter how many millions nominal you choose to call a quantity of stock, if there is no available resource from which to fill in its full value, it must presently sink, dragging with it multitudes into ruin, and for a time seemingly paralysing every industry, and leaving the nakedness of the land exposed to public gaze. This was precisely what happened in Germany. The people were going to conquer in trade as they had conquered in war, and woke up one morning to find that they had been fools for their pains.[1] But it by no means

[1] M. Ernest Lavisse, in an article in the *Revue des Deux Mondes* of November 15, 1876, produces some very significant figures regarding the sudden plunge into industrial and financial exploitations taken by the Germans in the effervescence of their victory and unity. At the outbreak of the French war, so little confidence had the Berlin financiers in the result, that Prussian Consols fell from 105 to 80, and the notes of the Prussian State Bank sank to a heavy discount as against silver and gold. All the more inevitable, therefore, was the rebound when an unexpected and far-reaching success crowned the efforts of the German arms. The French money and the German victories turned people's heads, and financial projects of every conceivable kind burst on the sanguine and delighted public. All kinds of schemes found supporters, and shares in

follows that Germany is not now wealthier than she was five years ago, nor is it true to say that the French indemnity has done her more harm than good. The receding wave of prosperity does not sweep everything away with it which has been deposited in its flow. A genuine stimulus has been given to some industries and to the production of wealth which tells when the excitement has gone by, and silently prepares the way for a large harvest of wealth at a future day, where the rush has not been madly self-destructive. And the French indemnity may contribute to this ultimate harvest in a very powerful fashion. Directly, it could not have done so at the time the speculators looked for its help, because very little of it immediately reached the people. Kolb gives, in his 'Handbuch der vergleichenden Statistik,' a very useful summary of the destinations to which this indemnity was apportioned, and from it we learn that out of a net total of about

---

them were carried to extravagant premiums. Stocks now quoted at 10 and 20, or unsaleable at any price, were run up on the Bourses of Frankfort and Berlin to 70 and even 90. Previous to 1870, forty-eight banks existed, some of them new, with an aggregate capital of about 42,000,000*l.*; but during the period 1871 to 1873 no less than ninety-five new banks were started, with a paid-up capital of 7,500,000*l.*, and a note circulation unsecured by metallic reserves attained the figure of 36,500,000*l.* There being no legitimate trade to absorb this new credit, it was at once devoted to the promotion of financial bubbles. From 1790 to 1870 only 300 joint-stock companies had been established in Prussia, but in 1871 and 1872 no less than 780 saw the light, or more than one new company per day. When the crash came the major part of them perished, involving frightful ruin. This is only one example of the speculation fever which overtook the young German Empire; many more will be found in the article cited, which is well worth perusal.

210,000,000*l.* which Germany had over after paying for the Alsace-Lorraine railways, merely a few hundred thousands could strictly be said to go at once into the pockets of the people. The whole of the money was, however, utilised in some form so as to tell after a fashion for their ultimate benefit. Where fortresses had to be built, or railways, it passed into their hands as wages; and where investments were made, as in the case of the Military Invalid Funds, the money was, as it were, lent for industrial uses;[1] but its influence as an augmenting force in the national wealth was at the best indirect and slow. Yet, again and above all, the in-

---

[1] A brief summary of the figures given in Kolb's *Handbuch* may be of interest to the reader. Of the total of 210,000,000*l.* given in the text, and which included the interest charged on deferred payments and the contribution of the city of Paris, 28,000,000*l.* was devoted to the invalid fund, 11,000,000*l.* to the completion of the German fortresses, 6,000,000*l.* to the fortresses of Alsace-Lorraine; to the imperial railways, particularly the strategic Wilhelm-Luxemburg line, 8,000,000*l.*; and to the war treasury 6,000,000*l.* Amongst smaller items, we may note as in some shape a direct contribution to the people, 300,000*l.* as an aid fund to the Germans expelled from France; but contributions to the navy, for the artillery, for rearming the fortresses, for maintaining the Alsace-Lorraine garrisons, &c., swallowed by far the largest figures. The wounded troops got a million and a half up to the end of 1872 as compensation, and about 5,000,000*l.* was devoted to paying compensations for war damages and services rendered. With these trifling exceptions, however, no less than 90,000,000*l.* of the total was swallowed up by the imperial requirements. The remaining 120,000,000*l.* was apportioned to the leading states of the empire, the lion's share, 79,000,000*l.*, going to the North German Bund, or, in other words, to Prussia, by whom it was mostly employed in civil and military objects. Except as the Governments had occasion to invest their funds, therefore, very little of this vast sum came within reach of the public, or helped to maintain credit at its most critical point, and no investments were likely to be made by the State in other than securities of the most approved order.

demnity has acted as a great factor in preventing a large increase of taxation, and thus slowly, no doubt, but also surely, brought great benefits to the people. The recovery of the nation may prove in the long run all the more solid and its prosperity greater that it found itself well armed, well fortified, and thoroughly provided with money—the sinews of war—without having contracted new debt or taken on crushing burdens in the shape of fresh taxes. It is clearly too soon, therefore, to say that Germany has not gained by the money she has got from France, or to suppose that because it did her no visible good in 1872, 1873, and 1874, it cannot do so over a series of future years. Looking at the matter purely in a pounds, shillings, and pence light, I should say that Germany has gained an immense permanent advantage as a producing and trading nation over her ancient rival by this transfer of capital, and that this will become obvious enough when the present depression has passed away.

Nevertheless, it seems to me that this money has strongly conduced to making the Imperial Government too independent and powerful, as against the nation, and has helped to enable it to impose its autocratic military system on the accretions to Prussia, which the new States incorporated in the empire virtually are. The money taxes have been kept lower, but the blood tax and the regulation of life by the laws of the barrack yard press upon the people with a weight which hardly any description could enable Englishmen to realise. Where every male without distinction is bound to serve seven years in the regular army, three of them at the depôts, and is after that liable on the outbreak of war to serve in either Landwehr or Landsturm, and where in time of peace an army of some 450,000 men is kept as it were under arms, it is not difficult to see that the blood tax must indeed be heavy. The total population of Germany is some 42,000,000, of which we may estimate 8,000,000 or 9,000,000 to be ablebodied men capable of bearing arms; and under the new military system of the empire 1,400,000 of these can be summoned for service, while all are liable to pass some portion of their lives in barracks. The exhaustion which such a system produces was no doubt one cause of the sudden collapse of Prussian financial and industrial progress after the war, and the drag which in the long run it places on industry is something which we cannot estimate with any accuracy. That the French indemnity has made this system all the more firmly rooted and independent of the public will, there can be no doubt, and the consequences are already very serious for the empire in more ways than one.

Passing from this question to the actual situation of German industries and of our trade with Germany, we shall, I think, find some encouraging features as to the future, though here also all is not unclouded. In fact, at present, nearly all kinds of industry are suffering from stagnation in Germany almost more than here, and none of course more than the iron trade. Since the spring of 1875 the great works of Herr Krupp, says a report on the trade of Germany, quoted by the Consul-General Crowe,[1] have been reduced by 3,000 hands, the number being latterly 9,000 instead of 12,100, and other large works show proportionate diminutions. And no wonder, for the fall in prices has been something that a poor country like Germany never knew the like of. Westphalian pig-iron has fallen nearly 75 per cent. since the beginning of 1873, and steel rails and bar iron more than 65 per cent., and other kinds in like proportion. This is not worse, perhaps, than with us, but we can stand the reduction much better than the Germans, especially as the cost of living has not risen nearly so suddenly or so far with us as in Germany.

The cotton industries are also in anything but a flourishing condition, as we learn from Ellison's report already cited. Germany, it appears, possesses, including Alsace and Lorraine, about 4,600,000 cotton spindles, but the spinners can only turn out coarse yarns, and both in yarns and goods find themselves unable to compete with England. Hence there has been a clamour raised in Germany for the imposition of a graduated scale of duties, so as to give the home manufactures some chance against this competition. This

---

[1] *Consular Reports*, Part V., 1876.

phenomenon is, in short, universal, where business is bad. It is somebody else who is ruining us, not we who have been foolish, and Government ought to help us in stopping that somebody's depredations. At present the Zollverein or Customs Bund of the German Empire levies a uniform duty on all cottons, which of course presses heaviest on the cheap kinds; while the finer sorts, of which English makers have now almost a monopoly of supply, are charged very lightly indeed in proportion to their value. In the report quoted by Consul-General Crowe, the proportion is given as about six per cent. duty on coarse goods, and two and a half to as low as one per cent. on finer qualities. Besides cotton, Germany had a considerable industry in linen, and it has grown somewhat rapidly of late years. There are now 326,000 spindles employed in linen yarn-spinning against 172,000 some eleven years ago, when the duty on imported yarn was reduced from 6s. to 1s. 6d. per cwt. At present, however, this trade is stagnant also, and the home manufacturer finds the production of the higher qualities of linen goods monopolised by England and Belgium. The same may be said of woollen goods. Germany is not able to maintain the command of the home market in any decided way, and only with isolated special articles can be said to command any foreign market. This is the broad, general fact, and it forms a subject of much discussion amongst German manufacturers at the present time, as involving the questions of higher or lower import duties. To an ambitious, pushing nation such as Germany has now become, it is a great aggravation to find itself hindered from making trade conquests abroad; and yet if the duties on imported articles are increased, the more enlightened amongst the people see that the chances of making these conquests must be lessened. On the other hand, if in many most important respects home makers are now unable to produce against foreign, in spite of the import duties, do they not run the danger of getting swamped altogether should these present slender protecting barriers be removed? These are very important questions, not for Germany only, but also for us, for there is no doubt that, as free trade or protection prevails, our commerce with Germany will be expanded or the reverse.

Before deciding from our English point of view which policy ought to prevail, I will lay before the reader a few of the statements made by the Germans themselves on this tariff question, in the report I have already alluded to, in order that we may be, if possible, able to judge the situation fairly, and as they see it. First in importance I would place some facts adduced with regard to the general comparative cost of production as between this country and Germany. As regards iron, for example, the protectionists say that we in England can produce rails 3s. per ton cheaper than the Germans, though not, it is added, of so good quality; but that cheapness wins the day. And as to steel, England is asserted to enjoy, what with shorter land carriage and cheaper sea freightage, an advantage over Germany equivalent to about 28*s*. per ton. Pig-iron must also of course in its degree be affected by the same causes, and as, at the date of the report (July 1876), 70 per cent. of the German smelting furnaces were out of blast, there would seem to be strong *primâ facie* grounds for the belief that the protectionists in this matter are right. There are considerations on the other side, however, to which we shall presently advert. Continuing, meantime, this summary, I find German cotton spinners and manufacturers dwelling on the advantageous position of England in possessing Liverpool—the European port nearest to the American cotton crops; and they contrast their scattered inland situations with the closely packed, highly organised condition of the industries of Lancashire. The German spinners, therefore, say they have, for these and other reasons, no chance of competing at home against England without protection. It also costs them more than it costs us to lay down spindles; they pay a commission of 3 per cent. more on their cotton; freights are against them, and, generally, their situation is a disadvantageous one: therefore they want to be still further clogged by a tax which will take vengeance on England for her provoking supremacy. This, however, is only half the question. It appears certain that the consumption of raw cotton has steadily increased in Germany in spite of the low duties, and some of the disabilities here enumerated are obviously such as enterprising traders could easily get removed. The differences of freight-charge as between Liverpool and Bremen on goods shipped in America should hardly be appreciable, and extra commissions ought to be capable of abolition; just as money might become much cheaper did not the people tend to over-trade and to over-mortgage the future. The most free trading amongst German manufacturers nevertheless advocate some sort of *ad valorem* duties, and complain that home cotton industries are at present at a disadvantage. To a less extent, because the industries involved are less, the same complaints are made regarding most other articles of manufacture except silk; but the only other important trade we need notice is the woollen. The German Handelstag Commission makes many strong statements about the way in which the native woollen manufactures are now hustled out of the market or trod under by those of England. Imports of English woollen fabrics are steadily on the increase; the Berlin manufacturers stating that the value of English cloth imported has risen from 1,000,000*l*. in 1868 to perhaps 8,000,000*l*. in 1875. Germany remains unable to compete with us, because of our facilities for selection of common wools, our cheap capital, and so forth, all of which require to be countervailed by a duty that cannot be under 8 to 10 per cent. *ad valorem*. English fancy goods have beaten all others out of the field, and although the Zollverein duty of 30 marks prevents much import of English broadcloth, Germans are quite unable to export any even to England, where there is no duty levied at all. It does not appear, however, that the strongest clamourers for protection have, as a rule, much hope either of selling to us or of competing against us in our greatest markets with any of what may be called their larger manufactures; but there is a strong demonstration made for what is styled protection at home. 'Keep the foreign goods out, at least,' is the common demand; and there can be no question that, should this demand be acceded to, our German trade must suffer considerably. This is by no means all that the more ambitious Germans aim at, however, nor, under a comparatively liberal trade tariff, is it all that they have attained; and in their efforts at establishing a foreign trade they have met worse obstacles than English cheap goods. They may not hope to beat us abroad; but they do not mean to let other countries shut them out from trying if retaliation will bring them to their senses. Even stronger complaints than those made against us are lodged against France, Belgium, Austria, and Russia, for their heavy and often prohibitory import tariffs; and the demand is not unnaturally made that, when these tariffs interfere with the export of German products, retaliatory duties should be levied on the imported goods of those countries which have the offensive tariff. The German trade policy advocated by many is, therefore, one of two parts—protection and retaliation—and it is not at all improbable that, in the present rather overbearing temper of the new empire, both may be attempted to be put into practice, although for the present, supported in the main as they are by Prince Bismarck, the free-traders have rather the best of it. The latter portion of the policy in any case cannot well be enforced against us, because we have no obstructive duties to be retaliated upon, but we stand in considerable danger of being hit by protective measures, unless German business revives before long.

It is easy to see that at present England controls, if she does not command, the markets of Germany for nearly every kind of spun and woven goods; and I believe that, where the Government does not see its own interests interfered with by the change, it may be quite ready to establish new and differential duties, to accord to German manufacturers and dealers in home produce the protection required. All the statements as to their disadvantages which I have summarised may not be true; but many of them obviously are, and the generally depressed state of business throughout the empire gives a colouring of truth to those that may not be.

In the case of iron, to which I will now again

revert for the sake of the argument it offers, I believe the Government had sufficient reasons of a selfish kind to make it desirous to see all duties abolished, and to these we probably owe it that since January 1, 1877, they have been so, in spite of the most strenuous opposition on the part of German ironmasters. Where other leading English articles are involved it is not improbable that we shall see modifications in the tariff calculated to equalise competing conditions, or, as we should hold, to curtail our market, although it is to be noted that Prince Bismarck rather pooh-poohs any attempt to retaliate on the exclusive policy of Russia. If the Government is right as regards iron it cannot be so when it seeks to raise the tariff to a protective level on other important articles of import; and notwithstanding the outcry in Germany, I believe the Government to be not only right in the iron duties, but that all experience in Germany itself proves them so. I shall point to one or two considerations in support of this statement, and in order to demonstrate that what is good in the one case must be good in all. And, first of all, it must be borne in mind that the iron trade of Germany, like most of its other trades, has been unhealthily stimulated since, I may say, 1868, and that it now suffers from the reaction from the fever. The effects of this reaction ought not, it is obvious, to be confounded with those arising from unrestricted foreign competition. All things in time find their level, and the shrinkage of German iron manufactures is merely an illustration of that trite saying. Further, it is admitted by the Germans themselves that they are now beginning to gain a footing in foreign countries for their iron machinery, and it follows from that fact alone that the true policy to pursue is to increase the effectiveness of that competition by reducing cost of production. At present the complaint is that wages are too high. The inflated rates paid when business was in the full tide of its unbroken credit have not been sufficiently reduced, and, on the other hand, the effective labour is less for the money. We find the same complaints rife at home here, but it would be curious to hear an English iron manufacturer clamouring on that account for the establishment of import duties on foreign pig-iron in order to protect them from the demands of their workmen. Of course it is said that we have no need to do this—we have so many natural advantages in production and manufacture that we can defy any sort of competition. But that is only partly true. We do not defy competition in very many branches of the iron trade, as our Customs statistics prove. Our imports of iron manufactures are steadily increasing in quantity every year, evidently because foreign engineers are more and more able to beat those at home in price or quality. Therefore the true policy of Germany is to secure cheapness of production as far as she can, and the best way to 'countervail' the higher wages paid—if they are higher, which I very much doubt—as against England is to remove all import duties. Nor is this all. In iron, as in other articles of German production or manufacture, successive reductions of the import duty have not only had no injurious effect upon the home industries, but the reverse. I append here a table illustrative of this, taken from the late Mr. David Forbes' 'Report on the Progress of the Iron and Steel Industries in Foreign Countries,' published in the second number for 1875 of the 'Journal of the Iron and Steel Institute.'[1]

From these figures it is at once obvious that low duty does not mean the destruction of native industry, but the reverse. It is the striking off of fetters. The truth of the matter is that the German protectionists have made too much use of causes which are general as if they were special and peculiar to Germany. All kinds of trade have been dull and are dull there, but so are they here also, so are they in the United States, in Austria—almost everywhere except, till within a few

[1] The production here given is that of the iron makers of Silesia only, but what has been good for them cannot have been hurtful for the rest of Germany.

	Pig Iron.		Iron Castings.	
	Duty. Silbergroschen.	Production. German cwts.	Duty. Silbergroschen.	Production. German cwts.
1847	10	1,249,207	45	772,094
1857	10	1,916,678	45	1,011,599
1867	7½	3,687,893	25	2,071,907
1869	5	3,913,783	25	2,686,399
1872	2½	5,829,758	17½	4,083,575
1874	2½	5,424,924	10	4,107,299

months ago, in France. And the iron trade in particular has suffered from two causes of a general kind: there has been much less railway building going on, and there is now a very extensive substitution of steel for iron on those railways already built. As steel lasts much longer in rails than iron, it follows that there is much smaller waste, and therefore that both the initial and the maintenance demands for railway iron have been of late materially less. The iron trade has thus passed not through a crisis merely, but through a revolution which has affected all its departments, and must still affect them. But this is no reason why one nation should need protection against another. Our iron rail makers at Middlesborough have as much need of protection as the Germans if the arguments which are framed on the depression of the trade are good in support of high duties or of any duties at all. The main arguments that apply in justification of the abolition of the German duties on iron and iron manufactures are, however, so general as to be of almost equal force against the imposition of import duties on any large staple in common use for manufacturing purposes.

In some of these also reductions in tariffs have not been followed by internal collapse, but by increased expansion, and what the German manufacturer has now justly to complain of is not the abolition of further import duties, but their maintenance, which injures him almost as much as the continuance of a policy of protection by his neighbours in France, Austria, and Russia. In all cases it may be said safely, moreover, that it is only special classes of goods which tariffs protect, and it is, therefore, only makers of these that can be injured by their removal. There is, therefore, in this view— and it is the right one—no such incentive in the long run to improvement of quality as the removal of so-called protective duties. The tendency when these are removed is for each country to find out what it can make cheapest and best of its kind, and manufactures thus differentiate without either deteriorating or involving permanent suffering to individuals. Competition does not destroy business, but rather increases and classifies it; and this is to some extent what is going on between this country and Germany now in cotton and woollen manufactures. Germany appears to be able to beat our makers both in quality and price in certain coarser sorts of textile fabrics; and our manufacturers might if they chose raise an outcry against the Germans on this very ground. Mill-labour, moreover, is cheaper at present in Germany than here, and not so closely hedged in by legislative restrictions, so that the manufacturers there have probably some advantage over us in that item of cost.

Assuredly then wherever the German Empire maintains or heightens duties upon articles that administer to the creation of wealth—that are staples of industry and not mere food luxuries—she cripples herself and retards the progress at which she aims. The bugbear of foreign competition ought not to blind German statesmen to the one plain irrefragable fact, that the shutting out of foreign goods, as against home, means the gradual closing of foreign markets to Germany, duty or not. All the statistics and facts gathered by the Handelstag Commission, and bearing on this subject, go to show that the comparatively low duties now levied hamper German trade abroad without doing it good at home—that home and foreign trade both grow as these duties recede; and if it be the purpose of Germany to become a great commercial as well as a great military nation, which no doubt it is, the sooner the tariff is stripped of much that it now contains the better for the entire German trade. This is, I may say, disinterested counsel, for although we should no doubt benefit in some sense by the adoption by Germany of free-trade principles, the Germans would gain much more. Their very poverty and frugal business ways would help them in some respects to become successful competitors against us.

No doubt the abolition of customs duties alone cannot make Germany our successful rival in the world's trading, because there are many other factors to be taken account of, which go to mar or make the competing capacity, but certainly the fewer the clogs on labour which taxation imposes, the easier that competition becomes; and the greater the social, military, or physical difficulties and disabilities to be overcome, the more the necessity that artificial hindrances should not be superadded. I regard the abolition of the German iron duties, therefore, as a step forward, and the endeavour to meet the wishes of manufacturers in other branches of German industry by the imposition of fresh taxes, should it be carried through, as a step backward in the progress of the country.

Of the immediate future of the trade between this country and Germany, it is at present very difficult to speak decidedly, on account of the chances of this see-saw policy, and because her crisis is not yet over; but I should imagine that it is a trade which will on the whole tend to enlarge. There are very many things which combine to draw the two nations together, and their very rivalry will probably cause them to do a growing business with each other, so long as they do not take to fighting. Just now, however, Germany is in many ways under transition, and her trade partially destroyed and disorganised by the changes the last four years have seen. It is not yet clear how her new gold currency is destined to operate on her trade and production, nor can we be sure of her continued capacity to stand the heavy blood tax which her military system entails, or of the influence on wages and the general capacity of the nation to sustain large industries which continued or extended emigration may have. But the people are industrious and pushing, they have many natural sources of wealth, and with peace they can hardly fail to make progress. Till they have got over the effects of the wild career of 1871, 1872, and 1873, we may possibly have to submit to a declining demand as at present; but, unless a vexatious tariff is imposed, I do not think the decline likely to be permanent, or that it will go much further. As it is, it affects only particular branches of business, and is not with Germany itself so bad as the trade figures make it appear. The transit trade has partially fallen off rather than our trade with Germany proper.

As to the extent to which Germany may become our competitor for the trade of other countries, little more can be said than the generalities already advanced. With countries contiguous to her we of course are in a measure out of the running, except where we have access to sea-ports, and even then much depends on the nature of the inland communications. As regards distant commerce, so long as we retain the bulk of the carrying trade of the world, the most profitable share of the general business must be ours. The effective competition of Germany for that carrying trade has little chance of becoming formidable unless European revolutions put her in possession of the harbours and colonies of Holland. One fact, however, deserves notice; Germans are now pushing their way into the centres of English business in all parts of the world. German houses swarm in London, and in many ways they are vicariously, as it were, possessing themselves of the advantages previously monopolised by Englishmen. The principal colonial wool brokers here are now, if I mistake not, nearly all Germans, and there can be no doubt that as time goes on these will tend to draw the centre of business towards their own country more than is the case now. The settlement of hundreds of thousands of Germans in the various English colonies must also have a tendency in the same direction. Should the new coinage measure prove a success, as it perhaps may, there will be a decided inducement by-and-by for German houses to draw bills on Berlin, Hamburg, Bremen, or perhaps on Amsterdam, rather than on London; and should anything happen in England to make capital temporarily dearer than in Germany, this patriotic inducement would be much supplemented by self-interest. Of course, as a manufacturing nation, Germany is at present very far behind us, being immeasurably poorer, more heavily burdened in ways that tell on the efficiency of labour, and far from thoroughly organised; but these disadvantages, partially counterbalanced as they are by lower rates of wages and longer hours of labour, will narrow as time goes on, unless the trade legislation of the Empire follows a mistaken course, and, by taking the retaliatory and *quid-pro-quo* line, effectually stops for an indefinite period all progress in this direction.

All that we can say therefore is, that Germany ought to be increasingly our customer in the future, and we increasingly hers ; and also that she may become more and more our trade rival; but that many considerations induce caution in forecasting her career in either direction. In the immediate future I look for a continuation of the dulness of the past four years, with probably an aggravation of it in some directions as regards some branches of business; but on the whole the trade between the two countries is decidedly sound and good, and will most probably continue so unless politics intervene, as indeed they may any day.

CHAPTER VIII.

FRANCE AND BELGIUM.

IF possible, people have been more astonished at the progress of France since 1871 than at the apparent retrogression of Germany. When the enormous fine which the Germans exacted at the close of Napoleon III.'s last mad war was first heard of, nearly everyone in this country cried, 'France cannot possibly find such a sum,' and the cruelty of the conquerors in exacting it was a favourite subject of declamation. It did, indeed, look a most outrageous exaction of blood money when reckoned up in the full view of a France still lying broken, disorganised, and bleeding at the feet of the new power that her own wrong-headed recklessness had helped to call into being. Not only were two of the wealthiest and busiest provinces of France to be torn from her, involving the abstraction from her resources of revenues amounting to more than 1,500,000*l*., and of an industry worth many millions a year to her commerce, as well as some of her steadiest sons and strongest fortresses, but the mutilated empire was to pay in addition sums which, when all added together, amounted to as near as possible 240,000,000*l*., including the local fines and the maintenance of German troops in the northern provinces held in pledge till these money indemnities were paid.¹ Where was a crippled, discredited country to borrow such a sum? The universal feeling seemed to be that it was a task beyond her strength.

When, therefore, France rose at once to the difficulty of her situation, raised the money sooner than had been stipulated, paid it, and got rid of the obnoxious invader; and, above all, when, in spite of an addition of something like 30,000,000*l*. to her budget, she worked herself out of deficits, without any apparent injury to her trade or serious clog on her producing capacity, the amazement and admiration became as great as the previous doubting pity. France was said to be the most marvellous country in the world, so rich, so patient and wise; she had profited by her misfortunes, and had extracted out of them an increased prosperity which was strikingly in contrast with the helpless poverty of her proud neighbour. The Germans, it was said, envied her this industrial triumph, and regretted that they had not exacted a larger sum of money, and in short, the stand-point of onlookers was entirely changed. The thoughtless—who usually speak most— rushed thus to another untenable extreme, and began to believe that France was capable of anything. Her

[1] Lord Lytton's Report on the Financial Situation of France, in *Legation Reports*. Pt. I., 1874.

prosperity, they said, could not suffer by what affected even England, so great was her wealth and thrift.

To my thinking both these extremes are about equally erroneous. I do not believe that France carries her great burden lightly, any more than I can assert that she did not pay her fine with a striking readiness. France no doubt toils on steadily, and does not grow sensibly poorer or weaker, but she is nevertheless loaded very heavily, and I am by no means sure that she can escape yet without something very like a commercial crisis, arising in part out of the troubles and debts of the war. At least, all is not so smooth with her as her admirers would have us believe, and the utmost I can admit is her ability to go on paying her way with a great effort and struggle. I recognise, too, that by-and-by the difficulties which lie across her path may grow less, but at the same time these considerations must not blind us to the facts; and not a few of them give, it seems to me, much cause for anxiety. This being so, I think the discussion of a few of the chief factors in her economic situation must possess some value. I do not desire to carry the reader through all the labyrinth of French finance, but it is impossible to be able to tell what her trade prospects are without first having a clear idea of what the last six years have done in the way of adding to the national burdens, as well as of the manner in which these burdens are adjusted to the shoulders of the people. Is the present taxation of France more than she can safely pay as a competing manufacturer and trader, or is the incidence of the taxation so distributed as to put nowhere a crushing weight on any particular class or industry? These questions are all-important in any attempt made to gauge the position and trading capacity of the country. Until we can give them an intelligible answer it is of no use to talk about imports and exports, and the marvellous fertility of French soil, or the equally marvellous industry of French workmen. I fear I must again inflict a few figures on the reader before I can clear the way towards an understanding of these questions, but I will be as sparing of them as possible.

First of all, we must get a conception of the debt, interest, and other national outlay of the country now as compared with a time not many years distant. The growth of the debt will be best shown by a short table; and as the previous growth of this debt, as well as the late war losses, may be fairly put down for the most part to the recklessness of the Emperor's administration, it will be best to begin the summary at the beginning of his reign. We shall thus see in a rough way what a charlatan Imperialism has cost France. I take the figures chiefly from Kolb's *Handbuch der vergleichenden Statistik*, and otherwise from official publications, French and English, such as Lord Lytton's report, already cited, and the French official *Gazette*:

THE DEBT OF FRANCE.

Date	Capital	Interest and Amortisation
1851	214,000,000*l.*	(about) 8,500,000*l.*
1861	389,000,000*l.*	14,000,000*l.*
1869	447,000,000*l.*	(say) 15,000,000*l.*
1874	906,000,000*l.*	48,000,000*l.*

From first to last the Second Empire has added nearly 700,000,000*l.* to the debt of France. Nor is this large addition by any means all that France has paid for the blessing of being presided over by a worn-out scapegrace of the house of Buonaparte. The city of Paris alone has now a debt of about 80,000,000*l.*, involving an annual charge of nearly 3,800,000*l.* The debt of London, taking the Metropolitan Board of Works stock and the City debt together, is less than 15,000,000*l.*; and as the population of Paris is considerably less than half that of London, we can easily form some estimate of what a crushing burden it is which the former has to carry, even after allowing for the fact that the corporation of Paris owns much more of the city property than the corporation or Metropolitan Board of London. Most of this dead weight also is due to the policy of the late Emperor, his half-strategic, half-stockjobbing transformation of Paris. No wonder that frauds are attempted on the *octroi* duties, that wine is adulterated, or that its consumption is growing gradually smaller.[1] And we do not sum up

---

[1] The wine consumption of Paris is about 180 litres per inhabitant; a larger average than that of any town in France, or that of provincial France generally, but it is an average which tends to decrease.

the local indebtedness of France in naming that of Paris. All over France communes have got into debt, and of the larger cities each has its permanent burden. By the instrumentality of the Crédit Foncier alone, a privileged lending institution which has lately been very much disgraced by its dealings in Egyptian bonds and Treasury bills, provincial France has got in debt to the extent of 54,000,000*l*. or so, independently of what may be borrowed by towns through other instrumentalities. Altogether the taxation which the French people have to raise every year at present for local and national purposes cannot be much less than 150,000,000*l*., of which the State requires 107,000,000*l*. to 109,000,000*l*., and the city of Paris about 8,500,000*l*.

Some idea of what the local burdens of France are may be formed by the perusal of a few statistics regarding the *octroi* duties of Paris as compared with the rest of the country. For example, we find that the duty paid on wine per head in Paris is about 23 fr. a year, while the average of all the other districts or communes is rather under 3 fr. a year. Altogether the municipal taxation of Paris involves a charge of nearly 47 fr. per inhabitant, of which 27 fr. comes from liquor taxes. For the rest of the country the mean pressure of local taxation is only a little over 13 fr. per head, of which about 5 fr. comes from drink. These figures show that Paris is, compared with the rest of the Republic, enormously burdened, but the comparatively modern *octroi* and other taxation of provincial France is not on that account to be treated as of no moment to the country. Added to the national requirements and the direct taxes, it suffices to make France on the whole the heaviest taxed country—head for head—in the world.

The burdens of France are therefore matter of very serious concern to her; but it would be unwise to jump at once to the conclusion that they are too heavy for the people. There are several mitigating circumstances in the situation which ought to be taken into account before coming to a definite opinion on that point, and we must remember that in any comparison with England the excess of the French population over ours must also be allowed for. France has nearly 4,000,000 more inhabitants than Great Britain, and has therefore by so much a greater tax-paying power. On a comparison of imposts per head, therefore, France has not so much more to carry than England; while, if we go back to the time of the Napoleonic wars, and compare what England had to face in the years 1812 to 1825 with what France has had to do since, we shall find that her task is not nearly so Herculean as that of England then was.

I cannot do better at this point than call the reader's attention to Kolb's excellent comparison of the burdens of France with those of England and Holland (*Handbuch*, p. 351). He shows that at the close of the last campaign against Napoleon I., or rather, in 1817, when the accounts of the war had been, as it were, finally adjusted, England had a debt of about 841,000,000*l.*, which had to be carried by a population of about 20,000,000, including that of Ireland. This gave a capital debt burden of 42*l.*, or 1,050 fr., almost a half more per head than the Imperial debt of France is at present. To be sure, the immediate burden of the English debt was not nearly so heavy as that of France, but this difference may be taken as incidental. By-and-by, when temporary arrangements run out or get abolished, the charges of the French debt will approximate our own very closely. For the most part France has borrowed as cheaply as England, and often, owing to the better financial policy which her ministers follow, more cheaply. An essential difference between the enduring capacity of France and England is, however, to be noticed in their widely different position as to colonial possessions and finances, but on that point I shall dwell further on. It is only a minor consideration, after all.

The growth of the French debt has been unprecedentedly rapid; yet when all is said its normal charge will not, within a few years, much exceed in actual amount that which England had to bear after the French wars at the beginning of the century, when the population was not within 14,000,000 of that which France has now, and when this country was much more exhausted. The interest alone on the present French consolidated debt is under 30,000,000*l.*, and the excessive charge which France has at present to bear is due in part to the exceptional obligations under which she lies for the repayment of a portion of the debt. In its straits the French Government got the Bank of France to advance nearly 60,000,000*l.* to help to pay the war charges; and this money was to bear interest at only 1 per cent. per annum, on condition that 8,000,000*l.* a year of the principal should be paid back till the debt was liquidated. This arrangement was, to some extent, disturbed in 1874 and 1875, but since then surplus receipts have enabled the Government to make up partially the deficiencies which had accumulated, so that we may consider the finances of France relieved of a heavy charge of 8,000,000*l.* per annum by 1880, should nothing untoward occur. The State Budget of France should, then, show an annual expenditure of not much over 100,000,000*l.*, if it be not below that sum.

When all is said these annual charges remain very onerous, however, and it becomes a question of much interest how the country is able to stand them, and what prospect there is that it will continue to do so as manfully as it has done. Before passing on to discuss how this great taxation affects French trade and competing power, it is therefore necessary to make one or two further general observations, so that we may comprehend a little the sources of the nation's strength. And, first of all, as to the manner in which the Rentes, or French debt, is held. There can be no question that this has a most important bearing on the tax-sustaining power of the community. To the Treasury, considered by itself, it may not apparently matter to whom it has to pay the annual interest or other debt charges, but to the people it is all-important whether the money thus paid by the Treasury goes out of the country, or comes back to them. Had the huge debt which England had to bear after her great anti-democratic wars been held mostly abroad, we should to-day have been in a position very different from the one we now hold. But, if we may use the expression, the nation happily owed its debt, for the most part, to itself; and the chief practical effect of this was that certain classes of the people grew rich with greater rapidity than they otherwise might have done, while others grew, perhaps, more hopelessly poorer. Our debt, no doubt, had thus a most substantial and, in many ways, hurtful influence on the social condition of the people, driving the majority who pay taxes, but who have no interest in the 'Funds,' towards poverty, and helping the minority to live in greater luxury, but otherwise it has as yet done no substantial harm. A national debt held at home perhaps impoverishes classes of the people, but it may increase the trading capacity of a country rather than otherwise, by the creation of a good medium of credit. Only in the sense of being an injurious social force, therefore, has our debt been hitherto any drawback upon the national prosperity; and it might be demonstrated that in some ways that prosperity has been materially augmented by the economic forces brought into play by the debt. It has been an enormous help to the capitalist, and has also tended to keep the labouring population on the whole well in hand.

Now, what is true of England is, in some respects, more true of France. The huge taxation rendered necessary by her debt is not even such a burden to the great majority of the people as ours is, still less such as it would be did none of the money paid as interest come back to them. On the contrary, a greater number of the people are interested in Rentes to an extent much beyond the taxes they pay than in any other country in the world, and still more get back as interest some portion of what they pay as taxes. Altogether there are nearly 4,500,000 holders of Rente inscribed in the books of the public debt, and their numbers are constantly increasing; and if we take these as on the whole representatives of families, we are safe in concluding that more than half the entire population derive some income from this source. This is a much greater proportion than in England, where, at the outside, not more than 230,000 people are holders of Consols, representing a fifteenth, or perhaps but a twentieth, part of the population as having an interest of some kind in the income thus obtained. Here, too, it is a declining interest, while in France it is a growing one. Obviously the results in France of this wide distribution on the tax-sustaining power of the community are proportionately greater. The French can thus afford, as a people, to pay higher taxes than probably any other nation in the world, because the taxes flow back to them in such large measure, and over so enormous an area, that it is, for a great number of people, a mere taking of money from one pocket to get it back into the other. This consideration is, therefore, of much value in forming a judgment upon what France may be able to continue to do under her seemingly overwhelming load.

Out of this important consideration there arises another on which too much stress cannot well be laid. That the French people stand in so advantageous a position is due to the social and agrarian changes of the first revolution. It is not necessary to repeat what everybody knows about the peasant proprietors and their hard, scraping parsimony. This class, forming the backbone and strength of the land, are, a great majority of them, holders of Rente, and all are hoarders. Some 52 per cent. of the entire population are, in one capacity or another, engaged in agriculture, including the cultivation of the vine; and there are nearly 4,000,000 occupiers, mostly freeholders, of small farms in the country. It is plain, therefore, that here we have the true source of the great wealth, the marvellous staying power, which France has displayed so conspicuously for the past six years. In England a privileged class of landed proprietors, few in number, and possessed of enormous privileges, intercept a very heavy percentage of the profits obtained from the cultivation of the soil, or levy from our citizens a tax such as would crush even Paris into insolvency. Call it ' rent,' or any name you like, this is the plain fact; and, therefore, by so much the capacity of the mass of the people of England for meeting the demands of the State is reduced. In France it is not so. Except in isolated instances, the State can obtain by taxation much of what goes in England to the owner of land as rent or game. We therefore find that the French agrarian system reacts in two ways to the advantage of the French State; it provides a very wide and strong tax-paying class, and it enables this class to draw back to itself a very perceptible portion of the taxes paid. The contrast between France and England in this respect affords food for much reflection, but I cannot now pursue the subject, nor is public opinion yet ripe for its discussion.

Here, then, we have two very important sources of strength in the economic situation of France, which must not be lost sight of in estimating her capacity to go on doing as she does now. An unprejudiced weighing of their value must lead the most despondent and doubting to be at least slow in concluding that France is overloaded, whatever temporary disturbance or depression of trade may yet arise out of the late sudden augmentation of debt. For my own part, I believe France might be able to bear continuously almost her present taxation, provided it were rightly distributed; and, therefore, if it is now pinching and crippling the country to any alarming degree, as I think probable, it must be because the incidence of it is unwisely distributed, or because the country has not at present recovered from the shock of conquest and sudden credit inflation; not because France has not strength to carry the load. The whole taxation of France is as nothing to what the non-improving, arrogant, semi-feudal and game-preserving landlords of England abstract from the urban and rural population here.

This question of incidence, however, bears directly on the subject in hand, to which the preceding remarks form what may appear to some a long-drawn-out introduction, for we in this country know very well that ill-regulated taxation may kill trade in spite of every natural element in its favour. On the question of the position of the trade of England with France, as well as that of France with England, the taxation of France has therefore the most direct bearing possible. Is it crippling, or the reverse? Here the answer seems to me to give very little cause for satisfaction. No two nations are more intimately bound together in trade relations than France and England. Broadly it may be said France supplies us with our luxuries, and we minister to her necessities. The heavy, solid utilities of commerce, the products of our power looms and engine shops, of our mines and smelting furnaces, are furnished by England; and from France we get in return many of our most useful as well as choicest wines, innumerable dainties and delicacies, objects of art, luxury, and most of the conceits of fancy and fashion with which we seek to lighten somewhat the staid surroundings of our practical English life. It would be difficult to conceive a case where the distinctive qualities of two races should better fit them for the freest possible interchange of produce with each other, because in no other instance that could be cited is each so completely supplementary of the other. There is nothing that we can supply better than France which France needs to be jealous of us for supplying, and very few things in the making of which her people excel ours in skill, taste, or natural advantages for which we need care to compete, or could effectively compete with her if we tried. Free trade between the two countries would, therefore, probably at once mean more business for both. There may be, of course, exceptions to this broad statement, as to all such, but taken generally it is true; and all the more is it to be regretted, therefore, if anything intervenes to prevent the full development of the barter trade between the two nations.

A good deal does intervene, unfortunately, and it is by no means certain that the situation in this respect may not grow worse between the two countries before it is mended. The Minister of Finance, M. Léon Say, might perhaps have been trusted, had he been undisturbed, to urge the nation towards free trade. It was his expressed aim to abolish pernicious taxes, to suppress disturbing bounties, and to open up France to the traders of other nations. But even he decidedly refused to entertain the proposals made by M. Gambetta, as chairman of the Budget Committee, which went in a general way towards a relief of the nation from heavy indirect burdens injurious to trade, seeking to substitute in their place, amongst others, a direct income tax. What he may do in the troubled state into which France has been thrown by intriguing clericals and Buonapartist freebooters, now that he has returned to power, we cannot predict. The fact is, French people have been so long habituated to pay most of their taxes indirectly that they will toil along under any weight of *octrois*, taxes on locomotion, monopoly prices, and such like, rather than submit to a heavy income tax, say, or a property tax, or to any far-reaching direct impost, such as a country so constituted should be willing to accept, as on the whole the most equitable and easiest borne load. This reluctance is the more astonishing that France is able to endure a personal tax, and does not even object seriously to pay an impost on windows, the very name of which carries us in England back to the days of the revolutionary wars at the beginning of the century. However explicable, the fact remains that there is great difficulty in abolishing the pernicious thing that exists for the less pernicious or beneficial that might well be substituted. Even the 'bounties,' as they are called, which M. Léon Say professed himself ready to abolish 'if they exist,' apparently cannot, so far as one great monopoly is concerned, be meddled with in any effective fashion. The sugar refiners of Paris seem able to defy the Government, and to continue in the enjoyment of what is practically a bounty of 3s. per cwt. on sugar exported, paid out of the general taxes of the realm. The cost of this single pernicious monopoly to the French people is rapidly approaching 1,000,000*l.* a year, which has to be paid out of the general taxation, and yet nothing is done by the Government to stop the mischief. The fair and true way to end it would be for Government to abolish the sugar duties, out of which the bounty arises; but while a heavy direct tax remains an impossibility they do not seem able to do this, and the next best thing, an adjustment of the scales under which the duty is levied and the drawbacks allowed, seems also beyond the power of the Government.

It is worth while, perhaps, to look into this sugar

question with some closeness, because it affords an admirable example of the quagmires into which some French industries seemingly very prosperous are in danger of falling. In some figures quoted in the autumn of 1876 by the Paris correspondent of the 'Times' it was demonstrated, for example, that the consumption of sugar has been almost stationary in France for many years, while in England it has gone on increasing with great steadiness and rapidity. As the French are unquestionably fond of sugar, there is little doubt that this abstinence is due to the heavy taxation, or rather to the vicious monopoly established under the shelter of the tax, and by means of which a few wealthy sugar manufacturers actually mulct the State now of some 800,000*l.* to 900,000*l.* per annum, in addition to the profits they obtain by selling their sugar for home consumption at a price beyond what the actual incidence of the Government duties would warrant. In all countries where sugar duties have been levied on the graduated scale of saccharine values, the consumer has suffered severely, and fraud in one form or other has tended to become chronic in the trade; but in France the mischief seems to be deeper-rooted than anywhere else. The French sugar duties and their concomitant bounties are indeed a most curious instance of the character of much French taxation, as well as of the difficulties which beset French financial reformers.

Established out of spite against England, to foster a native industry, they have ended by making that industry master of the situation at home to the serious injury of the people. The refiners are too powerful for the Government, else it would never permit so heavy a sum to go annually into their pockets out of the proceeds of the sugar taxes. The manner by which this is done is simple in the extreme. All raw sugars are taxed according to a graduated scale supposed to be in proportion to the amount of saccharine matter they contain, and the refiners merely contrive to have the raw French-grown beet sugar, which is entered in bond for refining, classed lower than its true saccharine value. When this sugar has been refined, 'if any of it is exported the refiners are entitled to get back the duty, and they accordingly demand a drawback equivalent to the full saccharine standard which the refined sugar shows, thus mulcting the State of the difference between the debit and credit. By this means two very divergent objects appear to be accomplished. The refiner, under pretext of the high duties, keeps up the prices of sugar at home and realises large profits. But abroad, by help of the Excise drawback, he appears as a cheap seller, and in point of fact has within the last few years almost driven English sugar refiners out of the market. In short, the higher the duty the bigger, as a rule, his profits both ways; for so long as his sugar is taken into bond by colour rather than by its true saccharine value, he obtains a larger profit on his drawback with every augmentation of duty, and rises into more supreme command of foreign markets at the expense of the tax-paying French public.

This curious monopoly, founded on fraud, has been much protested against in England, and sugar refiners here deprived of their trade have been urging our Government to put on what they call a 'counter-vailing duty,' so as to neutralise the effect of the bounty. This, however, would be a most foolish policy, not only because it might lead France to retaliate in turn with other vexatious duties, but also, even supposing she did not do so, because the quickest way to make France sensible of the mischief this irregular trade is doing her is to let her feel to the fullest extent its effects upon the people and the revenue. When the tax-payers begin to see what this huge sugar export business means, they may agitate for free trade in sugar and many things besides. We should be fools, indeed, to punish ourselves for the folly of others, however much temporary mischief that folly may do to us in isolated instances. A remedy will come, so far as our traders are concerned, presently; but for France it is impossible to say when the matter may be put right, just because the mass of her population is politically so ignorant that designing persons may always work upon it to their own profit. We can only help her, therefore, by steadfast adherence to our free-trade policy.

Obviously, at all events, we have here a large department of French trade placed on a most unstable footing, and should anything occur to sweep it away, or to expose it to fair competition, a considerable number of the French rural population now making a living by growing beet, as well as many hundreds of sugar-makers' workmen, would be seriously, and perhaps permanently, injured. Unless I mistake the signs, something of a crisis is at the present time threatening the French sugar trade. The planting of beet has been diminishing, the 'Economiste Française' tells us, especially in the North of France; and what is grown has for some time been, it appears, steadily diminishing in quality, owing to the manner in which the refiners grind down the prices allowed to the beet cultivators. Although the very limited home consumption may be easily met, and more, from the reduced yield, it will evidently be much more difficult for the refiners to retain their hold on foreign markets, for they will have to do so by the help of foreign raw sugar, the price of which they cannot control. We may, therefore, soon see the effects of this bad system abolished, in spite of the rather better beet-harvest in 1877. Were it not for the blindness of the French people, iniquities of the kind would not last a day.

It would not be fair to take this prominent example of French fiscal administration as an illustration of the generally unjust incidence of French taxation, and yet in their degree all protective duties work harm to the country protected and distort its commerce. They make a few people rich at the expense of the many, more than any form of internal tax can do, and France is no mean sinner in this respect, her Cobden treaty and Louis Napoleon's parade of liberal principles notwithstanding. So severe are the difficulties thus interposed between the traders and their markets for iron and for cotton and wool, that it is, after all, a question whether the agrarian system of France and the marvellous thrift of the people generally will win the battle against so many enemies to progress. Almost equally mistaken in a fiscal point of view, for instance, is the great tobacco monopoly, which produces a gross revenue of more than 9,000,000*l.* per annum, and the working of which is divided amongst sixteen manufactories. Not only is this method of producing revenue totally at variance with a wise commercial policy, but it is most costly to the people, were it for nothing else than the way in which it stifles commercial enterprise and spirit. Were the system of Excise to be introduced, and the growth and manufacture of tobacco liberated, as well as the import of the raw leaf rendered easy on payment of a high duty, it is more than probable that the resulting revenue would be greater, while the people would obtain their tobacco cheaper, and might become able to supply other nations to a much greater extent than now. Under the present *régime* healthy competition in quality and prices has no place, and an indigenous tobacco cultivation is fostered at probably considerable loss to the country, if not of ultimate danger to itself. Instead of cultivation following the natural demand and the capacities of the soil, it is more or less arbitrarily fixed according to the will of the Government, and foreign tobacco is only allowed to be imported at certain assigned depôts.

The treatment of iron is for us a much more vital matter, and it is just as bad. Were the iron duties of France simplified and reduced to, say, the level of Belgium—5d. per 100 kilos. of pig-iron—it is possible that France would do a larger business in the more artistic kinds of iron work than now, and she might even compete with English makers on more solid grounds. But at all events the people would be spared the imposition of a bounty on re-exports of iron from France, and we in England would probably find a better market for both raw iron and machinery. Certain it is that the bounties and the heavy import duties do not now enable French iron industries to bear up against the general depression of trade, and in foreign markets France is hopelessly beaten by Germany and Belgium, let alone England.

Strong as these facts may be, I fear that we must

not look very sanguinely for any immediate substantial advance of France in the path of free trade, and it is just possible that the continuance of a bad system may injure the staying power of the people by crippling the general trade, and so bring a commercial crisis. At present the taxes of France are raised from a great variety of sources, some of which, like the abortive match monopoly, are too insignificant for a great nation to trouble itself about, and many of which are obviously impolitic. We are concerned only with those that affect the course of international business, and when we compare the taxes and tariffs of France with our own, it is easy to see at what a disadvantage she places not us only, but herself. Not content with taxing her imports, France finds it necessary to tax exports and to levy duties on manufacturing industries and on transports—all tending to clog her trade—but the import duties attack us most intimately. The bold expedient tried by the United States of fining the foreigner, as is imagined, to the extent of the State's requirements, would not suffice in France, and cannot now be tried, I hope. Her necessities are so much greater that it would be impossible to overtake them by raised import duties alone. In justice to France, therefore, it must be said that her import tariff is very much lighter than that of the other countries we have yet had under review, except of course India and Germany. Her policy, bounties and monopolies apart, is to levy, comparatively speaking, a little here, there, and everywhere, rather than to extract a huge sum out of two or three preponderating duties. In this, no doubt, there is a certain show of wisdom, inasmuch as the wealth and resultant wants of the people are minutely distributed. But, for all that, in the aggregate the import duties of France are onerous enough, as a glance at the summary I subjoin will prove;[1] and there can be no manner of doubt that

---

[1] If we except the prohibited articles, such as tobacco, raw and manufactured, and matches, the articles on which French Customs laws weigh heaviest are the tissues of cotton, jute, hemp, and wool. All these are subjected to a carefully drawn up scale of duties, which progresses according to fineness. The lowest duty upon cotton is about 20s. per cwt., and the scale advances to upwards of 6l. per cwt., which is the duty on fine cloth containing forty-four threads and upwards to the 5 square millimètres. Sundry unbleached and printed calicoes are charged 15 per cent. *ad valorem*—a high duty—and altogether this tariff must be considered very unfair and unduly heavy. No doubt it owes its existence to the influence of the manufacturers of Alsace, now no longer in French territory. The duties on woollens are not quite so onerous, being for the most part 10 per cent *ad valorem*; but that is still very heavy, and especially when contrasted with the unrestricted freedom of England. Linen, hemp, and jute goods fare rather worse, fine cloths being rated as high as 8l. 3s. per cwt., and only the very coarsest kinds obtaining admission at low duties. Where *ad valorem* duties are charged, the usual rate is 15 per cent. *ad valorem*, and 'drills' pay 16 per cent. Silk escapes very lightly, many manufactures of it being admitted free. The other great staple of English export, iron, does not bear heavy duties, but yet they are more than free traders could be expected to tolerate patiently; and were France well supplied with coal and metal within her own bounds, they might be sufficient to turn the scale quite against us in her market, and to demoralise at the same time the French home trade. Oddly enough, if we except fire-arms, the highest duty is charged on needles; but all sorts of iron, almost without exception, are liable to a Customs duty. Rough cast iron pays only 9¾d. per cwt., but steel, sheet steel, sheet iron, bar iron, and all descriptions on which any labour has been spent, pay duties averaging from 2s. 6d. to 10s. 2d., the average duty for these descriptions being about 5s. Pins, fish-hooks, and pens pay from 20s. 4d. to 40s. 8d.

the very care with which they are spread over a great variety of articles is most injurious both to business and revenue. As contrasted with the English tariff, French customs duties are still either very burdensome, or else vexatious in their minuteness. We allow almost everything that France produces, except wines and spirits, and certain articles of luxury, such as prepared fruits or perfumes with alcohol in them, to enter duty free, but France taxes almost everything that we send her. There is, then, no fair reciprocity between the two countries; and notwithstanding that we are by far the most important customer that France has, her exports hither being twice the value of those to any other country, she has not done as much to unfetter the trade

---

Here again, therefore, the English free trader has much to complain of, inasmuch as the goods which we are best fitted to furnish to France in exchange for her exports to us are all more or less heavily burdened. Other metals suffer in a similar way, the duties on copper manufactures running from 4s. to 12s., but ore copper is admitted free; so is pig lead, pig and bar zinc, and ingots of tin. As compared with Austria, Spain, and Russia, the French tariff for all these articles is favourable, because not designed to be prohibitory; but as compared with Germany, Italy, Belgium and Holland, it is, as a rule, worse; and now that the German duties are reduced still further or abolished, it is time for France to think about revising her tariff. Amongst minor but still not unimportant articles, France charges a considerable duty on caustic soda (23s. 6d.), and levies duties of from 2s. to 3s. on other alkalies. Leather and leather goods are also subject to rather onerous burdens, and only raw hides and parchment are admitted free. Even articles of food do not escape, and besides sugar, already noticed, bacon and hams, cheese, salted butter, salted beef and pork, fish (especially cod fish, which pays 19s. 6d. per cwt.), and confectionery, all pay more or less duty. That on cocoa and chocolate is exceedingly heavy, no less than 40s. 2d. to 49s. 3d. per cwt. Here in England, where the duty on these articles is still retained, it only amounts to 2s. 4d. per cwt. on cocoa, and 18s. 8d. on chocolate.

between the two nations, as a wise selfishness on her part would dictate. As a consequence, we import from France very much more than we export to her. Though both sides of the account steadily increase, the imports do so by much the more rapid strides. For instance, in 1862 the two sides of the account, according to the 'Statistical Abstract,' nearly balanced; but since then the operations of the French tariff have been felt in the restriction of our exports to, and the gradual rise of our imports from, France, till the latter show a preponderance. With the single exception of 1871, when France was too disorganised to send us what we should have bought in ordinary times, and when her own abnormally stimulated necessities compelled her to be a more extensive customer to this country, the balance of trade has always latterly been in favour of France by many millions sterling a year. In 1875, the last year for which we have detailed accounts, the figures were—British imports from France 46,700,000*l.*, exports thereto, 27,300,000*l.*, showing a balance in favour of France of no less than 19,400,000*l.*, including the bullion movements. There is no doubt something of this discrepancy due to the different distribution of wealth in the two countries, but that allowed, it is, on the whole, mostly owing to the tariff; and it should, therefore, be the object of this country to strive for a more free interchange of commodities as a condition favourable to both countries. How important it is to us that France should become a bigger customer of ours in the future is illustrated not only by the present extent of the mutual commerce, but by the rapidity with which it has expanded within the present generation, or little more. In 1829, if we may rely on the very crude statistics then available in either country, we merely sent France a million and a quarter's worth of goods, and in 1854 the total of our exports thither was only just over 3,000,000*l.*, taking British and Irish produce alone, and perhaps about 5,000,000*l.* to 5,500,000*l.*, including all colonial products. By 1860 our total exports to France had risen to double that value, and since 1862 they have never fallen below 20,000,000*l.* There has, therefore, been a remarkable progress in spite of obstacles, and there is nothing which seriously hinders it from becoming greater in the future, save the tariff. The general purchasing power of the French people is likely to increase, whatever temporary financial troubles may overtake the country.

Yet at present there is not much chance, I fear, that the barrier will be perceptibly lowered. As I have already observed, even liberal French ministers of finance are peculiarly hampered by traditions and official habits, and find extreme difficulty in changing the modes of raising the necessary supplies. Recognising, as many of them do, the advantage of free trade almost as much as ourselves, they yet cannot adopt it, for the simple reason that the people, they are told, will not bear a greatly increased direct taxation. M. Gambetta's notions about establishing an income tax have met with no response in the country, and a French finance minister has accordingly to fight, probably against his strongest convictions, for the maintenance of all sorts of hampering, irritating customs, excise, stamp, and *octroi* duties, which the French people will rather suffer under than permit to be superseded by a few direct taxes, and one or two heavy excise or customs duties which would leave the way clear for reducing the tariff in other directions. M. Léon Say fought hard, for example, to retain his extra $2\frac{1}{2}$ centimes on salt, pleading that the budget could not afford to lose them, and although he lost his motion, he was probably, in a sense, right. Wherever there is a chance of obtaining a few hundred thousand pounds, in fact, it is necessary, under the present fiscal system, to try and get it in some indirect way; and the country is so averse to a heavy income or war tax that the finance minister is forced to put burdens on locomotion, for example, such as this country would not endure; to tax matches by making their manufacture a privileged monopoly, or soap and candles, salt and sugar; and, in short, to institute a minute ramification of stamp and other duties which lays hold of nearly every object capable of bearing the imposition of a *sou* or two. In the budget for

1876 the taxes on railway traffic alone were estimated to produce over 3,700,000*l.*, and the gross receipts of all the railways in France for the year 1875 were only 33,600,000*l.* This tax amounts, therefore, to more than 11 per cent. of the gross revenue. English railway shareholders, who have a perpetual interest in their property, while the French only enjoy leases, grumble when the Government tax they pay reaches 1 per cent. of the gross receipts, and cry out about the patent injustice they suffer. They little think what they enjoy. Where would our dividends and low fares with express trains be were the railways burdened here as in France? I do not believe that the French would grumble less than ourselves at taxes like these did they understand the meaning of them. Nay, I doubt whether all this outcry about the reluctance of the French people to bear direct taxes is based on a true statement of their feelings. If they are ignorant of the evil effects of bad taxes, they are equally so of the principles of sound taxation, and it is more than probable that the noise against a sound fiscal system is made by the interested few for their own ends, not by the people. If France had a Government strong enough, therefore, to take these carpers by the beard, and do the best it could for the country without regard to them, I am disposed to think that reform might be less difficult than it seems. Men of the Pouyer-Quertier stamp are found in every country, and do mischief everywhere. A strong Government for France means, however, a strong popular interest in politics, and that is, I fear, not yet to be counted on. In the meantime French commerce is injured by the necessity of raising taxes by and through it, and yet France makes progress, is growing in wealth, and bears her lot with what strikes an onlooker as a quite wonderful strength.

For all this, and the reciprocity argument apart, we cannot contemplate her situation without some misgivings. Very little would temporarily upset the towering fabric of credit on which her mere mercantile prosperity is reared, and it is becoming every year of more importance to the nation that it should enjoy free trade with the outer world. The working classes in towns, and also in some country departments where there is a large non-landholding class of *ouvriers*, are overborne by their many taxes, and the richer people are not bearing the share they should do. Other countries are stealing forward and opposing France in her special industries; our own colonies are seeking vigorously to enter the wine-producing category, and Hungary and Greece, as well as Italy, have made no mean progress in the same way. If France at once hampers her home producers and narrows the area of her foreign trade by the system now pursued, most serious consequences must by-and-by ensue. I am convinced that, comparatively mild though her present fiscal system may be when regarded fragmentarily, it is essentially thus tending to hurt the country's best interests, and that in the long run the people will suffer, however industrious they may be, and however a few may grow rich at their expense. Diffused as wealth is, there are large numbers of the nation who, whatever their thrift, are not able to save enough to make them insured, as it were, against the pressure of the taxgatherer and the changes of trade currents. Even in prosperous times these grow gradually poorer, and when any calamity overtakes the country, such as a bad wheat or grape harvest, or a deficient beet-root crop, or, worst of all, a financial panic and disorganisation, they must feel the dead weight that lies on them with crushing effect. The indirect taxes of a wealthy nation should as much as possible be levied through luxuries on wealth, and in times of financial pressure the State should endeavour to draw its main excess taxation from the richer classes by direct imposts, as not merely the best way to speedily raise the necessary money, but as the soundest course economically for the nation. As far as they dare, French financiers may have striven to do this by indirect taxation, and their operations show a skill and ability much beyond that usually found in England. They levy some 25,000,000*l.* from registrations, succession duties and stamps, and small sums from various direct sources, including a real and personal estate tax yielding about 9,000,000*l.* But a great deal more than a fair proportion of the hundred odd millions required annually presses on the poor, such as the salt tax, already instanced, the tax on slow railway travelling, on many articles of import, particularly cheap clothing fabrics and corn, the taxes on sugar, oils, &c., and even a variety of small taxes obtained from the stamps necessary to make transactions or manufactures legal.[1]

---

[1] The Paris correspondent of the *Times*, in his letter of January 7, 1877, gives the following very useful summary of the Budget of France for the present year, as finally adopted by the Chamber of Deputies:— 'Total revenue expected for 1877, 2,737,003,812 fr.—that is, 109,000,000*l.* sterling. Of this sum is collected from direct taxes, 412,470,600 fr.; from indirect taxes, 2,324,533,212 fr. The direct taxes are distributed as follows: Land Tax, 172,400,000 fr.; Personal Tax, 58,500,000 fr.; doors and windows, 40,761,000 fr.; patents, 155,938,400 fr.; mortmain, 4,975,000 fr.; dues from mines, 3,200,000 fr.; horses and carriages, 9,900,000 fr.; and other trifling items. The revenue raised from the indirect taxes is distributed thus:—Registration and mortgage duties, 466,370,000 fr.; stamps, 154,240,000 fr.; domains, 13,975,000 fr.; forests, 28,548,680 fr.; Customs, 268,445,800 fr., of which 39,200,000 fr. is paid on colonial sugar; 24,800,000 fr. on foreign sugar. The Excise on alcoholic drink amounts to 377,889,000 fr.; on home sugar, 122,842,000 fr. The match monopoly pays 16,000,000 fr.; paper, 12,000,000 fr.; oil, soap, and candles, 17,000,000 fr.; the railway passengers' duty, 75,900,000 fr.; *petite vitesse*, 22,500,000 fr.; tobacco, 312,400,000 fr.; powder, 13,094,000 fr.; and other sources of minor importance. The Post is expected to supply 116,126,000 fr.; the tax on income from personal property, 36,676,000 fr.; Telegraph, 16,600,000 fr.; and the revenue from Algeria, 24,483,400 fr. The expenditure for which this revenue is expected to provide amounts to 2,737,312,194 fr. This sum is distributed as follows: —Public debt and justice, 34,430,740 fr.; public worship, 53,919,745 fr.; foreign affairs, 12,720,500 fr.; interior, 81,569,586 fr.; marine, 186,709,786 fr.; public instruction, 49,211,282 fr.; fine arts, 7,417,480 fr.; agriculture and commerce, 19,762,988 fr.; ordinary public works, 79,234,988 fr.; extraordinary public works, 159,011,552 fr.; the charges of collecting taxes, 252,391,616 fr.; Algeria, 24,587,322 fr.; and reimbursements, 19,557,000 fr. The total of expenditure is 2,737,312,194 fr.; and the revenue 2,737,003,812 fr. The deficit amounts to 308,382 fr. There is also to be taken into account the Budget Rectificatif, comprising more

When added to the local dues of such an over-taxed city as Paris or even to the ordinary communal imposts, these various irritating, draining, and ever present Government requirements exercise a most hurtful influence. The weight of poverty becomes for great masses of the people nearly unbearable. The wealth which the peasant proprietors can produce in time of need should not, in short, blind us to the fact that there are very many poor people in France, huddled in the towns and villages, and that the money earnings of large classes are so small that relief from taxation may one day become for them a necessity of existence. In the country districts labourers are worse paid than in England, and can hardly be otherwise when a parsimonious class of peasant owners think they can spare little or nothing for hired labour. Although wages are higher in towns, as a rule, the increase is largely neutralised by the increased local taxes.[1] We do not in-

than 100,000,000 fr. of Supplementary Estimates voted in 1876, and which necessarily recurs in 1877. Against this is reckoned the addition to the revenue due to the increase of consumption since 1875, the receipts of which year are, according to usage, taken as the estimates for 1877.'

[1] The wages of the working classes in France have risen by large percentages during the Empire, but they are still in many districts very small, and agricultural labourers especially get but little absolutely or relatively. According to the careful official statistics compiled by M. Loua, the wages of workmen who are fed by their employers have risen 46 to 49 per cent. between 1853 and 1871, and the wages of nonnourished workmen 40 to 43 per cent. The maximum wages of the latter class of workmen in the departments exclusive of Paris, was 3·42 fr. in 1872, the latest return I have seen. This is equal to about 2s. 10d., and is much below the average rate of wages in England, although higher of course than the pay of the unskilled agricultural

deed find evidence that the pauper population of Paris has increased to any great extent in late years, but it

labourers in some parts of England still. The average wages of women appear to be from 1s. to 1s. 3d. a day in the provinces. Wages are much higher in Paris, men getting from 3s. 6d. to 4s. 2d. a day, and women from 2s. to about 2s. 6d.; but it must take the greatest possible thrift to make this go far. Of course no absolute comparison could be made with these figures, which are of the most general kind, but they do at least indicate that the money-earning facilities of the lower orders in France are comparatively low. This lowness is used by Mr. Hugh Mason in an able letter published in the *Times* of March 11, 1877, as a proof that with free trade France could beat us in some important departments of manufacture. His statistics are so interesting that I give them here in his own words: 'I need not enter upon any details to prove my statement that the French spinner is at no disadvantage whatever in the cost of building his factory and of fixing such plant as steam engines, boilers, and main gearing. When the factory has been built and fitted up, it must be fitted with machinery, and there is no doubt that French machinery of the present day is in all respects as good and as cheap as the English spinner can buy. Indeed, in a very few important appliances in the carding-room the French have lately taught the English some useful and practical lessons. Up to the point of the factory being ready to card the cotton and to spin the yarn, the French spinner is on a par with his English rival. The next thing to be considered is the wages of the operatives, the production or the turn-out of yarn, the quality of the article, and the cost. On these essential matters I shall deal only with facts. My statements on the English factories can be easily tested, and as regards the French factories I will give statements upon which implicit reliance can be placed. Until now I had no idea that French wages were so very much lower than the English. I will tabulate the list of wages for easy comparison.

Weekly Wages.

	France.	England.
Men in cotton-room	13s. 0d.	24s.
Grinders and strippers	10s. 0d.	24s.
Under carders	24s. 0d.	30s.
Can tenters	11s. 0d.	16s.
Drawing frame tenters	13s. 0d.	16s.
Self-actor minders	23s. 9d.	34s.
Roller coverers	19s. 0d.	30s.

'Let me carry into further detail one extensive department of labour, the minding of the self-actor mule or jenny. In a factory of 50,000 spindles certainly shows no signs of diminishing. I have not the figures of the pauperism of Paris for a date suffi-

thirty minders will be required, giving 1,680 spindles to one minder. There is no difference in the two countries in the number of spindles put under the control of one minder. The French pay their thirty minders in wages the sum of 1,852*l.* a year. The English pay their thirty minders 2,652*l.* a year. Let the same tests be applied to other departments of labour, and the result will show that the French capitalist will make good profits when the English capitalist would be ruined. I have made this comparison (so far very unfortunate to the English spinner) on the basis that the English and French factories are equal in hours of labour. When, however, the actual hours of work are counted, the contrast becomes startling. The English factory works 56 hours a week, or 2,912 hours a year. The French factory works 66 hours a week, or 3,432 hours a year. Here it is that the dead weight of high-priced labour becomes so burdensome to the English spinner. The French pay the thirty minders 1,852*l.* for working 3,432 hours, and the English pay 3,125*l.* for the same number of hours. This is in one department of labour only. The question must now be asked—Do the French get off as much work in the same hours as the English? I emphatically answer—Yes. A well-managed French factory can produce No. 32's yarn, English counts, at less than threepence per pound. The best-managed modern factories in Oldham cannot produce the same counts for less than threepence and one-eighth per pound. In the French calculation of cost every item, without exception, is added, including 5 per cent. interest on capital, and also item, which an English spinner does not reckon in prime cost—namely, a substantial reserve to meet bad debts, break-downs, &c. Coal is an important item of cost, and in its economical consumption the French are in advance of the English. The higher price in France has necessitated the use of the best appliances for the economic raising of steam, while the English are extravagant in the consumption of their low-priced coals. France is now a heavily-taxed country, but is England less heavily taxed for national purposes? What chance have we of supplanting the French spinner in his own country? And yet the French Government not only favours a French spinner by prohibiting our yarns by high protective duties, but he possesses the natural advantages which we cannot rob him of—the cost of transit, which, alone, is equivalent to 15 per cent. MM. Balsan and Duval, in their recent report to the French Government, confessed "that the cost of production is only 3 or 4 per cent. greater in France than in England, and that even that difference is often compensated for by carriage expenses paid for goods sent to compete in the French market." The French spinner, like the ciently recent to enable an exact comparison to be made, but my impression is that the absolutely pauper population of London is not more than one-half that of the sister city, reckoning the numbers per thousand inhabitants.[1]

We must now take leave of this subject, however,

French sugar refiner, is allowed to raise the prices of his special productions for his own private gains, and to the serious loss of the majority of the people of France. Is it not for the English spinner to consider seriously either to take his capital to France, where the reward for the use of it is so much greater, or to bring the French workmen to Lancashire to moderate the excessively high price paid for labour? The English home market is very limited, and the trade depends mainly on foreign demands. An outlet abroad for English yarns must be found, or the cotton industry in Lancashire will seriously suffer. In my comparison of English and French factories I have not taken extreme cases; I have compared a well-managed modern factory in Oldham with a similar factory in a well-known town in France, and my comparison will be found to be a fair one for three-fourths of the entire trade in the two countries.'

I believe there is great truth in these statements, and yet I maintain that with free trade the English spinner would have nothing to fear, were it for no other reason than that it would at once stimulate him to a greater economy and at the same time probably raise the cost of production in France. I doubt, indeed, whether that be so low now as Mr. Mason makes out. Wages are always the bugbear of the English manufacturer—wages and hours of labour; but we have never yet found that he suffered appreciably for the shorter hours of the one or the higher money value of the other. Mr. Mason does not see that the French tariff just stops the competition where it would do most good, viz., in the markets other than French, and therefore that it unduly reduces the money-earning power of the French labourer. His point about the cost of transport has more force, and our English railways will have to become much more liberal in their dealings.

[1] The French have no Poor Law to curse their labouring poor with perfunctory doles such as we disgrace our civilisation by in England, but the corporations and communes all over France distribute considerable amounts yearly in hospital and other assistance. The poor of Paris alone, according to statistics published in the municipal accounts, reached 127,000 in 1875, and the number of those who got out-door relief was 312,544.

and turn to one or two other matters of interest. In reviewing the hindrances and disabilities which the trade of France may be considered subject to, it is necessary to take note of the position of the Bank of France, and the large paper circulation it possesses. Like the United States when overwhelmed with war, France had to resort to large issues of inconvertible paper, and it was only by means of these that the Bank was able to make advances to the Government. The suspension of cash payments thus caused has continued till now, but it cannot be said that French trade has materially suffered in consequence, and in nothing has the skill of French financiers been more conspicuously shown than in the delicacy with which the balance of credit has been adjusted so as to prevent a heavy and disastrous depreciation of the inconvertible paper. Resumption has been kept steadily in view, and every opportunity which the balance of the trading account, or of financial dealings, gave, has been seized to increase the bullion reserve of the Bank. Thus, although the paper created or afloat has reached as high a figure as 108,000,000*l*., the premium on gold has never been appreciable, so far as the smaller commerce of the country was concerned. It has never been, practically, more than one or two francs per thousand, and for a long time past the notes have been at par. This is not astonishing when the Bank lately held bullion to the extent of upwards of 93 per cent. of the total note circulation. The only manner in which France can be said to have suffered by the suspension of specie payments, therefore, has been by its exclusion from the international bill-broking and discount market. The world's bullion dealing and the exchange business founded thereon has all centred in London, no doubt to the serious loss of some French financial houses and banking establishments, a loss which some of them have, however, contrived partially to escape from by opening branches in London, where they engage vigorously in the competition for this kind of business with our own financial houses. What with French houses, represented by French or Polish Jews, and German Jew houses, all fighting for the crumbs which a dull trade and cheap money leaves them, the old-fashioned English broker finds his occupation gone, or hardly worth retaining. How far the shutting off, to which France herself is now financially subject, touches her general commercial interests indirectly, it would be difficult, if not impossible, to say, but I am disposed to think at least as little as the inconvertible paper currency does her bill dealing.

The Bank of France, then, may be considered a thoroughly sound and admirably conducted institution which has done not a little to protect France from the worst evils of a forced paper currency. The same cannot, however, be said of many of the other banks in France, and the situation of some of them is, it appears to me, calculated to excite no little anxiety and alarm, lest the nation should be enveloped before long in a monetary and mercantile crisis which may prove more injurious to her than that of Germany or Austria. The French joint stock banks nearly all do what is called 'finance' business, *i.e.*, they furnish money to float companies, traffic in unplaced railway or foreign State bonds, and generally play the *rôle* undertaken in England by a class of people known by the not very savoury names of 'promoters' and 'loan mongers.' They thus often contrive to get large amounts of money locked up, which under no circumstances could they recover were anything suddenly to cause it to be required. Fenced round by privileges and official support, as some of these credit institutions are, and upheld by a sort of mutual *camaraderie* in the race for inordinate wealth, they, nevertheless, cannot in the long run escape the consequences of transactions of this kind; and at the present time it is a moderate estimate which places the dubious liabilities of a few prominent members of the group at from 40 to 50 millions sterling. Some of these credit institutions are known to be in a very weak condition, and should one go there is likely to be a panic, and a general collapse. This is, to my mind, the most obvious danger to which France is at present subject. The republic has inherited from the empire a crowd of not very reputable 'financiers' who have unquestionably led the French public into a great many ruinous projects, for which, sooner or later, a day of reckoning must come; and when it does come the huge gap which it will reveal is not unlikely to take many a day to fill up. There is more need on this account also that France should do her utmost to unshackle her general trade, on which alone the country can rely in a time of financial depression. Whatever expands that, whatever opens fresh markets for French produce, breaks the monopolies of the few wealthy capitalists, and facilitates the cheap acquisition of what Frenchmen want at home, must most materially assist the nation to tide over its troubles. There is a mass of rottenness in the financial speculations of the country which has got to be cleared away sooner or later, and the country, however sound at the core, must suffer while this is getting done. Her burdens being at the same time just as much as she can well carry in quiet and prosperous days, her future cannot be considered without danger till this cleansing process has been gone through. France will not escape finally from the reactionary wave which has overtaken other nations, however much her industry may give her a recuperative force, and her mercantile laws may seem to enable her to stave off the evil day.

As regards other features of the general foreign trade of France at the present time, there is not much more to be said. It is fairly satisfactory; and her imports especially might seem to prove that the present fiscal system of the country is no great hindrance to her general trade. England last year, however, felt the effect of these more sensibly, perhaps, than ever before; and accordingly we find that many important departments of our exports to France show a diminution. As a general rule it may be said that France is now buying from us less manufactured goods and more materials either crude or half-manufactured, such as wool and woollen yarns, coal, and pig-iron: and this alone proves that the protective system which she at present trades upon is sensibly diverting the trade between England and France from the courses it would naturally pursue. And it needs no demonstration to show that France cannot be the gainer by that diversion; she has to pay for it in dearer materials made at home, and in trades founded on the dangerous basis of duties which prevent her from sharing the foreign business of her neighbours, and which, therefore, keep them in an eminently precarious position. The exports of France, taken generally, show a falling off last year, and the two sides of her trade account are now showing a debit balance against France, instead of as in former years a large balance to her credit. No doubt the dulness of trade in other countries may account for the smaller demand for French productions, and when trade grows more active over the world generally, her business may revive. But the trade policy of France cannot be considered as a help to this revival. The increase which last year's import trade exhibits, is indeed due mostly to higher imports of food and of raw material used in home manufactures, which, although a direct result of the trade tariff, is not a sign of sound progress. It is not sensibly owing to a heightened demand for foreign industrial products such as would come were France growing really richer by her foreign trade, and therefore we cannot be sure that the decline of French exports is not ominous of a coming contraction of her trading power.[1] A continuance of this adverse balance might, indeed, in no long time lead to the diminution of the bullion reserves of the bank and the consequent postponement of a return to specie payments; and should the harvest of 1877 necessitate any large import of corn, as seems not improbable, this bullion efflux may be almost counted upon.

[1] The following telegram, dated Paris, January 16, 1877, gives the official estimate of the French foreign trade for the past year:

According to official returns published to-day, the value of French imports during the past year amounted to 3,950,000,000 fr., against 3,537,000,000 fr. for the year 1875. The exports in 1876 amounted to 3,570,000,000 fr., as compared with 3,873,000,000 fr. for the preceding year. This increase in the imports and decrease in the exports, compared with 1875, occurs chiefly in the following articles:

Imports.

	1876	1875
Provisions imported	950,000,000 fr.	747,000,000 fr.
Raw materials imported	2,310,000,000 fr.	2,154,000,000 fr.
Manufactured goods imported	496,000,000 fr.	467,000,000 fr.

Exports.

	1876	1875
Raw materials exported	1,449,000,000 fr.	1,528,000,000 fr.
Manufactured goods exported	1,932,000,000 fr.	2,140,000,000 fr.

The best argument for a further advance in the direction of free trade is however, after all, to be found in the manner in which French foreign trade as a whole, as well as with England alone, has advanced during the last sixteen years—since Cobden succeeded in persuading Louis Napoleon to adopt an ameliorated customs tariff. In 1860 French imports, exclusive of the transit trade, were only 76,000,000*l*, in value: by 1864 they had risen to over 100,000,000*l*., and in 1874 they reached over 140,000,000*l*., which was, besides, lower than the values imported in any one of the preceding three years. At the same time the exporting power of France, instead of decreasing with the removal of high duties, has increased till last year even faster than its importing power; and this, at all events, proves that the free-trade policy of England has hitherto done her nearest neighbour no harm. No doubt the increased wealth, the development of habits of luxury, and the passion for display which the present and the passing generations have exhibited in this and other countries, have had a powerful influence in stimulating the production of those articles of taste and fancy which France excels in making; but when that is admitted it remains the fact that these do not form all the substantial portion of French trade. Toys, silks, leather goods, jewellery, works of art, and ornaments, may give employment to workmen of Paris and several of the larger cities; but it is her wine, her fruits and vegetables—the choice products of her soil and her fisheries, in fact, which form the solid staples of her export business. She cannot in my opinion, even with free trade, enter into competition with England as a great manufacturing country, partly because she has not the facilities for doing so, nor the working capacity perhaps, but also because England permeates the world with her traders while Frenchmen stay at home. Our trade is, therefore, conducted on a much more extended basis than that of France can be. In the matter of iron, moreover, France is comparatively poor, and at present, notwithstanding the depression of business which her ironmasters feel, as well as ours, she is not able to provide raw iron enough for home consumption. Last year, in spite of the duty, she imported about 95,000 tons of pig-iron from England alone. She is still worse off for good coal, and required from us last year as much as 3,250,000 tons—the largest quantity, I believe, which France has ever imported in any one year. Wanting these all-important constituents of production, France can never in my opinion be a great manufacturing centre, and, therefore, whatever forces her into competition in that direction, must be in the end injurious to the prosperity of the country. Her business is obviously, in the main, to supply the luxuries of other nations, and the more of their solid articles of utility which she buys the larger customers for these will they become.[1] Along these lines she has undoubtedly prospered beyond any precedent since the treaty of 1862, and a further step in that direction must, I believe, lead to a further development of her trade. It should therefore be the endeavour of her law-makers to set her commerce more absolutely free. The true aim of all tax-gatherers should be to try and cheapen the means of living in the first instance, to free manufactures, and to enable products of all kinds to circulate freely. That done, their aim ought to be so

---

[1] The *Iron and Coal Trades Review* of January 5, 1877, states, in its French iron trade report, that only such firms as Schneider's at Creuzot, and Wendel's at Hayonge, who have a good name, can run their works with anything like regularity, and at full time. And the report proceeds as follows:—'The French manufacturers complain greatly of the competition, for English makers with their cheap iron are preventing them getting remunerative prices for native iron. The importations of foreign iron during the first eleven months of 1876 amounted to 271,000 tons, against 263,000 tons during the same period of the previous year, while the exportations were only 199,000 tons as compared with 200,000 tons in 1875. This showing must be considered very unsatisfactory—an increase in importations with a decrease in exportations, and that, too, when the native manufacturers are doing their utmost to keep foreign iron out of the market. The coal trade is quite as unsatisfactory as the iron trade; no break in the black cloud of depression appears, and prospects are everywhere regarded as very gloomy. It is many years since the French coal trade was in such a condition as it is at present, and there is no saying whether it may not be worse. In October it was thought that business would be tolerably good throughout the winter, but, so far, the trade has been much below an ordinary one, and colliery owners are resolved upon reducing the output, more especially those in the Nord and Pas-de-Calais, it being out of the question to go on raising coal and putting it into stock, particularly when the extraction of the coal involves a loss.' This statement about the coal trade is very significant when placed beside the fact I have stated regarding the heavy French import of English coal. It proves that the winning of French coal is so expensive that England can beat the native article on its own ground after all freights are added.

to impose taxes that they would clog no industry but bear only on the spending resources of the individual. No system of taxation that can be devised would be absolutely just; but the kind of taxation which makes the poor pay more heavily than the rich, which strikes at the sources of wealth, which lessens the value of the wages of the employed more than the wage-paying power of employers, and restricts the movements of articles of commerce, is the most pernicious of all.

Had France, however, manufacturing advantages— which it is evident she has not—there is still one cardinal fact in her political situation which must prevent her from building up a foreign business in any but those articles which she can produce cheapest and best. She has practically no colonies that are worth anything to her. Algeria, of which she makes such a parade, does not pay her any appreciable amount either directly or indirectly, and never will do so, notwithstanding the money and labour spent upon its colonisation and improvement, nor does it offer a large outlet for her products, manufactured or other. Her other small settlements scattered over the world—shreds of a shattered dream of world dominion—are about equally profitless and insignificant.[1] To a progressive

[1] Besides Algeria, with a population of about 1,050,000, France possesses Martinique, Guadaloupe, and sundry small islands in the West Indies having an aggregate population of about 300,000. French Guiana, on the north-east coast of South America, has only some 17,000 inhabitants. The Isle of France, in the South African Ocean, near Mauritius, has a declining population which in 1872 did not exceed 194,000 souls.

nation, French Guiana, Martinique, Guadaloupe, Pondicherry even, and above all the settlements at Saigon, in Cochin China, might form the starting-points of great conquests, of a civilising influence which would benefit it indefinitely. But to France these settlements are of comparatively little use because she is not, in this sense, at all progressive. A blight has apparently lighted on her fecundity, and her efforts at colonisation are miserably inadequate So also is the return which she gets from what foreign possessions she can call her own. Her West India colonies send her some raw sugar, and with the whole of them she of course does a certain amount of trade, but it is not trade that can expand very far, because the colonial policy of France, like that of Spain, does not allow any offshoot

The colonies in Senegal are more important, and do a trade with the mother country worth about 700,000*l.* or so a year, while their population is perhaps about 450,000; but there is no other possession of which France can boast which is of the least importance, except perhaps Saigon. The five isolated points still retained in India are utterly useless to the nation, and the settlements on the Society Islands and in New Caledonia are almost equally valueless. French Cochin China is capable of becoming a splendid possession, and is the most populous of all her foreign settlements, but it is managed so as to be of little or no use to her. The largest part of the commerce which it possesses goes off in foreign vessels, and the country is full of misgovernment, squalor, and misery. Some cynic said that the only memorial the French would leave behind them when they evacuated the country would be the palatial Government House at Saigon, built on a desolate flat plain so as to be visible from the far retired dens of squalor honoured with the name of town. In short, the French have no genius for colonising, and no colony they ever planted permanently succeeded. To this day no English subjects are more difficult to lift above the level of their poverty than the French Canadians, remnant of an effort of old France to emulate the conquests of Spain.

to develop its energies in freedom. There is thus before her colonial trade no great future; and in nothing is the commanding position of England, the sources of her greatness and power, more manifest than in the mighty position she holds as head of the most flourishing and progressive offshoots and colonies that were ever planted by any nation. Against us, if we foster these colonies and use them well, Frenchmen, with their inaptitude as colonisers, their second-rate capacities as practical traders, and their lack of great natural centres of demand, cannot hope to compete. Their truest interest is therefore to link themselves as much as they can on to the commercial greatness of their neighbour, so as to be able to draw to themselves some of the wealth which flows to her shores. Our business with France must always be large, but it cannot grow as it ought to do till she has recognised and given effect to this cardinal truth. The longer it remains unrecognised, the greater the danger that France may yet have to struggle through times of depression and misery of which she takes now no account. The war indemnity is not paid yet, and good harvests may not always so favour French agriculturists as they have done since 1871. It is too early yet to say therefore that France has overcome her troubles and is again strong.

Many things press on her, too, besides her tariff. She has not yet mastered the militarism which has cursed her since the days of the First Napoleon's 'whiff of grape-shot,' and the cost of her big army weighs heavier on her head than even that of the Germans. It abstracts from her working power, and, worse almost than that, it makes defiance of law and order possible to martinets like MacMahon and political marauders like M. Bardy de Fourtou. But for this army one might predict many things of France; but in presence of that huge fighting power which the folly of the nation has raised up within itself and above itself, one can predict nothing. All that remains to us is to hope that France may yet see the error of her ways. On the other hand, one cannot but fear that she may come anew into the hands of the spoiler.

Before passing on to other and in some respects more important countries, it may be well to look for a moment at the mercantile position of Belgium. To us that little kingdom, created by compromise and treaty, is chiefly known as a competitor in iron, and we have every now and then been scared by the news that such and such a Belgian firm had obtained a contract over the head of English competitors. And this is no doubt the most important aspect under which to view that country; but it has others which deserve notice, if not for their actual importance, at least for what they may become. For instance, the port of Antwerp has been rapidly advancing in importance within the past few years as an entrepôt for South Germany, and its wool market already attracts no inconsiderable portion of the South American clips which formerly found their way to London. Germany has thus in its rise stimulated the commercial importance of its little neighbour. As a sign of the times, this change in the current of trade seems to me very important; and it is naturally followed, though to a very limited extent, by the course of manufacturing industries.

The metal industries of Belgium are still, however, supreme over all the rest, and if it be any consolation for Englishmen to think that others are as badly off as themselves, the present state of the Belgian iron trade must be to them a source of much comfort. Notwithstanding cheaper labour than we can get in England, measuring labour by mere money wages, notwithstanding enormously long hours of labour, and the employment of women in mines to an extent that we are not supposed to tolerate in England, the Belgian iron trade has long been fully worse than our own. Exports have fallen off, prices have declined, and dulness has everywhere prevailed. Her iron masters might be able to make engines and locomotives cheaper than these could be made in Glasgow or Newcastle, but they did not succeed in extracting a profit from the sale of them, and consequently trade has gone from bad to worse. More than half the blast furnaces of the country have been blown out. Formerly, Belgium did a great trade in iron rails, but it has been broken down and revolutionised through the cheapness of steel, until bankruptcy has overtaken some of her most prosperous concerns. The Americans might be disposed to cite this state of things as an example of the bad effects of the lowness of the Belgian tariff, but the plain fact of the matter is that Belgium is overtaken by troubles which are universal. She profited exceedingly by the inflation due to railway building, and was within her small limits no mean competitor against England; but when the tide of this speculation turned, she suffered more heavily than her neighbours because of her very weakness.

What may be the future fortunes of this little community—the whole population of Belgium is not much larger than that of London—I can hardly venture to predict; but I think it probable that it may be a considerable time before it finds a fresh field for its industries. The larger neighbours it has are likely to overshadow it in iron-making were the iron trade brisker than it is, and its population may have to take to other ways of getting a living. They are considerable cotton manufacturers, and may extend business in that direction and in woollen industries, both with Germany and France, should France be disposed to give them fair play. But unless attached to a larger nation by closer ties than those of trade merely, I do not think that Belgium can count for a great deal at any future time amongst manufacturing communities.

Its foreign trade must always be for the most part dependent on facilities granted by foreigners. Its population is in part debased by superstition, and its realised wealth is on the whole insignificant. It has next to no mercantile marine except in coasting trade, and is, in short, only a sort of dependency on France and Southern Germany. As a separate nation Belgium has probably seen its best days. The best thing that could happen to it, short of political extinction, would be, in my belief, fiscal autonomy with France on a free-trade basis. Its largest trade is with France now, and its greatest possibilities for the future lie also in that direction. Such a union would undoubtedly increase the commercial importance of both France and Belgium. It would give France the command of iron and coal which her tariff now shuts partially out, and it would give Belgium a wider basis for its trade and larger wealth to work upon. It may be said that this would injure our home interests, but that I do not believe. Always provided that we do our work honestly and well, that we study to supply our markets with what is best suited to their wants, and that we stick to free trade, we have nothing to fear from the growth of competing powers elsewhere. The absence of competing power always means poverty, and poverty means bad trade for all concerned. Apart from France, I do not think Belgian competition of any importance ; but in fiscal union with France and with free trade, Belgium might undoubtedly do something to compete with us in some of our markets. I think it probable also that we should ourselves use much more of Belgian products than we do now, and that, on the other hand, her powers of buying from us would also be increased.

At the present time the total trade between Belgium and England amounts to about 25,000,000*l.* a year, and s on the whole wonderfully steady. Much of this is of course transit trade, but probably more than half represents the actual products and wants of Belgium. Our principal import thence is silk manufactures and not, as many might suppose, iron; and in these there has, as we might expect, been latterly a considerable falling off. Our import of iron, raw and manufactured, has never amounted to much more than 600,000*l. per annum*, and it is more than balanced by her purchases from us. Her purchases of cotton and woollen goods also nearly balance her sales to us—a clear proof that there is nothing to fear from her competition. The more export trade Belgium does, no matter in what, the greater, in short, should her purchases be. Except flax or linen yarn, the rest of her trade to this country is made up mostly of articles of food and luxury, such as wheat, fruit, hops, lace, sugar, potatoes, watches and the like; and she buys from us mostly manufactures. A better basis of trade could not well be found, and whether we look on it as native Belgian trade or as mere transit business, we have good reason to be satisfied. The late depression in Belgium has affected this trade on both sides of the account to some extent, but not so much as might have been expected, probably because of the increasing commerce of Germany, and it may revive again when the dull times pass away. We at any rate cannot accuse ourselves of being the direct cause of the inflation in Belgium. We have invested money in her railways and iron works indeed, and have lost part of it, but we have not stimulated the nation to wild spending by any gigantic loan; and as the trade between the two countries has been governed rather by our own inflated demands at home than by the extravagance of Belgium, it will probably revive when our general trade revives. Large or small, it is a trade that we ought to cherish as we cherish that of France, and the more we can persuade Belgium to knock its fetters off the better will it by-and-by become for both countries.

END OF THE FIRST VOLUME.

LONDON: PRINTED BY
SPOTTISWOODE AND CO., NEW-STREET SQUARE
AND PARLIAMENT STREET

UNIVERSITY OF CALIFORNIA LIBRARY
Los Angeles

This book is DUE on the last date stamped below.

APR 24 19

PLEASE DO NOT REMOVE
THIS BOOK CARD

University Research Library

www.ingramcontent.com/pod-product-compliance
Lightning Source LLC
Chambersburg PA
CBHW050847300426
44111CB00010B/1167